TRAVELER

provence
& the côte d'azur

provence
& the côte d'azur

by Barbara A. Noe
photography by Gérard Sioen

National Geographic
Washington, D.C.

CONTENTS

Pages 2–3: La Roque Alric
Left: Lavender festival in Sault

TRAVELING WITH EYES OPEN

Alert travelers go with a purpose and leave with a benefit. If you travel responsibly, you can help support wildlife conservation, historic preservation, and cultural enrichment in the places you visit. You can enrich your own travel experience as well.

To be a geo-savvy traveler:

- Recognize that your presence has an impact on the places you visit.

- Spend your time and money in ways that sustain local character. (Besides, it's more interesting that way.)

- Value the destination's natural and cultural heritage.

- Respect the local customs and traditions.

- Express appreciation to local people about things you find interesting and unique to the place: its nature and scenery, music and food, historic villages and buildings.

- Vote with your wallet: Support the people who support the place, patronizing businesses that make an effort to celebrate and protect what's special there. Seek out shops, local restaurants, inns, and tour operators who love their home—who love taking care of it and showing it off. Avoid businesses that detract from the character of the place.

- Enrich yourself, taking home memories and stories to tell, knowing that you have contributed to the preservation and enhancement of the destination.

That is the type of travel now called geotourism, defined as "tourism that sustains or enhances the geographical character of a place—its environment, culture, aesthetics, heritage, and the well-being of its residents." To learn more, visit National Geographic's Center for Sustainable Destinations at *national geographic.com/travel/sustainable.*

provence
& the côte d'azur

ABOUT THE AUTHOR & THE PHOTOGRAPHER

Author **Barbara A. Noe** earned a B.A. in French and International Relations from the University of California at Davis, with a year of study at the Université de Bordeaux, France. After receiving an M.A. in Journalism from the University of Missouri School of Journalism, she moved to Washington, D.C., for an internship with *National Geographic Traveler* magazine. Years later, she is now the senior editor of National Geographic Travel Books and, having returned to France many times since her first visit, her favorite region is still Provence.

Gérard Sioen has traveled around the globe since 1974. His pictures appear in numerous photography books, including *Vive le Pays Cathare, Californie, Egypt, Camargue,* and *Provence.* His gallery is located in Carcassonne.

Christopher Pitts wrote the Hotels & Restaurants, Shopping, and Entertainment, and Activities portions of the Travelwise section.

Charting Your Trip

With 12,124 square miles (31,401 sq km) and six *départements,* Provence and the Côte d'Azur can't be covered in a week—not, at least, in a way that it deserves. The key to enjoying this lavender-scented region, after all, is to take your time and literally smell the roses. Stroll through the produce-filled markets, luxuriate in the shade of centuries-old plane trees, and sip pastis in an old village square. Pick either the Quintessential Provence tour, centering on the charming towns of Avignon, Aix, and Arles; or the French Riviera tour, a celebration of beaches, contemporary art, and glitzy nightlife. A crammed-in "Best of Both" itinerary is outlined as well, for those who want to do it all at Parisian rather than Provençal speed.

Getting Around

If you're flying into Provence, you'll land in either Marseille or Nice. Or, you can fly into Paris Charles-de-Gaulle and catch the TGV *(raileurope.com)* south, a delightful three-hour trip via high-speed train. Once in the region, you'll definitely want to rent a car to drive around "Quintessential Provence." That's the only way you'll be able to explore tiny villages tucked away in the countryside. If you're sticking to the French Riviera, however, you feasibly could get by with taking the train, which snakes along the coastline from place to place. This is fine if you want to touch only on the coastal towns. To go farther afield—to Grasse, St.-Paul-de-Vence, as well as the corniche roads—you'll need a car. Driving in Quintessential Provence is manageable, though roads can be narrow and twisty; driving in the French Riviera becomes a little more crazy, with high traffic volume and fast speeds. If you're traveling on the A8 tollway (and any other tollway), be aware that France has removed the human tollbooth, and many of the machines accept only credit cards with a microchip (see Travelwise p. 205); at the very least, if your card doesn't have a microchip, make sure you have sufficient change with you.

Quintessential Provence

Begin in up-and-coming Marseille, to see for yourself the urban renewal taking hold in France's second city. Must-sees include the MuCEM, the dramatically renovated waterfront, and the café-filled Panier quarter. On **Day Two,** drive north about 30 minutes (20 miles/30 km) to Aix-en-Provence, with its lane-noodled old town, fabulous Musée Granet, and fountain-dotted cours Mirabeau, considered the most beautiful street in Provence—if not all of France.

Ceramic cicada

On **Day Three,** drive west about 30 miles (50 km) into the Luberon, basing yourself in one of the hill towns (Gordes and Bonnieux are favorites), or perhaps in a vineyard-surrounded villa (called *mas* or *bastide* in these parts). Spend a day (or two, if you can) exploring the country-side, dipping into such picture-perfect villages as Bonnieux, Lacoste, Ménerbes, and Gordes. Ride a bike on countryside lanes, visit local markets, shop for linens, lavender, and pottery in darling little shops—whatever you do, take your time.

On **Day Four,** go farther west about 60 miles (95 km) to Roman-centric Arles, home to the fabulous Musée de l'Arles et de la Provence Antique, which showcases Roman antiquities including a recently discovered bust of an aging Julius Caesar. You'll want to explore the beautifully preserved Roman amphitheater, as well as the not-so-well-preserved theater (though it still gives you a good sense of the architecture and history). Van Gogh lovers must follow in the disturbed artist's footsteps—here he cut off his earlobe and checked himself into the hospital, now the Éspace Van Gogh.

> ## NOT TO BE MISSED:
>
> **The Abbaye de Sénanque's lavender fields in bloom 59**
>
> **Ducking into wine caves at Châteauneuf-du-Pape 74–75**
>
> **The amazing Pont du Gard 85**
>
> **Van Gogh's Arles 95**
>
> **Taking in Marseille's cultural metamorphosis 116–123**
>
> **Hearing the monks chant at Île St.-Honorat 139**
>
> **Singing Picasso's praises in Antibes 152–154**
>
> **Nice's Italian-infused old town 166–167**
>
> **Checking out the faïence shops in Moustiers-Ste.-Marie 196**

Day Five brings a splendid drive north about 15 miles (24 km) through the Alpilles, with perhaps a stop at Les Baux and olive-oil tasting in the surrounding countryside.

Visitor Information

Before leaving home, visit *atout -france.fr* or *rendezvousfrance.com* for helpful planning information. Nearly every town and village has a tourist office (*office de tourisme*) offering local information, and many make hotel reservations. Here are some more helpful websites:

aixenprovencetourism.com
arlestourisme.com
avignon-tourisme.com
cannes-destination.com
frenchriviera-tourism.com
marseille-tourisme.com
nicetourisme.com
provenceguide.com
visitprovence.com
visitvar.fr

Spend the night in charming St.-Rémy, where there's not much else to do but play *pétanque,* see where Nostradamus lived, and peruse the weekly market (one of the best in the region); van Gogh fans will want to visit St.-Paul de Mausole, where the mad artist admitted himself for a year and, on good days, painted such pieces as "Olive Trees With the Alpilles," "Starry Night Over the Rhône," and "Irises." Across the street at Glanum are some amazing Roman ruins.

On **Day Six,** drive north about 12 miles (20 km) to Avignon, home to the sublime Palais des Papes, along with a handful of other important museums. After a day of sightseeing, enjoy an apéri-tif in the bustling place de l'Horloge.

On **Day Seven,** catch a train north to Paris, or meander back to Marseille to close the loop.

Tipping Tips

Most restaurant bills include a 15 percent service charge. Look for *service compris* at the bottom of the menu. If in doubt, ask: *Est-ce que le service est compris?* It is usual to leave a small additional tip for the waiter if the service has been good. It is customary to tip taxi drivers 10 to 15 percent. It is usual to give porters, doormen, and tour guides a tip of 1 to 2 euros, ushers and cloakroom attendants 5 euros, and hairdressers 10 percent. There is no need to leave a tip for hotel maids unless you have required out-of-the-ordinary service.

French Riviera

If you prefer the glitz and glamour of the legendary French Riviera, this itinerary is for you. Fly into buzzing Marseille, where you definitely should stay at least one night to take in this world-class city. Then head east along the coast. You can rent a car—advisable especially if you want to explore some of the nooks and crannies along the way—or hop on the train, which follows the coastline fairly closely all the way to the Italian border.

On **Day Two** head for Cannes, the über-celebrity hub on the sparkling sea. It's 110 miles (180 km) to get there along the A8 tollway, but if you have the time, take the more leisurely route along the coastline, poking into Fréjus and St.-Tropez along the way. Once you arrive, lie out on the beach; stroll along La Croisette, the city's famed esplanade; visit the movie sights; or simply chill out on monk-owned St.-Honorat island, just 15 minutes offshore by ferry.

The next day, **Day Three,** explore the surrounding inland countryside, especially devoting some time to the nearby hill town of Grasse, where you can make your own perfume, and St.-Paul-de-Vence, another hill town famous for its artist heritage. Stop by the hill town of Mougins, where the new Musée d'Art Classique de Mougins is the much-talked-about attraction. Moneyed Antibes, the former home of Picasso, is another popular destination in the vicinity; his art museum here, housed in the ancient Grimaldi castle, is a huge draw, and the beaches are some of the country's best. Spend the night in one of the towns.

Day Four brings you to Nice, 14 miles (22.6 km) east of Antibes, a pastel showcase of Italianate architecture with its newly transformed Place Masséna, sun-blessed old town, and contemporary art scene. You'll want all day to stroll, take in Chagall and Matisse at their eponymous museums—or simply sunbathe.

When to Go

The best months are May and June, when the temperatures are warm and tourists few. Spring brings blooming almond and cherry trees and fields of red poppies. September and October are also good months to visit, with the *vendange* (grape harvest) beginning September 15.

Winter can be cool; the *cueillette des olives* (olive harvest), however, takes place mid-November through early January, and ski season in the Alps of Haute-Provence is Christmas through March.

Summer is often brutally hot, though the lavender fields bloom late June to late July. August can see sudden storms and frequent rain showers.

Keep in mind that the cold, northerly mistral wind blows on average 100 to 150 days a year, often reaching 60 miles (100 km) an hour and dropping temperatures as much as 20°F (6°C). It is strongest in winter and spring, when it can last for several days at a time.

Sanary-sur-Mer's port protects a large collection of *pointus,* or traditional wooden boats.

On the next day, **Day Five,** enjoy fabulous sea views along one of the coast's three famous corniche roads, each one offering a different-level perspective over the mountains and sea. Regardless of which one you take, you'll end up in Monaco, 12 miles (19 km) east of Nice. Visit the palace, the cathedral where Princess Grace and Prince Rainier are buried, and legendary Monte-Carlo.

On **Day Six,** head 5.5 miles (9 km) farther east, ending near the Italian border in lovely, sun-drenched Menton, said to enjoy the sunniest weather of all Riviera resorts—316 days a year. It's famous for its gardens, lemons, and the artistic legacy of Jean Cocteau. You can head north into the Southern Alps from here, stopping by charming hill towns along vertiginous roads, including Conte, Coaraze, and Peille.

On **Day Seven,** head back to Marseille for your flight or train home.

Best of Both

If you truly want to make a whirlwind tour to "see it all," you'll have to rent a car. Begin in Marseille on **Day One,** taking in the Vieux-Port and the MuCEM. On **Day Two,** drive west to Arles via the A7 and A54 (55 miles/90 km) and spend the afternoon exploring Roman and/or van Gogh sights. The next day, **Day Three,** drive north (25 miles/40 km) through lovely olive-dotted countryside, through St.-Rémy, to Avignon. On **Day Four,** amble east through the Luberon, less than an hour away (25 miles/40 km to Gordes), where you can explore the hill towns. Spend the night in Bonnieux or Gordes. On **Day Five,** head east, stopping in Aix for lunch. Continue east on the A8 to starstruck Cannes (138 miles/223 km). On **Day Six,** continue east 33 miles (53 km) to Nice, stopping at your choice of sights along the way: perhaps Grasse, St.-Paul-de-Vence, and/or Antibes. On the last day, **Day Seven,** if you don't need to leave right away, drive one of the corniche roads through Monaco, ending 18 miles (30 km) from Nice in sunny Menton. ■

History & Culture

The Marseillais fought fiercely against the Royals during the French Revolution.

A Provençal evening in Gréoux-les-Bains

Provence & the Côte d'Azur Today

To deal cards the Provençal way is to throw them down on the table to mix them up as much as possible. This practice aptly describes Provence itself: a jumble of orchard-dotted valleys and snowy peaks, turgid rivers and bubbling springs. Mixed in are Roman ruins, pebbly beaches, bird-filled marshes, and dark forests. There are lively cities like Nice and Marseille, and sleepy medieval hill towns. Old and new, traditional and modern, natural and man-made all combine to create this enchanted land, a varied and contradictory realm indeed.

There's one thing, however, that's universally agreed upon. Cross into Provence and you succumb to its charms. The translucent light, the dazzling blue skies, the exquisite scenery all work together to seduce you. Sitting at the Café de France's terrace in Lacoste, sipping an apéritif and overlooking the patchwork fields far below, Bonnieux's golden medieval buildings rising on a hill beyond. Coming upon a field of blooming lavender on the plain near Buoux, the tiny buds creating an effervescent blue-violet aura. Watching a *santonnier* meticulously paint a tiny terra-cotta figure in the elegant town of Aix-en-Provence, as artisans have for centuries. Sampling a bowl of savory bouillabaisse by Marseille's raucous fish market. Scanning the Camargue sky for flocks of flamingos ...

> **The translucent light, the dazzling blue skies, the exquisite scenery all work together to seduce you.**

Provence is a glorious place, celebrated for its fruity wines, abundant fruits and vegetables, Romanesque architecture, yearlong calendar of festivals, friendly people, lilting accent, famous beaches ... all good reasons to explain why everyone from ancient Romans to movie stars have been lured here.

There's a certain je ne sais quoi about the Provençal style, a flair that is both rustic and sophisticated, traditional and elegant—and nothing is accidental: The stone for the walls is faded by centuries of sun, the bright and distinctive fabrics for table and bed come from designers working in a centuries-old tradition, the pottery and glassware are the product of local craftsmen.

Even those who haven't visited know Provence's joyful vibrance, thanks largely to the parade of artists who have passed through: Matisse, Renoir, Picasso, Bonnard, Chagall, and Aix-native Cézanne, to name a few. But the artist most affected by the landscape was certainly Vincent van Gogh, who moved to Arles in 1888 and frenetically painted more than 150 canvases over the next two years. It's these tableaus that have given us the most quintessential image of Provence: the bold, colorful irises, sunflowers, starry nights, outdoor cafés. He wrote his sister Willemien in 1888: "Nature in the south cannot be painted with the palette of a mauve for instance which belongs to the north ... how the palette is distinctly colorful, sky blue, orange, pink, vermillion, a very bright yellow, bright green, wine and violet."

But, as with most things, there's more than meets the eye.

Marseille's übermodern MuCEM sharply contrasts the age-old Cathédrale de la Major.

Purple waves of lavender roll across the plateau de Puimichel. Cutting machines do most of the work these days, though some smaller, older fields are still harvested by hand.

Mother Nature

Porous limestone is the basic ingredient of the Provençal landscape, nurturing an arid vegetation that features silvery olive trees and prickly succulents, the thick maquis and *garrigue* (shrublands). Water is greatly cherished, noted by the myriad fountains in towns and villages. In a few days, or a few hours, it can rain here as much as it does in Paris in a year. Then the mountains blur into torrents, as the water races toward the Verdon, the Durance, the Rhône, the Mediterranean Sea. After, the land can remain parched for months. Adding to this hardship, the mistral wind rages down from the north more than a hundred days a year, ravaging farm crops, influencing the positioning of houses, and affecting people's moods. It overturns cars, rips off roof tiles, uproots trees. Provençal writer Marcel Pagnol eloquently portrayed nature's fury in *Jean de Florette* and *Manon des Sources,* the story of a kind farmer's demise due to conniving neighbors who hide the source of a nearby spring from him, and his daughter's revenge upon his death.

Agricultural Paradise

"How can this rocky, seemingly forsaken land give us such richness?" asks food writer Patricia Wells in the introduction to her book, *At Home in Provence.* Indeed, the hardy

Provençaux coax an Eden of produce from this brutal climate: exquisite truffles, luscious red cherries, quinces, pears, olives, rich wines, pungent goat cheeses. The farmers markets are always full of such delicacies, along with bundles of sunflowers, *coquelicots* (red poppies), or whatever other seasonal flowers are blooming in nearby fields.

Such bounty defines the root of the Provençal character—resilient, hardworking, making much from little. Historically farmers and fishermen, the Provençaux have always been tied close to the earth. Rather than dominating, they have adapted, planting trees for shade from the hot Midi sun, facing houses away from the relentless north wind, adding heavy shutters to their homes to keep out harsh temperatures.

The rural way of life was jeopardized after World War II, when Provence, with the rest of France, embraced industrialization. The economic focus moved to Concorde supersonic aircraft, nuclear power, and other pursuits. Farmers were encouraged to modernize their equipment. Many went bankrupt, since their small farms were not suitable for new tools designed for larger plots. In the early 1980s, only 10 percent of the Provençaux worked as farmers, compared with 35 percent before World War II.

But then a global trend toward organic, biologically sound produce came to the rescue. People could not get enough fresh, organic pressed olive oil, herbs, wines—Provence's forte. Provence reinstated the family farms, a back-to-tradition trend that persists to this day. Indeed, Provence holds the top spot in France for the production and exporting of produce.

All this is not to say that modernity is bypassing the region. Not at all. Nuclear research continues at Cadarache, while La Gaude is world famous for its contributions to

All in a Word

Strolling the streets of Provence, you may see signs written in a language that doesn't look quite French. Avignon is written as Avignoun, for example, and "welcome" is *benvengut* (instead of *bienvenue*). You are a firsthand witness to the Provençal dialect, still spoken by a minority of people in southern France. Here's the story. The French language is a product of the Roman conquest. The Romans brought both classical Latin and the colloquial Latin of soldiers and merchants. The latter drove out Celtic and evolved into the Romance vernacular known as French. However, a single language did not take root. Various dialects in the south evolved (Provençal, Aquitain, Languedocien, Auvergnat, and Dauphinois), collectively called the *langue d'oc,* while in the north arose a separate set of dialects, called the *langue d'oïl.* The subjection of the southern provinces in the 13th century assured that the northerner's langue d'oïl would dominate—this is today's French language. Provençal survived as a regional spoken language, but its literature died out until its 19th-century revival.

electronics. Marseille devotes much energy to biological research, while atomic and meteorological exploration takes place on Mont Ventoux, as well as at Michel-de-Provence and Nice. The Fos-Lavera-Berre industrial and port complex, specializing in petrochemicals, polymers, and fine chemicals, is one of the major chemical platforms in Europe.

And you will hear much about Marseille's Euroméditerranée project. Unique to Europe, this fully fledged urban development operation, covering nearly 740 acres (300 ha) in the city's heart, has brought major professional and technology companies together in one place. In addition, new cultural venues and modern housing have been built, museums renovated, and fine restaurants opened. The city buzzes with hyperactivity.

> **Each village has its own coat of arms ... its own fruits, cheeses, wines, and specialty sweets.**

The Heart of Tradition

Wrapped in heirloom lace, the Queen of Arles speaks fluent Provençal, the traditional regional dialect—a distinction much more important than beauty. Elected every three years by a panel of seven judges, l'Arlesienne, as she is called, epitomizes the region's enduring devotion to tradition, embedded throughout the Provençal culture in myriad ways.

Each village has its own coat of arms, for instance, its own fruits, cheeses, wines, and specialty sweets. The yearly calendar is filled with local festivals, many including traditional dance, music, and costumes. Most are religious—the festival in Les-Stes.-Maries-de-la-Mer, for example, which venerates the Gypsies' patron saint—or tied closely to the earth around the harvests of lavender, wine, olive oil. Some are obscure. Take Gorbio's snail-lantern festival, in which townspeople wander through the streets carrying empty snail shells aglow with flames. Or Nice's gourd festival, symbolizing the end of winter and a time to make public amends to one's spouse after having been cooped up together all winter.

Of all the festivals that embody Provence's singular traditions, however, the most cherished is Christmas. It all starts with the *gros souper,* the large supper served before midnight Mass on Christmas Eve. The family gathers around a table decorated with sprigs of myrtle and St.-Barbe's wheat and lentil sprouts, which are symbols of prosperity. Additional places are laid for the poor or for parents who have died, and for three days the table is not cleared, so as to allow angels to take part. Everywhere you see Nativity scenes populated with *santons,* the colorful, meticulously carved wooden or clay figures of the Christmas story that have been a traditional craft since the 18th century.

But perhaps what best defines Provence are its daily traditions, suggesting that the people who live here know how to take life slowly, to take the time to enjoy friends and family, and never get too harried. Shops and businesses (and most museums) close between noon and two or three, even four, as their owners enjoy a

long lunch and siesta. Dinners are often long conversational affairs as well, starting with an apéritif—perhaps pastis, the region's popular licorice-flavored liqueur, or a glass of Muscat—and negotiating through several courses of dishes prepared from the freshest of local ingredients.

Provence, it seems, has stayed Provençal by existing separately from the world, creating a special essence all its own. And yet southern France has drawn the world to its borders since the Greeks arrived in 600 B.C. Centuries ago, West Indies traders brought the bold ornamental cottons called *indiennes,* for instance, today so instantly recognizable as Provençal. The salt cod, so prevalent in local dishes, originally came from New England. Marseille, long a mondial crossroads, is a city of immigrants, with a quarter of its population of North African origin.

And that's the beauty of this beguiling land. There's more than meets the eye. You could spend a lifetime getting to know it. And you should. ■

Laid-back Provence can be found at the local *pétanque* court (every village has one), here in Fontvieille where old-timers whittle away Midi afternoons playing the traditional game of bowling without pins.

Cuisine du Soleil

In every Provençal town, market stalls burgeon with sun-kissed goods that hint at the region's simple, aromatic, healthy cuisine. Based on the seasons and on age-old tradition, it's a Mediterranean gastronomy, an ode to olives and garlic and tomatoes, that stands apart from the rest of France. Elements hark back to the Greeks—indeed, the Greeks introduced the first olives to the region—with an even greater influence coming from its proximity to Italy. But the Provençaux have ensured that their *cuisine du soleil* is distinctly their own.

Goat cheese from Banon has been prepared the same way since Gallo-Roman times.

There are three essentials to Provençal cuisine. Garlic anchors most dishes, providing a tangy (and healthy) kick. Olive oil is regarded nearly as highly as wine, some even possessing their own AOC (Appellation d'Origine Contrôlée). Finally, Provence's wild herbs—basil, thyme, and rosemary especially—season all kinds of dishes, from chicken to gelato.

The region's singular sauces and condiments are working variations of these basic ingredients. The most famous is aioli, a garlicky mayonnaise that's served with codfish, raw vegetables, or soup. *Anchoïade* is an anchovy paste made with garlic and olive oil, while tapenade is a black-olive-based purée seasoned with garlic, capers, anchovies, and olive oil and served on toast or celery.

Prevalent vegetables include spring asparagus, *aubergines* (eggplants), *courgettes* (zucchini), young artichokes, tomatoes, and mushrooms. Ratatouille is a savory mixture of onions, tomatoes, aubergines, and courgettes stewed with green peppers, garlic, and *herbes de Provence*. Stuffed vegetables are also popular, including *aubergines farcies à la provençale,* eggplant stuffed with meat, onions, and herbs in a tomato sauce; and *fleurs de courgettes farcies,* stuffed zucchini flowers. From Nice comes *salade Niçoise* (containing most of the following: tomatoes, cucumbers, hard-boiled eggs, onions, green peppers, green beans, olives, sometimes tuna, but never potatoes) and *pissaladière* (onion tart with olives and anchovies). Grilled tomatoes with garlic and bread crumbs is a common side dish throughout Provence. *Soupe au pistou* is the signature soup, a hearty vegetable, bean, basil concoction served with *pistou* (a basil, garlic, and olive oil sauce that's stirred in). And no list is complete without *truffes*—truffles—Provence's black gold (see sidebar p. 55).

The greatest meat delicacy is *agneau de Sisteron,* lamb roasted with herbs and listed on menus as *gigot d'agneau aux herbes.* Game includes rabbits, hare, wild boar, and birds including snipe and thrush (served in stews and *saucissons*). Beef is served in rich, slow-cooked *daubes.* In the Camargue, you'll come across *taureau* everywhere—bull's meat served grilled, stewed in red wine, or in *boeuf à la gardiane.*

Along the coast, fresh fish is the treat: anchovies, cod, sea bass, sea bream, and whiting, to name a few *délices,* while inland you'll be treated to freshwater trout. In fishing ports west of Marseille you'll find *oursins* (sea urchins), *violets* (sea squirts), and bowlfuls of *bulots* (whelks). But the queen of all seafood dishes is bouillabaisse, Marseille's classic seafood stew that's available up and down the coast (see sidebar p. 121).

Provence is celebrated for its fruits, among them Luberon cherries, Cavaillon cantaloupes (grown here since the Avignon papacy), apricots, table grapes, and sumptuous late summer figs from Marseille. The best place to find the seasonal specialties is at a local farmers market—most towns hold one at least once a week.

As far as cheeses go, goat cheese (*chèvre*) is Provence's forte. Banon is the most famous. *Picodon* is a small, tangy goat cheese, while *pelardon* is similar, but ripened and firm. *Brousse* is typically a soft and mild sheep's milk cheese, used in ravioli or served as a dessert with olive oil and honey.

For desserts, see sidebar p. 184. ■

EXPERIENCE: Cook the Provençal Way

Take home the secrets of Provençal cooking by joining a local chef to see how it's done. All kinds of cooking classes are offered throughout the region, most of which include a trip to the market for the freshest produce possible, as well as an end-of-the-preparation sampling. Here are a few of the best.

• Iconic cookbook author **Patricia Wells** (*patriciawells.com*) opens her 18th-century farmhouse a few weeks a year for personalized cooking classes.

• At Avignon's **La Mirande** (*la-mirande .fr*), the region's best chefs offer gastronomic cooking classes in the hotel's 19th-century kitchen. The pastry classes are the most sublime (for example: chocolate cocooning and macaron).

• Three-Michelin-star chef Gérald Passédat, famed for his unique Mediterranean fish dishes, offers cooking classes at his latest Marseille endeavor, **Le Môle Passédat** (*lemole-passedat.com*). A personal vegetable garden supplies necessary accoutrements.

• Star-rated chefs teach you the secrets of French cooking at **Les Apprentis Gourmets** (*lesapprentisgourmets.com*), a high-tech cooking school in the heart of Cannes. The flagship course is the express lunch formula—a 30-minute lesson for €17.

Provence's Wines

Provence's fecund soils and sunny climate—with a dash of brutal mistral wind—are ideal for grape growing. The Greeks brought the first vines, introducing the Syrah, a grape variety originally from Shiraz, Persia. Since maceration wasn't known, it was a rosé that became Provence's quintessential summer swill. Though the region is France's second largest wine-producing area, its quality hasn't always been highly acclaimed. Indeed, "tourist pink" and "hard-to-swallow red" are more common descriptions than "fine" or "rare." But that's all changing, as a new generation of winemakers has begun to emphasize quality.

Grape gathering near Cotignac, Côtes de Provence

The River Rhône is one of the world's greatest wine rivers, nurturing some of the world's finest wines along its banks. In Provence, these appellations include Tavel, Muscat de Beaumes-de-Venise, and the fabled Châteauneuf-du-Pape. Farther east, the Côtes de Provence is where most of Provence's rosés derive, while pocket vineyards along the Côte d'Azur coastline produce an assortment of wines, including Cassis' illustrious, salt-air-tinged whites. Here is a primer on some of Provence's better known appellations.

Côtes du Rhône This appellation, focusing mostly on reds, extends through six

départements and three regions, covering more than 148,300 acres (60,000 ha). The southern half, known as *vins méridionaux*, is Provence's segment, located north of Avignon along the Rhône's eastern bank.

The most celebrated vintage in the Côtes du Rhône is the landmark region of Châteauneuf-du-Pape, harking back to papal days (see pp. 74–75).

Other highly regarded reds from the area include hearty and robust Gigondas. From the vicinity, too, come the delicate fruity reds of the 17 Côtes du Rhône villages, noted for their good soil and microclimates. The wines are best when made by the traditional barrel fermented

Reading French Wine Labels

Wine labels reveal a lot about what's in the bottle, including the winery name, vintage, alcohol content, bottle volume, and regional designation and classification of the wine, the latter of which is broken down into three different tiers:

Appellation d'Origine Contrôlée (AOC) Taking into account the geographic origin of a wine, including its soil, climate, and geography that combine to create its unique character (known as terroir), the AOC is awarded to regional producers following strict standards of growing, harvesting, blending, and labeling. This classification is broken down into Grand Cru, the absolute highest classification of

French wine, and Premier Cru, denoting either a superior vineyard plot or the highest tier within the Grand Cru classification. Provence has nine major wines with AOC designation, with Côtes du Rhône being the largest.

Vin de Pays This higher-class table wine, meaning "wine of the land," is guaranteed to have originated in a certain region.

Vin de France This is basic French table wine, labeled simply as coming from France.

AOC vs. DOC France recently instigated a new system to align with the overarching EU designations. So you may see AOP (Appellation d'Origine Protegée) for AOC, and IGT (Indication Geographique Protegée) for *vin de pays*.

---

techniques and not the newer carbonic maceration technique.

Provence's most famous (and expensive) rosé is Tavel, originating 8 miles (13 km) west of Châteauneuf-du-Pape. Dry, full-bodied, it's best enjoyed as young as possible. Domaine de la Forcadière and Domaine de la Genestière produce some of the most excellent Tavels.

Finally, Beaumes-de-Venise makes a sweet, fortified muscat that's been entitled its own AOC; it's served as a popular apéritif.

Côtes de Provence Provence's principal AOC (annual production a hundred million bottles), and France's sixth largest, it comprises roughly 50,000 acres (20,250 ha) between Nice and Aix-en-Provence, including the Varois hinterland and bordering the Mediterranean from Hyères to Fréjus. Its diversity of terroirs and climates—ranging from coastal maritime to inland hills—means that the appellation covers a wide range of wine types. The majority—89 percent—is fresh and fruity rosé, with the rest being multiflavored reds and the much rarer whites. Côtes de Provence is always drunk young and served at a crisp 46°F to 50°F (8°C–10°C). Excellent producers: Domaine Gavoty and Domaine Richeaume.

Bandol Bandol is famed for its round,

deep-flavored reds, produced from the dark-berried Mourvèdre grape that requires a minimum of 18 months to age in oaken *foudres*. It's good for immediate consumption but is best known for its *grands vins* that need aging. There's also a rosé produced for local demand, aged a minimum of eight months in wood (unusual for a rosé), giving the wine an orange tinge.

Cassis The tiny seaport of Cassis (see p. 124) is renowned for its crisp, nutty whites (75 percent of production), Provence's very first appellation (1936). They perfectly match such local specialties as sea snails with garlic mayonnaise. Clos Ste.-Magdelaine produces one of Cassis' most distinctive whites, its grapes grown on a sunny sliver of limestone soil on the edge of the Mediterranean.

Tasting, Visiting, & Buying You can buy directly from the *domaine* (wine-growing estate) of the *producteur* (wine producer) at a lower price than most shops. Most places offer *dégustations* (wine-tastings). The best wine-touring is in the Châteauneuf-du-Pape area (see sidebar p. 75), Les Dentelles (see pp. 66–67), and the Varois hinterland near Les Arcs (see pp. 130–131). To visit the wineries, phone ahead to confirm opening days and times.

History of Provence

Peaceful, picture-perfect Provence is a product of conflict—cities against cities, province against crown, authority against individual, Catholics against Protestants, borders shifting all the while. Along the way, a fierce nationalism took root, renewed by Frédéric Mistral at the turn of the 20th century, and, later, Marcel Pagnol and Jean Giono, and surviving today in a regional loyalty toward all things Provençal—including its proverbial cuisine, traditions, and language.

Prehistoric Times

Provence's strategic position along the Mediterranean made it attractive to visitors early on. The first arrived in the Monaco area about a million years ago, where they etched drawings on the Grotte de l'Observatoire. Modern man—*Homo sapiens*—arrived more than 900,000 years later, leaving behind weapons in the Grimaldi grottoes. About 20,000 B.C.—the peak of the last ice age—hunter societies left ornate wall paintings of bison, seals, and ibex in caves such as the Grotte Cosquer in the massif near Cassis. The Neolithic period—aka New Stone Age—arrived as early as 6000 B.C., during which time the first fixed populations appeared, raising sheep and cultivating crops, and building drystone houses called *bories*.

> **Western civilization came to Provence in 600 B.C. in the form of Greeks, who settled at Massalia (Marseille).**

It's difficult to pinpoint the origin of the Ligurians, but the term generally refers to anyone living in the Mediterranean area as the Neolithic Age spilled over into the Iron Age. Beginning about 800 B.C., this disparate group built fortified villages on hilltops, today referred to by the Latin name *oppidum*. About the same time, waves of Celts, a Germanic tribe, invaded Provence from the north. They intermingled with the Ligurians, eventually forming a fierce tribe called the Celto-Ligurians.

The Greeks (600 B.C.–118 B.C.)

Western civilization came to Provence in 600 B.C. in the form of Greeks, who settled at Massalia (Marseille). Over a couple of centuries, they established trading colonies at Antipolis (Antibes), Nikaia (Nice), Olbia (Hyères), Monoïkos (Monaco), and Glanum (near St.-Rémy). Their introduction of grapevines and olive trees established an economic base that would serve Provence for millennia to come.

As the Romans began their centuries-long domination of the West, the Massalians allied with them, if only because their common enemies included the Etruscans, the Phoenicians, and the Celts and Ligurians. When Hannibal, the famous general of Carthage (North Africa), crossed the Alps with elephants to attack Rome, the Massalians were quick to join forces with the Romans. In 212 B.C., Massalia switched over to a Roman form of municipal government.

The alliance reached its apex in 125 B.C., when Celto-Ligurians, who had been waiting for just the right moment, banded together to attack Massalia from Entremont. The overwhelmed Massalians called on their friends in Rome for help. The Romans destroyed Entremont, establishing the Roman stronghold of Aquae Sextiae Salluviolum (Aix-en-Provence) at its base. Addressing the need to protect their trade route to Spain, the Romans established garrisons in towns between the Alps and the Pyrenees, and the huge Provincia Romana—the first Roman province outside Italy—was born.

Provincia Romana (118 B.C.–A.D. 476)

After Julius Caesar's total conquest of Gaul in 58–51 B.C., the Romans created a prosperous province, where they would remain for 600 peaceful years. Nîmes, Aix, and Arles became important Roman cities, while colonies at Glanum and

Drystone dwellings, called *bories*, have been built in the Luberon since prehistoric times.

Vaison-la-Romaine thrived. Throughout Provincia Romana, enormous monuments and landmarks were built, including amphitheaters, arenas, bathhouses, temples, and stadiums, many of which remain standing in well-preserved glory. Roman engineering was applied to transportation (including a road system that spread from Italy to Spain) and the water supply (the Pont du Gard near Nîmes being one of the most striking reminders).

Meantime, Massalia, in recognition of its support for Rome, was allowed to stay an independent state within the Roman territory. Alas, the city made the lethal mistake of siding with Pompey rather than Caesar during Rome's civil war in 49 B.C. After Caesar rose to power, he punished the town by taking away its independence and transferring its possessions to Arles, Narbonne, and Fréjus. The city nevertheless went on to flourish as an intellectual center whose universities rivaled those of Athens—the last outpost of Greek culture in the West.

The conversion of Constantine the Great to Christianity in A.D. 312 marked the beginning of the end for the Roman Empire. The new religion reached Provence, and soon monasteries and churches were replacing Roman temples.

Age of Invasions (Fifth–Tenth Centuries A.D.)

The Western Roman Empire expired in A.D. 476, heralded by invasions from several Germanic tribes: the Burgundians (of Scandinavia), Ostragoths (East Goths, from the Black Sea area), and, most notably, the Visigoths (West Goths, from the Danube Delta region in Transylvania). In the sixth century, another Germanic tribe, the Franks, gained the upper hand. Marseille, Arles, and Avignon rebelled and were brutally squashed, and Provence

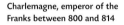

Charlemagne, emperor of the Franks between 800 and 814

was absorbed into a mix of duchies and kingdoms of western and central Europe that would form the historic kernel of modern-day France and Germany.

Provence remained under Frankish rule beneath the great Carolingian rulers (including Charlemagne) until 843, when the Treaty of Verdun broke up their kingdom. The ninth and tenth centuries saw further invasions, by the Normans, and even the Hungarians, who sacked Nîmes in 924.

But it was the Saracens—a generic term for Muslim invaders—who raised most havoc. Although Provence at first formed an alliance with this marauding force to fight the Franks, skirmishes soon erupted between the forces that lasted for centuries. The villagers withdrew to hilltops where they built fortified towns—many of Provence's *villages perchés* (perched villages) come from this chaotic time. The Saracens were defeated in several battles, but only in A.D. 972, when William the Liberator (Guillaume le Libérateur), count of Arles, attacked their stronghold at La Garde-Freinet in the Massif des Maures, was their threat eliminated once and for all.

Medieval Provence (1000–1300)

In 1032 Provence was absorbed into the Holy Roman Empire. With the power base so far away in southern Germany, however, towns became fiercely independent, and battling barons and shifting alliances occurred with little interference from overlords.

One bright light was the huge expansion of churches, led by Marseille's Abbaye de St.-Victor. This was the era of pilgrimages, especially to St.-Trophime in Arles and St.-Guilhem near Aniane, while the Crusades were launched in 1095. At the same time, Provence (as elsewhere in Europe) experienced a spectacular flowering of architecture, poetry, and music. Traveling from castle to castle, troubadours sang Europe's first lyric poetry.

Sometime in the 11th century, a small dynasty awarded itself the title of counts of Provence. When the line died out in 1113, the title passed to the counts of Barcelona. The clever Raymond Bérenger V (1209–1245), the first Catalan count to reside permanently in the new Provençal capital of Aix, had high hopes of creating a great Mediterranean empire. He married his daughter Béatrice, heiress of Provence, to Charles d'Anjou, brother of Louis IX (St.-Louis), king of France. After Bérenger's death in 1245, the Comte de Provence (county of Provence) passed to the House of Anjou.

The Pope's Jews

In medieval times, when Jews were forced to convert to Christianity throughout Europe, they found a safe refuge in the papal enclave of Comtat-Venaissin—a place where Protestants, heretics, agnostics, and atheists were not allowed. Granted, they didn't have complete freedom: They were limited to three trades (secondhand textiles, used furniture, and limited money lending); men had to wear a yellow badge and women a piece of yellow fabric on their bonnets; and they lived in crammed quarters in Avignon, L'Isle-sur-la-Sorgue, Cavaillon, and Carpentras. Life was not fabulous by any means, but the pope's protection allowed them to survive—and to openly practice their faith. For more than five centuries, their services ended with a prayer to "exalt our sovereign and Holy Father, the pope."

The Popes Come to Avignon (1309–1417)

Fed up with bickering in Rome, French-born Clément V (R. 1305–1314) moved the papal court to Avignon in 1309. Eight more popes followed, ruling the Roman Catholic Church until 1376 from this vassal city of the Holy See. The third pope, Benoît XII (R. 1334–1342) began work on the Palais des Papes (Palace of the Popes). His successor, aristocrat Clément VI (R. 1342–1352), found the palace austere and simple, and so he built a second, more elegant one.

During this time, Avignon and the surrounding area, called the Comtat-Venaissin, experienced a cultural renaissance, with the expansion of new industries such as glassmaking and paper manufacturing and the rise of an artistic school, now known as the Provençal Primitives or the Avignon school. At the same time, the venality of the papal court caused the city to become infamously corrupt.

Pope Grégoire XI (R. 1370–1378) finally succeeded in reestablishing the Holy See in Rome, in 1377. The French cardinals, however, selected their own pope, Clément VII, which led to the Great Schism of the Occident. During this time there were two popes, one in Rome and one in Avignon. The schism lasted for nearly 40 years, until 1417, when Martin V established himself in Rome.

More Medieval Happenings (1348–1536)

The Black Death entered through the port of Marseille in 1348, decimating the city's population. At the same time, feudal despots such as the seigneurs of Les Baux added to a general sense of fear and confusion.

By 1409, however, things seemed to be improving. Louis II of Anjou, a most capable ruler, founded the University of Aix. His son, Bon Roi René of Anjou (Good King Rene; 1409–1480), brought an artistic revival to his court, and during his reign, Aix became Provence's star city. René was the last count of Provence to rule, and, after his death, Provence became part of France. Holy Roman Emperor Charles V took the opportunity to invade Provence between 1524 and 1536 as part of the French-Italian Wars.

Wars of Religion & Beyond (1545–1720)

Brought on by the Reformation, the Wars of Religion between the Catholics and "heretic" Protestants occupied the latter part of the 16th century. Protestant enclaves had taken hold in Orange, Haute-Provence, the Luberon, and especially in Nîmes, where three-quarters of the population became Huguenot (French Protestant). The Catholics became determined to rout them all out. Shocking massacres ensued, along with the wholesale destruction of churches (including St.-Gilles).

Hostilities ended with the 1598 Edict of Nantes, in which Henri IV guaranteed Protestants civil and religious liberties. The uneasy peace lasted until 1685, when Louis XIV revoked the edict and persecution of Protestants ensued again.

In the 17th and 18th centuries, regional alliances decreased as a national awareness grew. Towns expanded with elegant town houses (*hôtels particuliers*), and châteaux proliferated. Despite economic development in the textile industry and the growth of the ports at Toulon and Marseille, this was a tough period for many, culminating in the devastating plague of 1720. Introduced in Marseille, the plague killed more than half of the city's population and spread as far as Aix and Arles.

> In the 17th and 18th centuries ... towns expanded with elegant town houses (*hôtels particuliers*), and châteaux proliferated.

Revolution (1789–1795)

Sharing the general population's discontent with the royalty, the Provençaux enthusiastically joined forces with the revolutionaries in 1789. In Marseille a guillotine was set up along La Canebière, which some say saw as many royalist heads rolling as the one in Paris. One of Provence's biggest contributions came from Marseille's National Guard, who, as they marched north to Paris, sang a cheery little tune composed several months earlier during the war against Prussia, called "Chant de Guerre de l'Armée du Rhin" ("Battle Hymn of the Rhine Army"). Later it was rechristened "La Marseillaise" and adopted as the French national anthem.

During this time, anarchy reigned throughout France. Many châteaux were destroyed, while churches were desecrated and cathedrals turned into temples of reason.

Territorial Reshufflings (1790–1860)

In 1790 Provence was divided into three départements: the Var, Bouches-du-Rhône, and Basse-Alps (Lower Alps). France's annexation of papal Avignon and the surrounding Comtat-Venaissin two years later paved the way for the creation of another département—the Vaucluse.

Revolutionary forces seized Nice from Italy in 1793, as well as Monaco, which heretofore had been recognized as an independent state ruled by the Grimaldi family. The British, taking advantage of the confusion, occupied Toulon in 1793, only to be chased away by 24-year-old Napoléon Bonaparte. The young Corsican would go on to take power in 1799 (see pp. 156–157).

In 1814 France lost the territories it had seized in 1793. Nice and its surrounding lands went to Victor Emmanuel I, king of Sardinia. The next year, Napoléon escaped from his exile on Elba, stepping ashore at Golfe-Juan with his boatfuls of supporters. They marched north (on what's today called the Route Napoléon) to Paris, where he returned to power.

Revolting against high taxes, Menton and Roquebrune declared themselves independent from Monaco in 1848. In 1860 Charles III, king of Monaco, ceded rights to these towns to France in exchange for Monaco's recognition as an independent state.

The last major territorial shift saw Nice and its hinterlands returned from the House of Savoy in 1860.

Belle Époque (1840–1910)

With the Second Empire (1852–1870) came the effort to revive the Provençal culture and language, spearheaded by Frédéric Mistral. He was one of seven young poets who in 1854 began the Félibrige Movement, devoted to the cause (see sidebar p. 35).

At the same time, industrialization was transforming the region. The Suez Canal's opening in 1869 and the expansion of France's colonies brought increased port traffic—and wealth—to Marseille. The coastal railway, an engineering marvel with its tunnels and high bridges, reached Toulon in 1856, Nice in 1865, and Monaco in 1868. In 1864 work began on the road between Nice and Monaco.

Above all, this era saw the development of coastal Provence as the playground of the rich and famous. First came the English gentlemen on their culture-polishing Grand

---

EXPERIENCE: Help Restore History

For more than 45 years, Henri and Simone Gignoux have lovingly worked on restoring St.-Victor-la-Coste to perfection—using solely traditional techniques. You can join the volunteers who arrive every April through October at this medieval village located between Nîmes and Avignon to help repair the castle ramparts, build pathways, and clear the terrace garden. No experience is required. You'll stay in bare-bones but cozy quarters right in the historic village, with meals cooked from local ingredients and served under the shade of fruit trees. A typical day involves working in the morning, relaxing in the heat of the afternoon, with Thursdays off to explore the surrounding region. The cost is $500 per week, including accommodation, meals, and activities. For more information, contact **La Sabranenque** (www.sabranenque.com).

REMPART (rempart.com) offers similar programs at heritage sites throughout France.

Members of the maquis Résistance, who helped fight the Nazi garrison in Marseille before the entry of Allied troops, celebrate the city's liberation in September 1944.

Tour, followed by wealthy French, English, Americans, and Russians who built grandiose winter villas in Nice and Hyères. Nice's chic promenade des Anglais was created in 1822, and in 1834, Lord Brougham, former lord chancellor of England, was held over in the small fishing village of Cannes and declared that he liked it so much, he would build a villa there. His friends and countrymen followed.

Royalty, too, wintered along the Riviera, including Queen Victoria, Aga Khan, and Empress Eugénie, the wife of Napoléon III. After Stéphane Liégeard published the first guidebook to the French coast in 1887, titled *La Côte d'Azur,* the region had a name.

World War I & the Interwar

Provence lost one out of every five men in World War I. The bright side was that, with the south's reliance on tourism rather than industry, the 1920s and '30s saw the explosion of glitz and glamour, with regal hotels built in Nice and Cannes. Socialites Sara and Gerald Murphy built Villa America on Cap d'Antibes and invited their friends—including Ernest Hemingway and F. Scott Fitzgerald—to frolic in the summer sun, thereby inventing the Summer Season. The first casino opened in 1929 in the Palais de la Méditerranée in Nice, the creation of American railroad magnate Frank Jay Gould. A paid summer vacation under the Socialist Front Populaire in 1936 meant even more tourists flocked to the region.

World War II

After Paris fell in June 1940, the south became part of the *zone libre,* or free zone (though Menton and its northern Vallée de la Roya were occupied by the Italians). The Côte d'Azur, especially Nice, became known as a safe haven from occupied France, and by 1942 some 43,000 Jews had come to seek refuge. Monaco remained neutral throughout the war.

With Nazi Germany's invasion of Vichy France in 1942, Provence was at war. German troops occupied the south, and the southern Résistance became active.

When the Nazis moved to confiscate French warships at Toulon in 1942, the French scuttled the major portion of their fleet to prevent Germans from seizing them. The Germans responded by invading Toulon, while Italians took over Nice. In January 1943 Hitler gave the 40,000 residents of Marseille's Le Panier quarter—a popular refuge for Jews and Résistance leaders—24 hours to pack up and leave, or face incarceration. The whole neighborhood was duly razed.

Provence was finally freed ten weeks after D-Day, on August 15, 1944, when Allied forces landed in a two-pronged attack centered on the Var. The Italian-occupied Vallée de la Roya was finally returned to France in 1947.

Modern Provence

Cannes's International Film Festival in 1947 brought back a sense of normalcy to postwar Côte d'Azur, as well as rocketing Cannes into the role of Europe's film capital. Over the next couple decades, the Côte d'Azur went on to become known worldwide as the glittery enclave of stars, money, and high living. Prince Rainier III's fairytale wedding in 1956 to Hollywood film princess Grace Kelly added to the mystique.

Provence was finally freed ten weeks after D-Day, on August 15, 1944, when Allied forces landed in a two-pronged attack centered on the Var.

Algeria in 1962 achieved independence, sending some 750,000 impoverished, newly homeless *pieds noirs* ("black feet," as Algerian-born French people were known) to France. Many settled in Provence, especially in Marseille, Toulon, and Nice, setting off a wave of strong anti-immigrant sentiment. More and more outsiders (mostly British) began coming to Provence in the late 1970s to restore charming old *mas* (farmhouses), exemplified by Peter Mayle's *A Year in Provence*—whose publication in 1990 brought even more hordes, especially to the Luberon.

Corruption reigned in the 1980s and '90s, topped off with the antics of Jacques Médécin, Nice's right-wing mayor who, during his 38-year stint, was found guilty twice of income tax evasion. Socialist President François Mitterand, elected in 1981, created regional governments across France—a major turning point in the centuries-old pursuit of Parisian centralism.

In the mid-1990s, the extreme-right Front National (FN), spearheaded by Jean-Marie Le Pen, won victories in municipal elections in Toulon, Orange, and Marignane in 1995, and in Vitrolles in 1997. The FN failed to make any headway in national politics until the 2002 presidential elections, when Le Pen stunned the nation by earning 4.8 million votes (16.7 percent) in the primary election. Since then, Le Pen's daughter, Marine, has taken the helm.

With the new millennium came the opening of the TGV Méditerranée, cutting travel time between Paris and Marseille to three hours. The whole region is already feeling the effects of the Euroméditerranée free trade zone, of which Marseille has been chosen to be the central hub. As part of this international economic initiative, the city has been well funded to transform itself into a booming business center and tourist attraction—a far cry from the rural image that has been associated with Provence since its beginnings. ■

The Arts

Provence's exquisite landscape, ever shining sun and blue skies, and traditional culture have long inspired artists and writers, all of whom have striven to interpret this magical place in their own style, their own words. The result: An extraordinary wealth of works that celebrate Provence by the likes of such luminaries as van Gogh, Cézanne, Dufy, and Picasso (to name a few).

Architecture

Provence's greatest architectural influence came from the Romans. During their 600-year occupation of Provincia Romana, they built classical-style aqueducts, fortifications, marketplaces, temples, amphitheaters, triumphal arches, and bathhouses using large blocks of limestone. While they copied Greek architectural forms, they added their own flourish—massive rounded arches, vaults, and domes, for instance. Some of their buildings still exist, including the great amphitheaters at Nîmes and Arles and the theater at Orange.

Invaders chased villagers to hilltops beginning in the Middle Ages, where they built towns protected by fortified walls and gates. These *villages perchés* have survived as today's picturesque hill towns—Bonnieux, Gordes, and Grimaud among them.

A religious renewal in the 11th century allowed Provence to develop its own distinct architectural approach, called Provençal Romanesque. Combining the classic order and perfection of Roman design with new styles from northern and southern Europe, it featured round Roman arches, barrel vaulting, heavy walls with few windows, and little ornamentation. The best examples include the three Cistercian abbeys: Sénanque (1148), Le Thoronet (1160), and Silvacane (1175).

Ironwork Bell Towers

Skeletal bell towers grace Provence's church steeples, a centuries-old design that yields to damaging mistral winds. Gusts blow right through the light, open, wrought-iron framework, carrying the bells' melodic tolling far and wide. Some bell towers are highly ornamental, others plain and simple, but all are exclusively Provençal.

The Gothic style, which flourished throughout northern France in the mid-12th through 16th centuries, did not make much headway into southern France. Avignon's Palais des Papes is the south's supreme showcase, while other important examples are the Val de Benediction Charterhouse in Villeneuve-lez-Avignon, the basilica at St.-Maximin-de-la-Ste.-Baume, and Carpentras's Cathédrale St.-Siffrein.

The Renaissance and its illuminating rebirth of culture likewise barely touched Provence. During the 1600s, citadel architecture, spearheaded by Sébastien le Prestre de Vauban (1633–1707), was the period's most notable contribution (see sidebar p. 152).

Moving into the 18th century, the Italian baroque spilled over Provence's eastern borders, especially into the churches of Menton and Nice. With classic architecture as a base, the style dripped with a profusion of paintings, sculptures, and gilded adornments. Nice's St.-Jacques and Cathédrale Ste.-Réparate and Menton's St.-Michel show off full-blown baroque style.

Beginning about 1740, neoclassicism encompassed a renewed interest in classical

Great military architect Vauban oversaw the construction of Entrevaux's 17th-century hilltop citadel.

forms normally associated with antiquity—columns, simple geometric shapes, traditional ornamentation—that showed stability and permanence during increasingly turbulent times. In domestic buildings it's seen in elegant facades graced with elaborate doorway carvings and windows (as in the buildings of Aix's Mazarin Quarter).

Belle époque architects—who reigned between 1870 and 1914—made play with all historical styles according to their fantasies: Arabesque palaces rose beside medieval and neo-Gothic châteaus, "wedding cakes" beside "chocolate boxes." The extravagant trimmings often included decorative stucco friezes and trompe l'oeil paintings. The finest collection of belle époque villas is found in Nice (see sidebar p. 168).

France's most celebrated 20th-century architect is Charles Édouard Jeanneret, aka Le Corbusier (1887–1965), one of the major instigators of the International Style. Le Corbusier interpreted objects akin to cubist painters, pioneering a philosophy of functionality summarized in his famous dictum: "Buildings are machines to live in." His greatest work in Provence is Marseille's massive Cité Radieuse (1946–1952; see p. 123).

Peille's vaulted passageways and cobbled lanes epitomize the architecture of medieval *villages perchés.*

More recently, ultramodern styles have been used for many art galleries, most notably the Musée d'Art Moderne et d'Art Contemporain in Nice (1990), Sir Norman Foster's Carré d'Art in Nîmes (1993), and Rudy Ricciotti's Musée des Civilisations de l'Europe et de la Méditerranée (2013) and Musée Jean Cocteau–Collection Séverin Wunderman (2011) in Menton.

A discussion of Provence's architecture is not complete with touching upon the vernacular—seen most prominently in the traditional stone-built *mas* (farmhouses) speckling the countryside, as well as the *cabanes* of the Camargue *gardians.* In both, thick, stone walls, small windows, heavy shutters, and reinforced doors ward off the brutal mistral wind and relentless summer sun.

Provençal Literature

Beautiful writings have graced Provence's culture since the Middle Ages, when troubadours sang lyrical poems throughout the region's courts. Writing in the ancient *langue d'oc* (see sidebar p. 17), Provence's most celebrated troubadours included Bernart de Ventadorn and Raimbaut de Vacqueyras. Provençal literature declined after Provence was annexed to France in 1481 and French evolved into the official language. Some writers, however, continued to write in the ancient tongue. Among the more notable was Grasse native Louis Bellaud, better known as Bellaud de la Bellaudière (1532–1588).

The name most closely related to the Provençal movement is that of poet Frédéric Mistral (1830–1914), who wrote solely in the ancient language and was also largely responsible for the late 19th-century revival in Provençal literature (see sidebar opposite).

Provence's French-Language Literature: Physician and astrologer Nostra-damus, born in St.-Rémy in 1503, became famous with *Les Centuries* (1555), a book of more than a thousand prophesies in verse quatrains. He died in Salon-de-Provence in 1566, of gout, as he had predicted.

The controversial Marquis de Sade (1740–1814), who owned a castle at Lacoste in the Luberon, led a life of criminal debauchery for which he was condemned to death in 1772. He passed his sentence both at the Bastille and the Vincennes dungeon, writing his best known works: *Justine, ou les Malheurs de la Vertu; Juliette, ou les Prospérités du Vice;* and *La Philosophie dans le Boudoir.* Though many consider his writings licentious and obscene, some critics stress his importance as a precursor of Nietzsche's Superman.

Nîmes-born Alphonse Daudet (1840–1897) spent a considerable amount of time with Mistral in Maillane, though he wrote in French, not Provençal. His Romantic drama *L'Arlésienne* was later set to music by Bizet, but the novelist is chiefly remembered for *Lettres de Mon Moulin (Letters from My Windmill),* a collection of sentimental yet humorous sketches portraying Provençal life and culture that was published in 1866.

In the 20th century, Jean Giono (1895–1970), a native of Manosque, celebrated the Provençal Alps and their people in rich poetic language. Among his most famous works is *Le Hussard sur le Toit (The Horseman on the Roof),* made into a movie in 1995. His contemporary, playwright Marcel Pagnol (1895–1974), was only incidentally a novelist. In 1952 Pagnol filmed *Manon des Sources* near La Treille, and the movie was so successful that he wrote a novel, *L'Eau des Collines* (1962), comprising *Jean de Florette* and *Manon des Sources.*

The early writings of St.-Tropez resident Françoise Sagan (1935–2004) addressed the rebelliousness and cynicism of her peers in French bourgeoisie. Her 1954 novel, *Bonjour Tristesse (Hello Sadness),* was set on the Côte d'Azur.

Expats Answering Provence's Muse: Many foreign writers have succumbed to Provence's allure. The earliest was Italian poet Petrarch (1304–1374), who moved to Avignon with his father at age nine. There in 1327 he cast eyes on the lovely but married Laura de Noves, to whom he wrote 366 love sonnets and ballads. Tortured by his unrequited love (and fed up with papal corruption),

Frédéric Mistral

Early on a lover of the Provençal traditions and language, poet Frédéric Mistral (1830–1914) devoted his life to preserving Provence's age-old ways. While presenting the purity of the Provençal language in his writings, he extolled the beauty of Provence's countryside and people. Among his most famous works are *Mirèio* (1859), the epic story of two star-crossed lovers, and *Calendau* (1867), about Provençal fishermen. Over 20 years he also compiled a dictionary of the Provençal language, dialects, beliefs, and traditions, the *Lou Tresor doù Felibrige (Treasury of Félibres).* With six other writer friends, Mistral in 1854 founded the Félibres, a group of militant Provençal writers determined to save southern France's original language. He went on to win the Nobel Prize in literature in 1904 and used his prize money to establish the Museon Arlaten in Arles that same year. Although there are vestiges today of a lively Provençal literature, it's increasingly the language of the past.

he moved to Fontaine-de-Vaucluse, where he wrote his *Canzoniere* songbook for her. With that, he became one of the greatest Renaissance poets and, along with Dante, among the first to write in vernacular Italian.

Many centuries later, during the "great days" of the 1920s and '30s, British novelist Somerset Maugham lived on Cap-Ferrat. He set little of his fiction in Provence, however, apart from two short stories: "The Three Fat Women of Antibes" and "The Facts of Life." American F. Scott Fitzgerald (1896–1940) is probably the most famous expat author. He and his wife, Zelda, spent summers on Cap-Ferrat, playing and partying with Ernest Hemingway and other Americans.

Painting

Provence's first painters were Upper Paleolithic–era inhabitants who adorned the Grotte Cosquer, near Marseille, with dozens of painted and etched horses, stags, bison, auks, and human hands. Any significant contribution to the painting movement, however, didn't come about until the 14th century, when the popes moved to Avignon (1309–1417) and hired some of Italy's finest artists to decorate their

Vincent van Gogh captured a clear St.-Rémy night in "Nuit Etoilée" ("Starry Night"; 1889), just one of his flurry of canvases completed during his stay in Provence in 1888–1889.

Palais des Papes. Foremost among the talented group was Simone Martini of Siena (1280–1344) and his assistant, Matteo Giovannetti of Viterbo. Their magnificent frescoes fuse Italian naturalism with French Gothic in a refined, elegant style that became known in Western European courts as International Gothic.

The Avignon school developed in the early 15th century, assimilating International Gothic with the precise techniques of Flemish masters and producing some of the greatest paintings in the history of French art. Two northern masters headed the movement, Enguerrand Charenton (or Quarton; circa 1416–1466) and Nicolas Froment (1435–1486). Charenton's tragic "Avignon Pietà," his best known work, now hangs in the Louvre, but one major painting survives in Provence: his panel of "Le Couronnement de la Vierge" ("The Coronation of the Virgin"; 1453), now in Villeneuve-lez-Avignon's Musée Municipal. Froment is best known for his "Le Buisson Ardent" ("Burning Bush"; 1475–1476), a minutely observed triptych hanging in Aix's cathedral (see p. 110).

The Bréa family, above all Louis Bréa (1450–1523), dominated the school of Nice, which flourished in the 15th and 16th centuries and marked the transition between medieval and Renaissance art (Nice was then a part of Italy). They illuminated the altarpieces of many churches in Nice and the nearby countryside. Louis's first known work is a triptych of the Pietà (1475), in the parish church at Cimiez.

An interest in sentiment and emotion in the 18th century rooted itself in the painting world as Romanticism, headed by Eugène Delacroix and Jean-Auguste-Dominique Ingres. Provence's virtuoso romantic painter was Grasse-born Jean-Honoré Fragonard (1732–1806). Fragonard's fame heightened in 1771, when he painted for Louis XV's pleasure-loving court. Some of his works are on display at the Villa-Musée Fragonard in Grasse.

Postimpressionism & Modern Art: In the 19th and 20th centuries, artists discovered Provence's luminescent light and unparalleled scenery. One of the most influential artists of this time is Paul Cézanne (1839–1906), of Aix-en-Provence. Having spent some time in Paris and Auvers-sur-Oise, he returned south in 1870 to escape the Franco-Prussian War. Here the Impressionist contemporary entered a later phase built around a few basic subjects: still lifes of studio objects focused on recurring elements such as apples, statuary, and tablecloths; studies of bathers; and, above all, successive views of nearby Montagne Ste.-Victoire. He captured this stark limestone mountain on canvas more than a hundred times, trying to see the "cylinder, the sphere, and the cone in its form," a thought process that heralds cubism. Though no major Cézanne works are in Provence, a handful of minor ones are found at Aix's Musée Granet.

> ## Van Gogh's greatest paintings were done during his two years in Provence, including "The Night Café on the Place LaMartine, Arles."

Vincent van Gogh's (1853–1890) greatest paintings were done during his two years in Provence, including "Le Café de Nuit Sur l'Endroit Lamartine, Arles" ("The Night Café on the Place Lamartine, Arles") and "La Maison Jaune" ("The Yellow House"), painted in 1888. He came to Arles from Paris that year, in the hopes of establishing an Académie du Midi. Fighting his own demons, he threatened his friend and mentor Paul Gauguin (1848–1903), whom he had convinced to join him in Provence, on the street with a razor and cut off part of his own ear. He was taken to the Hôtel-Dieu (now Éspace Van Gogh), then in May 1889 voluntarily confined himself to an asylum in St.-Rémy. Here he painted flowers (including his famous "Irises") and views of the asylum garden. He left for Auvers-sur-Oise in May 1890, where the disturbed artist, at the height of his genius, produced 76 more paintings before allegedly committing suicide on July 27.

When Henri Matisse and André Derain happened upon some of van Gogh's paintings at the Galerie Bernheim-Jeune in Paris in 1901, they were inspired by his simplified forms and vibrant colors. Along with Georges Rouault, Maurice de Vlaminck, Raoul Dufy, and Kees van Dongen, they showed their own van Gogh–inspired works— mostly painted along the Côte d'Azur, especially La Ciotat, Cassis, and L'Éstaque—at the Salon d'Automne in 1905. An art critic described the room as a *cage aux fauves* (cage of wild beasts)—the term "fauve" was born.

Other artists discovered the Côte d'Azur's allure around the turn of the 20th century. In 1892 pointillist painter Paul Signac (1863–1935) visited St.-Tropez and was so bedazzled by its beauty that he bought a house there. One of the founders of the Nabis, Pierre Bonnard (1867–1947) lived in Le Cannet for more than 20 years until his death. During this time he developed a style that united color and light, offering a transition from Impressionism to abstract art.

> **Probably the south's most influential artist in this world of influential artists was Pablo Picasso (1881–1973).**

The biggest name of this period, however, was an aging Pierre-Auguste Renoir (1841–1919), who visited the coast in the late 1890s for health reasons. The Impressionist eventually bought a house and studio at Cagnes-sur-Mer, where he painted "Les Grandes Baigneuses" in 1887.

Interwar & Beyond: Henri Matisse (1869–1954) began developing an interest in color after seeing a group of Impressionist works in Brittany. His real discovery, however, had come when he visited Paul Signac in St.-Tropez in 1904, which inspired his "Luxe, Calme, et Volupté." The next year, Matisse went to Collioure in Roussillon with his friend Derain, where he created the first major work, "Le Bonheur de Vivre" ("The Happiness of Life"). From there, he took his own road, full of color and Middle Eastern mystique. He first visited Nice in 1917 and, enchanted by the brilliant and sensual environment, began spending his winters there two years later. His crowning achievement was the Chapelle du Rosaire in Vence, a chapel that he designed in its entirety.

Inspired by Cézanne and early cubism, Fernand Léger (1881–1955) developed a distinct style in which he used simple lines and blocks of color to depict urban and machine imagery, as well as scenes of proletariat life. Upon his death, his wife opened a museum devoted to him in Biot.

Probably the south's most influential artist in this world of influential artists was Pablo Picasso (1881–1973). The flamboyant Spaniard came to Antibes in 1945 where, beneath the brilliant Midi sun, he produced exuberant masterpiece after masterpiece. The standout is his "Joie de Vivre" ("Joy of Life"; 1946), a lighthearted, whimsical depiction of his latest lover, Françoise Gilot, as a dancing woman-flower bathed in light and

Sporting a bullfighter's hat, Pablo Picasso (center) enjoys a mock bullfight in Vallauris in 1955 with artist pal Jean Cocteau (to his right). Picasso revitalized the town's ceramics industry.

surrounded by flute-playing centaurs and fauns. Most of his works, including "Joie de Vivre," hang at the Château Grimaldi in Antibes, where he had his studio.

French-Russian painter Marc Chagall (1887–1985) is best known for his joyful illustrations of folk tales and Bible stories, though he also worked as a designer of book illustrations, stage sets, and stained-glass windows. He moved to Vence in 1950, where he first attempted painting and modeling ceramics and, a few years later, created his first mosaics. Nice's Musée National Message Biblique Marc Chagall showcases his interpretations of the Bible on vast, colorful canvases. He is buried in St.-Paul-de-Vence.

Hungarian-born Victor Vasarely (1908–1997) was a major pioneer of op art, a style that uses hard-edged black and white or colored patterns that appear to vibrate and change their shape as the viewer looks at them. The Fondation Vasarely in Aix-en-Provence showcases 42 of his works.

Eventually, as the focus of art shifted across the Atlantic, Provence lost its artistic limelight. There are still pockets of innovation, however. In the 1960s, Nice became the center of nouveau réalisme, the French version of pop art. Leading members were Yves Klein, Martial Raysse, and Arman, all of whose works can be seen in Nice's Musée d'Art Moderne et Contemporain. The geometrically abstract Support, Surface Group emerged in Nice in 1969, founded by Claude Viallat (1936–). And today, the region's devotion to contemporary art is alive and well, in part thanks to the efforts of BOTOX(S) *(botoxs.fr),* an association devoted to defending, representing, and promoting contemporary art.

Grace Kelly and Cary Grant lounge on a beach in the 1955 classic *To Catch a Thief.*

Cinema

When cinematography pioneers Auguste and Louis Lumière showed their two-minute reel of a train pulling into La Ciotat's train station *(L'Entrée d'un Train en Gare de La Ciotat* or *The Arrival of a Train at La Ciotat Station),* moviegoers were startled out of their seats. The year was 1895, the place their father's Château Lumière in La Ciotat, and Provence has been involved in the film world ever since.

Seeking greater independence, Hollywood producer Rex Ingram (1893–1950) bought Victorine film studios in Nice in 1925. His first silent movie, *Mare Nostrum* (1926), was a spy story involving German submarines. Writer and director Marcel Pagnol (1895–1974) built studios near Marseille in 1934, and over the next decade he devoted himself almost entirely to making films, with dialogue written for the southern accent—including *La Femme du Boulanger* (*The Baker's Wife,* 1938).

Cannes donned its cloak of glamour in 1946 when movie stars hit La Croisette during the first Cannes International Film Festival. Every May, the city still fills with stars, as films from all over the globe are judged. But it is also a serious marketplace, where much wheeling and dealing of films and talent take place.

After a wartime slump, Provence's movie industry perked up in 1956 with *Et Dieu Créa la Femme (And God Created Woman),* a low-budget flick starring an unknown Brigitte Bardot. The movie proved to French film financiers that young directors could make commercial successes, helping to pave the way for the *nouvelle vague.* Aggressive, unorthodox, influential, these "new wave" directors have become some of the film industry's biggest names: Jean-Luc Godard, François Truffaut, Louis Malle. The breakthrough came in 1959 with Truffaut's *Les Quatre Cents Coups* and Alain Resnais's *Hiroshima Mon Amour.*

Though the new wave has lost its edge, Provence continues to be a favorite backdrop among filmmakers and a playground for the stars. ■

Fabled Provence, with vineyards, lavender, burgeoning market stalls, and Roman ruins abounding throughout

Avignon & the Vaucluse

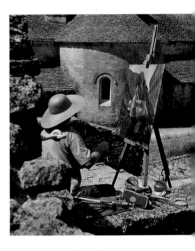

Capturing the Abbaye de Sénanque on canvas

Avignon & the Vaucluse

Named after the closed valley that harbors the Fontaine-de-Vaucluse, this dreamy region of perched villages, ocher cliffs, rocky limestone mountains, and endless vineyards fans out north and east from its capital of Avignon. The Romans left behind columns, bridges, and triumphal arches, but it was the arrival of the popes in the 14th century that changed the area forever.

Snuggled inside ancient city walls along the River Rhône, Avignon is the area's largest town, its high point being the impressive Palais des Papes, the popes' lavish residence for nearly a century. Known for their ostentatious lifestyle, bringing grapes, melons, and an entire new outlook on art, architecture, and theater, the popes heralded a new era of culture and good living that's still celebrated today. But there's much more here, including several art and cultural museums and a famous theater festival every July.

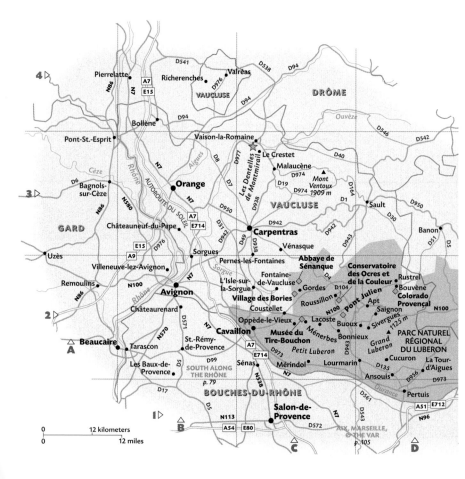

The Luberon

Eastward lies the fabled Luberon, the idyllic countryside that everyone pictures at the mention of Provence, with its vibrant fields, blooming flowers, and toylike hill towns. The Marquis de Sade left his imprint in Lacoste's château (bought by Pierre Cardin for summer theater and a private residence), while the villages of Ménerbes, Bonnieux, and Oppède-le-Vieux have their own charms. Lesser known Luberon includes tiny hamlets far off the tourist track, including Lourmarin, whose château is known as the "Médicis Villa of Provence" for the number of writers and artists it has fostered through the years.

Brilliant red ocher tinges the soil around Roussillon, where a short trail wanders through the whimsical formations of a disused ocher quarry. Gordes has perched on its clifftop aerie since the 16th century, its Renaissance château towering above. The nearby Village des Bories is a small settlement of drystone dwellings dating from the 17th century (though the technology is much older), while down the road, the Abbaye de Sénanque, founded in 1148, is an iconic lavender destination.

NOT TO BE MISSED:

Avignon's grandiose Palais des Papes 45–49

Sipping an apéritif at Lacoste's Café de France 54

The vibrantly colorful Sentier des Ocres in Roussillon 57

The Abbaye de Sénanque's lavender fields in full bloom 59

Finding antique treasure at L'Isle-sur-la-Sorgue's Sunday market 62

Wine-tasting in the Dentelles 66–67

Taking in Orange's ancient Roman theater 68–71

Ducking into wine caves at Châteauneuf-du-Pape 74–75

North of Avignon

The towns of L'Isle-sur-la-Sorgue and Fontaine-de-Vaucluse grew up on the River Sorgue. The former is best known for its antique markets, while the latter's mystique swirls around the seemingly endless spring that feeds the river. How deep is it? No one knows. Both are picturesque but touristy towns, with Fontaine-de-Vaucluse offering a plethora of museums, including one devoted to former resident Petrarch and another to the Résistance movement during World War II.

Roman ruins abound in Vaison-la-Romaine, a picturesque town with an upper and lower village, spanned by an ancient Roman bridge. Vaison is the starting point for a drive around Les Dentelles de Montmirail, showcasing the hilly, vine-striped beauty of the Côtes du Rhône countryside. More Roman relics await in Orange, including Europe's best preserved theater, where performances still are held. ■

ALPES-DE-HAUTE-PROVENCE

D951

N96

D13

D4

N100

Forcalquier

D13

ALPES PROVENÇALES
p. 185

N96 A51

E712 D4

Valensole

Manosque

N96

D952

D23

VAR

AVIGNON &
THE VAUCLUSE

ITALY

Area of map detail

E

Avignon

The popes built the Palais des Papes—Avignon's Gothic fortress-palace—in the 14th century to rule the Roman Catholic Church from here. Today, a lively university city bustles in its empty shadow. A longtime papal tradition, the city's devotion to the arts springs alive every July with the joyful Festival d'Avignon.

The Palais des Papes harks back to Avignon's early days as the papal center of power.

Market Days

Daily except Mon.

Avignon

A 42 B2

Visitor Information

✉ Office de Tourisme, 41 cours Jean-Jaurès

☎ 04 32 74 32 74

avignon-tourisme.com

DISCOUNT CARD:
Available at the tourism office or participating stores, the Avignon Passion card provides ticket reductions to monuments and museums.

Avignon's role as Vatican of the north began in 1309, when Pope Clément V fled Rome to escape political infighting. His successor, John XXII, chose to stay in town, and the third pope, Benoît XII, built the magnificent palace. Over the next several decades, the ecclesiastical lordships held extravagant court with much feasting, arts, and culture as befitting their high office, while the city became an international meeting place of pilgrims, diplomats, ecclesiasts, and courtiers. The acclaimed poet Petrarch spent much of his early life here, but Simone Martini, the

great Sienese painter, served the pope most effectively. He and his assistant, Matteo Giovanetti, decorated the palace and cathedral with refined, elegant frescoes in a style that became known as International Gothic. In 1376, when Pope Gregory XI was persuaded to return to Rome, Avignon elected its own rival pope—setting off a schism that split the Christian world. The struggle ended in 1417 with the disbanding of the papal cult in Avignon.

Medieval walls surround Avignon, and you will most likely enter the city through the **Porte** de la République, where cours Jean-Jaurès (which becomes rue de la République) bisects the town, leading straight to the **place de l'Horloge.** This lively, vibrant square, with its cafés, restaurants, and belle époque merry-go-round, is the city's tourist heart. One of its most beautiful buildings is the **Opéra-Théâtre,** finished in 1847. Boasting a year-round bill of theater and opera performances, it showcases some of the most important plays during the annual Festival d'Avignon (see sidebar this page). Here, too, 2015 heralds the arrival of the **Carré du Palais** (carredupalaisavignon.com), featuring wine-tasting, a wine bar, a gourmet restaurant, shops, and guest rooms in the former Banque de France.

To visit the papal heart of the town, head uphill from the place de l'Horloge.

Palais des Papes

Part fortress, part showplace, this vast stone residence—once crammed with paintings, sculptures, tapestries, and silverware—has little furniture or artworks to visually illustrate the pope's once luxurious way of life; the audio guide and videos throughout the palace help bring the fascinating history to life.

The Palais des Papes comprises two palaces—the Palais Vieux (Old Palace), built by Benoît XII on the east and north sides, and the Palais Nouveau (New Palace) expansion, a graceful Gothic residence that Benedict's successor, Clément VI, built on the south and west sides. Linking the two is the **Cour d'Honneur** (Courtyard

of Honor), the main venue for Avignon's festival since 1947. From here the tour begins, exploring the lower level on Circuit One, then continuing with the upper level on Circuit Two.

Circuit One: From the courtyard, enter into the **Salle du Consistoire** (Reception Room), a long dark hall with four tall, narrow windows along the east side. The pope sat on a dais against the southern wall, with his assembly perched on wood-paneled stone benches along the walls. The hall was used as a tribunal, as well as an audience, where the pope would receive visitors, sovereigns, and ambassadors, plus hear legal, theological, and political matters. Don't miss the small **Chapelle de St.-Jean** (St. John's Chapel) with its richly hued frescoes by Giovanetti, painted between 1346 and 1348 and narrating the lives of St. John the Baptist (on the north and east walls) and St. John

Palais des Papes

 Place du Palais

☎ 04 32 74 32 74

$ $$$. Combined ticket available with the Pont St.-Bénezet: $$$. Audio guides available.

palais-des-papes.com

A Theatergoer's Dream

More than 120,000 theater lovers flock to Avignon for three celebrated weeks every July, when 40 new French and foreign drama and dance productions are unveiled in 20-some venues throughout the city during the Festival d'Avignon. The tradition dates back to 1947, when actor-director Jean Vilar performed a play in the courtyard of the Palais des Papes. Alongside this official festival (dubbed "le In"), a popular fringe festival also takes place at exactly the same time, with more than 1,200 unique shows (called "le Off"). For more information: *festival-avignon.com* **and** *avignonleoff.com.*

Cour Palais Vieux

Grand Tinel

Cour d'Honneur

Palais des Papes

Main entrance

Tour de la Gâche

the Evangelist (on the south and west walls).

Proceed to the **Salle de Jésus** (Jesus Hall), where faint monograms of Christ (I.H.S., Latin abbreviation for "Jesus, Hominum, Salvator") still adorn the walls. This room was a kind of antechamber where cardinals awaited the pope before entering into the Consistory.

Next you visit the **Chambre du Camérier** (Chamberlain's Chamber), once divided into several rooms but now one large room featuring eight masonry vaults in the floor, where valuable documents were hidden. The chamberlain was the church's highest ranking dignitary after the pope and oversaw the Apostolic Chamber.

Now peek into the ornate **Revestaire**

Chambre du Parement

Grande Chapelle

Grande Audience

Pontifical (Papal Vestry), with its pale green and gold decorations featuring cherubs and coats of arms. In this small room the pope put on his consistorial robes: the amice, the alb, and the stole, along with red sandals, a cape adorned with a breast plate, gloves, red velvet cape, and white miter.

INSIDER TIP:

Don't miss Les Luminessences d'Avignon, an extraordinary summer evening sound-and-light show in the Palais des Papes.

—CHRISTEL CHERQAOUI
National Geographic Books

Go down the stairs to enter the enormous **Grande Trésorerie** (Great Treasury Hall), where the Apostolic Chamber took care of the popes' financial matters—including accounting for taxes taken from Christendom's religious establishments, the minting of pontifical coins, and other aspects of the treasury's responsibilities. Down more stairs is the **Trésor Bas,** with its subterranean coffers that once held coins as well as beautiful objects of gold and silver.

From here, detour to the **Pontifical Gardens,** once the domain of the popes' vegetable garden, as well as a menagerie of lions, camels, wild boar, and stag.

Circuit Two: Backtrack through the Trésor Bas and climb the staircase along the Cour Palais Vieux to continue a visit to the upper floors.

You'll be led to the vast **Grand Tinel,** where banquets were held on feast days. Beside the fireplace you enter the **Grande Cuisine** (Upper Kitchen), devoid of the grills and spits that once cooked the piles of meat that formed the centerpiece of medieval banqueting. Be sure to peek into **Chapelle St.-Martial** *(undergoing restoration),* which features more elaborate murals painted by Giovanetti between 1344 and 1346. These portray scenes from St. Martial's life.

Next you enter the **Chambre du Parement,** the antechamber to the pope's chambers. Parement was used to describe the tapestries that covered the walls and seating (the ones hanging now are Gobelins). Here is where the pope and cardinals held secret consistories.

The adjacent **Studium** (Study Tower) boasts the palace's only original 14th-century floor: Green and brown tiles alternate with decorative scenes of critters and geometric designs.

Up some stairs, the **Chambre du Pape** (Pope's Bedroom) gives an idea of the popes' devotion to lavishness, with its frescoes of intertwining vines and oak leaves against a rich blue background.

Next up, the **Chambre du Cerf** (Stag Room), was Clément VI's study and bedroom. Its walls are covered with frescoes of a stag hunt.

Down some wooden stairs awaits the **Sacristie Nord** (North

Sacristy), where the pontiff changed vestments during ceremonies in the adjoining Great Chapel.

Hold your breath as you enter the heavenly **Grande Chapelle** (Great Chapel), with its soaring ceiling and light-filled space. Clément VI was behind this magnificent room—measuring 170 by 49 by 65 feet (52 x 15 x 20 m). Despite the threat of Black Death, the chapel was completed in less than a year, in 1348. Of its 16th- and 17th-century frescoes, only a handful faintly remain.

The circuit continues with the **Chambre Neuve du Camérier** (Chamberlain's New Room), with paintings and a film about sculpture in the palace.

From here, you are given some choices. Straight leads to the **Chambre des Notaires,** showcasing paintings of all the Avignon popes. And the stairs to the left climb up through the **Tour de la Gâche** to an amazing panoramic view over the palace, Avignon, and beyond.

You are then led to the **Loggia,** overlooking the Court of Honor, where the pope gave his triple blessing to the crowd below. Downstairs is the dark **Grande Audience** (Great Audience Hall), a two-nave hall that housed the court of apostolic causes; thousands of appeals were heard here, against whose judgments no appeal was possible. Giovanetti graced these walls in 1352 with frescoes of the prophets, of which only one remnant is apparent in one corner, with traces elsewhere.

Detailed carvings grace the 1619 Hôtel des Monnaies, one of Avignon's best examples of baroque style.

Follow signs to a shop selling popes' wines and onward to the gift shop and exit.

Around the Palais

Next door, the newly renovated **Cathédrale Notre-Dame des Doms** was built in the 12th century atop a paleo-Christian basilica and has been remodeled many times since. It contains the Flamboyant Gothic tomb of some of the apostate popes. The gold statue topping its steeple is the Virgin, from the 19th century.

Farther up the hill, on the north end of Palace Square, is the **Musée du Petit Palais.** Built for Cardinal Bérenger Frédol circa 1318–1320, it holds two collections: the Avignon school paintings from the Musée Calvet, and a large group of Italian paintings from the 13th to 16th centuries. You'll want to stop and study many of these fine works, but be sure to seek out the "Virgin and Child Between Two Saints and Two Donors" (Room XVII;

Cathédrale Notre-Dame des Doms

✉ Place du Palais
☎ 04 90 82 12 21
🕐 Treasury: Open by appt.
cathedrale-avignon.fr

Musée du Petit Palais

✉ Place du Palais
☎ 04 90 86 44 58
🕐 Closed Tues.
💲 $$
petit-palais.org

Pont St.-Bénezet

✉ Rue Ferruce

☎ 04 32 74 32 74

💲 $. Combined ticket with Palais des Papes: $$$.

Musée Lapidaire

✉ 27 rue de la République

☎ 04 90 86 33 84

🕐 Closed Tues.

💲 $

musee-lapidaire.org

1450–1455) by Enguerrand Quarton, one of the founders of the Avignon school. Its simplicity and use of light in the construction of form are typical of the Avignon school in its attempt to bridge Flemish realism and Italian abstract style. Other masterpieces include "Virgin in Majesty" by the Master of 1310, an altarpiece showcasing the masterwork of early 14th-century Italian painters (Room III); the "Virgin of Mercy" by Pietro di Domenico da Montepulciano (Room VIII); and

Pont St.-Bénezet, Avignon's famous bridge

the graceful "Virgin and Child" by Botticelli (Room XI). Take a cup of tea or coffee in the delightful garden café.

Outside the Petit Palais, a ramped walkway leads up to the **Jardin du Rocher des Doms** (Garden of the Rock of the Lords), a 19th-century public park with splashing fountains, classical statuary, a rock grotto, and a duck-dotted pond. Overlooking the River Rhône where it splits in

two, this spot was strategic as far back as the Neolithic age. During papal times, it was the private aerie of cardinals and bishops.

Take the staircase down to the River Rhône and the **Pont St.-Bénezet,** Avignon's famous bridge *("Sur le pont d'Avignon, on y danse, on y danse …")*. No one knows who built the original bridge, but the story goes that a young shepherd was instructed by voices to build a bridge over the Rhône at Avignon. He finally convinced the bishop—by performing the miracle of moving a boulder all by himself—and he became a hero. It's a miracle any of the bridge survives: Built between 1177 and 1185, it was destroyed in 1226 during the siege of the city, rebuilt, then endured more flood damage and repairs until 1660, when the Rhône swept away half of it—only 4 of its original 22 arches survive. Also surviving is the bridge's little **Chapelle St.-Nicholas,** which preserved the remains of St.-Bénezet until they were lost in the French Revolution.

Avignon's Museums

Wandering the labyrinth of Avignon's little streets, you'll come across a handful of delightful small museums. Facing rue de la République, the **Musée Lapidaire,** the Musée Calvet's archaeological annex, is housed in the 16th-century chapel of the Collège des Jésuites. Several different civilizations are featured here: Greek and southern Italian; Etruscan; and Roman, Gallo-Roman, and paleo-Christian.

INSIDER TIP:

Jardin du Rocher des Doms offers spectacular views of the Rhône, and the park benches are perfect for an afternoon snack—or even a nap.

—DAVID KENNEDY
National Geographic contributor

Nearby, near Église St.-Denis, is the **Musée Angladon,** a former *hôtel particulier* featuring the magnificent art collection of Jacques Doucet—the celebrated Parisian haute-couture designer who cultivated several young artists, including Pablo Picasso. The ground floor's modern, stark white walls are the backdrop for 19th- and 20th-century masterpieces, including several Picassos ("Arlequin," 1915; "Nature Morte Cubiste," 1920; and "Nature Morte à la Guitare," 1919) and Provence's only van Gogh—the dark "Wagons de Chemin de Fer," painted in Arles in 1888. You'll also spot works by Degas, Manet, Cézanne, and Sisley. Upstairs, rooms furnished in 18th- and 19th-century period style show rare antiques and objets d'art.

Another fine art museum, housed in another beautiful hôtel particulier, is the **Musée Calvet,** located across rue de la République on tiny rue Joseph Vernet. Originally the varied collections of Avignon physician and scholar Esprit Calvet (1728–1810), its wide range of—and ever expanding—works include European paintings and sculptures from the 15th to 20th centuries, decorative arts and anthropological artifacts, and arts from Asia, Oceania, and Africa. Three magnificent rooms display the Egyptian antiquities collection, including the "Head of a Vizier." Upstairs, the Vernet Gallery pays tribute to the illustrious Vernet family of painters, while a new room of modern art features the likes of Bonnard, Manet, Sisley, Vuillard, and Camille Claudel. The garden, restored to its original splendor, is a popular venue for the Festival d'Avignon.

Papalines

For a heavenly treat, try these chocolate truffles filled with Comtat liqueur distilled from 60 herbs picked from nearby fields.

Down a few crooked streets is yet another museum in a hôtel particulier, the **Musée Louis Vouland,** featuring a quirky collection of 17th- and 18th-century decorative arts collected by businessman and art collector Louis Vouland (1883–1973). You'll find faïence from Moustiers and Marseille, Asian porcelain, and furniture (including four Regency armchairs from 1736 depicting fables by Jean de la Fontaine), all the while serenaded by songbirds in the garden outside.

Finally, the growing **Collection Lambert** showcases the contemporary art collection of famous Parisian gallery owner Yvon Lambert, ranging from the sixties to today. ∎

Musée Angladon
- ✉ 5 rue Laboureur
- ☎ 04 90 82 29 03
- 🕐 Closed Mon. & a.m. mid-June–Nov., closed Mon.–Tues. & a.m. rest of year
- 💲 $$

angladon.com

Musée Calvet
- ✉ 65 rue Joseph Vernet
- ☎ 04 90 86 33 84
- 🕐 Closed Tues.
- 💲 $$

musee-calvet.org

Musée Louis Vouland
- ✉ 17 rue Victor Hugo
- ☎ 04 90 86 03 79
- 🕐 Closed Mon. & a.m. Nov.–April
- 💲 $$

vouland.com

Collection Lambert
- ✉ 5 rue Violette
- ☎ 04 90 16 56 20
- 💲 $$

collectionlambert.com

Luberon Villages

Medieval *villages perchés,* honey-hued farmhouses, vineyards, bounties of cherries, melons, and goat cheese, and fragrant fields of red poppies, sunflowers, and lavender: The Luberon is classic Provence.

The Luberon's splendid lavender fields burst into bloom in July.

Luberon Villages
⚠ 42 C2–C3, D2;
    43 E2

The fecund expanse ranges from Cavaillon in the west and Manosque in the east, and from Apt south to the Durance River. Dominating the landscape is the Montagne de Luberon, the rocky, oak-covered massif for which the area is named. This powerful barrier is broken only in one place, at the Combe de Lourmarin, creating the Grand Luberon—rising to 3,691-foot (1,125 m) Mourre Nègre—to the east, and the Petit Luberon to the west. Much of the area is preserved as the Parc Naturel Régional du Luberon, established in 1977.

The hill towns hark back to a time when Ligurians, Romans, then Saracens settled here. The most dramatic period, however, came in the 1500s, during the Wars of Religion, when the Vaudois (a Protestant sect), who had taken refuge in the Luberon, were persecuted by the Catholics. Villages were razed, and whole populations were decimated.

Petit Luberon

In the shadow of the Luberon massif, tiny lanes wander through a potpourri of vineyards, cherry orchards, and lavender fields to some of Provence's most delightful *villages perchés*. Enjoy this charming niche at a leisurely pace, taking time to visit farmers markets and to stop in some of the more esoteric museums, including one devoted to corkscrews (*tire-bouchon*) and another to bread.

INSIDER TIP:

Consider renting a car in Avignon to go "village hopping" in the Luberon. There are some tight roads, but it's still driver friendly.

—DAVID KENNEDY
National Geographic contributor

Oppède-le-Vieux is a virtual ghost town now, its empty buildings and silent streets begrudgingly giving away secrets of its past. The town's name belies its former importance as a Roman stronghold. Indeed, among artifacts that have been found here are coins, tiles, and an altar for worshipping Mercury (now at the museum in Cavaillon; see p. 76). Its entire Vaudois population was massacred by Catholics in 1545, in the throes of the Wars of Religion; afterward, its remaining residents left the old village for the plains below.

You will have to leave your car in the parking lot at the base of the village and follow the picturesque path up the hill. Upon entering the village, climb timeworn cobblestone lanes past empty noble facades to the top of the hill. Perched at the village's highest point, the **Collégiale Notre-Dame d'Alidon** was built in the 16th century on the site of an ancient church. Romanesque in style, it received Gothic touches in 1592. In the simple interior, nearly all ornamentation comes from frescoes, some of which have been restored. Above the altar is a 17th-century painting by Reynaud le Vieux, portraying Mary handing a rosary to St. Dominic and St. Catherine of Siena. Above the church are the broken-down walls of a château-fort constructed in the 13th century under Raymond VI of Toulouse and enlarged in subsequent centuries.

Follow little lanes 3 miles (5 km) east of Oppède, past cherry and fig trees to pretty **Ménerbes.** Another ridgetop fortress town, its old château sits atop the highest point (*closed to visitors*). The castle was considered impregnable, yet during the 16th-century Wars of Religion, 120 Protestants entered by ruse in 1577 and sheltered here for more than a year. The Catholics took it back using similar methods. Despite the unwanted fame bestowed upon the town thanks to Peter Mayle, who lived here from 1986 to 1993 and wrote about it in *A Year in Provence*, Ménerbes remains an unassuming, friendly place. Devoted to truffles and wine, the **Maison de la Truffe et du Vin du Luberon**

Weekly Markets

Ansouis: Sun.
Apt: Tues. & Sat.
Bonnieux: Fri.
Cucuron: Tues.
Gordes: Tues.
Lacoste: Tues.
Ménerbes: Thurs.
Oppède: Sat.
Roussillon: Thurs.
La Tour-d'Aigues: Tues. & Thurs. (July–Aug.)
marches-provence.com

Bonnieux

42 C2

Visitor Information

✉ 7 place Carnot

☎ 04 90 75 91 90

**tourisme-en-luberon
.com**

Apt

42 D2

Visitor Information

✉ Office de
Tourisme, 20
av. Philippe de
Girard

☎ 04 90 74 03 18

luberon-apt.fr

(*place de l'Horloge, tel 04 90 72 38 37, vin-truffe-luberon.com*) is the place to go to sample a truffle menu, taste wine, and shop for local products.

In the valley nearby, you can visit the **Musée du Tire-Bouchon** (*Domaine de la Citadelle, Le Chataignier, chemin de Cavaillon, Ménerbes, tel 04 90 72 41 58, closed Sat.–Sun. Oct.–March, $, domaine-citadelle.com*), established by Yves Rousset-Rouard, former village mayor, former MP, and movie producer. It presents more than a thousand different corkscrews dating from the 17th century to the present. You'll see an early French corkscrew, hand-forged from iron in the 1600s, and more modern corkscrews, some several feet tall. Wine-tasting is included at the end.

The infamous Marquis de Sade retreated to his castle crowning **Lacoste,** 4 miles (6 km) east of Ménerbes, in the late 1700s between various prison terms, where he hosted wild parties. The French nobleman's perverse sexual preferences and erotic writings gave rise to the term "sadism"; his best known work is the notorious novel *Justine* (1791). Designer Pierre Cardin bought the ruined castle and converted it into an open-air lyrical arts theater; the Festival de Lacoste (*tel 04 90 75 93 12, festivaldelacoste.com*) now takes place within its walls every summer. The town itself is beautifully restored, with steep cobbled lanes winding up to the castle. Be sure to enjoy an apéritif at the **Café de France** (*opposite town hall, tel 04 90 75 82 25*), with its sublime views across farmlands to the hilltop village of Bonnieux.

The biggest of the Petit Luberon villages is magnificent **Bonnieux,** its sand-colored buildings clinging to a pyramidal mound that rises up to the 12th-century **Haute Église.** You'll have to climb 86 steps, past tiny plazas and fine old houses, to reach the often closed church—the views, however, are amazing, taking in an Impressionist patchwork of vines, lavender, and fruit trees set against the Monts de Vaucluse. Tucked away on a quiet street hides the **Musée de la Boulangerie**

Oppède-le-Vieux, topped by its ancient feudal château

(*12 rue de la République, tel 04 90 75 88 34, closed Tues., $*), complete with period bread oven. At the base of the hill is the newer **Église Neuve,** built in 1870.

Nearby, on the D149, the three-arched **Pont Julien** is the only remaining bridge on Via Domitia, the old Roman road between Italy and Provence.

Grand Luberon

The wilder brother to the Petit Luberon's gentleness, the Grand Luberon is a deeply forested, canyoned land dotted with small bourgs lost in time. **Apt,** its major hub, however, possesses an industrial air. The city's beauty lies in its old town, with its ancient vaulted passageways and fountains. On Tuesdays and Saturdays, the open-air market unfurls on place Lauze de Perret. Hidden away in a courtyard off rue des Marchands is the **Maison du Parc Naturel Régional du Luberon,** with a museum focusing on the area's natural history, as well as helpful tourist information. The bones of Ste.-Anne, the Virgin Mary's mother, were supposedly discovered in the town's eighth-century crypt, inspiring the construction of **Cathédrale Ste.-Anne** in the 11th century. Look for the saint's shroud among the treasury's reliquaries, and admire the set of 14th-century stained-glass windows at the end of the apse that describe her life. The town's major museum, the **Musée de l'Aventure Industrielle du Pays d'Apt** (*14 place du Postel, tel 04 90 74 95 30*), housed in an old

candied fruit factory, presents the regional industries of crystallized fruits (perfected for the popes' sweet tooth), ocher mining, and ceramics.

Wee roads south of Apt wander through some of the Luberon massif's wildest lands, with forests stretching to the horizon and every imaginable Provençal herb scenting the air. Follow the GR92 to lovingly restored **Saignon.**

Maison du Parc Naturel Régional du Luberon

- ✉ 60 place Jean-Jaurès, Apt
- ☎ 04 90 04 42 00
- 🕐 Closed Sun.
- 💲 Museum: $

parcduluberon.fr

Here, *boules* players while away hot afternoons in the shade of plane trees, and *le rocher de Bellevue*—what's left of the old château—offers sublime 360-degree views over fields, mountains, and villages (follow signs for "Le Rocher").

Nearby are the peaceful bourgs of **Sivergues,** offering a popular trailhead for hikes up the Grand Luberon, and **Buoux,** in the middle of lavender fields. Buoux's

Cathédrale Ste.-Anne

- ✉ Rue de la Cathédrale, Apt
- ☎ 04 90 74 36 60
- 🕐 Treasury: Open July–Sept. Guided tours only, at 11 a.m. & 5 p.m. Mon.–Sat. & 11 a.m. Sun.

Lourmarin
◮ 42 D2

Visitor Information

✉ Office de
Tourisme,
place Henri
Barthélémy
☎ 04 90 68 10 77
lourmarin.com

Château de
Lourmarin
☎ 04 90 68 15 23
🕐 Closed Jan.
Mon.–Fri.
💲 $$
**chateau-de-
lourmarin.com**

Ansouis
◮ 42 D2

Visitor Information

✉ Mairie
d'Ansouis,
place St.-Elzéar
☎ 04 90 09 83 79
ansouis.fr

fortress, which provided refuge to the Vaudois during the religious wars of the 16th century, was destroyed in 1660 by Louis XIV—only pieces of the rampart and chapel walls survive today.

The twisty D943 brings you farther south to **Lourmarin.** Its Renaissance **château** has lorded over town since the 16th century. Since restoration in the early 1900s, it has received writers and artists in residence, earning it the title the "Médicis Villa of Provence." The village has been turned over to chic restaurants and cafés, boutiques and antique shops, frequented by well-coiffed clientele. Nobel Prize–winning writer Albert Camus (1913–1960) was a longtime resident; he and his wife rest in peace at the village cemetery, his tombstone planted with rosemary, hers with lavender.

Another castle (*rue Cartel, tel 04 90 09 82 70, closed Tues. March–Nov.,* open Sun. only rest of year, $$, chateau ansouis.fr*) rises from the vineyards in **Ansouis,** southeast of Lourmarin via the D135, dating from the tenth century. The tour takes in the kitchens with their shiny copperware, the salons with their Flemish tapestries, plus the Room of Saints, devoted to the family's St.-Elzéar and Ste.-Delphine. The saintly couple married in 1299 and vowed to live together in chastity—no doubt made easier by the fact that he rarely spent any time at home. The terrace gardens are magnificent.

The village is charming, with tiny streets lined with boutiques and artisan workshops. Look for the **Musée Extraordinaire** (*rue du Vieux Moulin, tel 04 90 09 82 64, open p.m., $*), an eclectic assemblage of life-size sculptures, paintings, shells, and fossils, and the **Musée de la Vigne et du Vin** (*Château Turcan, rte. de Pertuis, tel 04 90 09 83 33, $, chateau-turcan.com*), whose display of viticulture tools includes ancient glassware and huge winepresses.

Scenes for Ridley Scott's *A Good Year* were filmed in quiet **Cucuron,** east of Lourmarin (the film also takes place in Bonnieux and Gordes). Walk through the 18th-century ramparts to see the **Église Notre-Dame-de-Beaulieu,** with a baroque altarpiece and Gothic side chapels, and the medieval donjon of **St.-Michel** (*closed to public*). The **Musée Marc-Deydier** (*tel 04 90 09 87 61, open p.m. weekends*) houses 3,000 photographs of the Luberon and of the Vaucluse, taken between 1885 and 1917.

On the Grand Luberon's eastern fringe, the town of **La**

EXPERIENCE:
Countryside Cycling

Pastoral, bird-serenaded lanes wind through the Luberon's farms, vineyards, fields of sunflowers, and ocher valleys, making this sun-blessed region one of the most coveted cycling lands around. For a grand 147-mile (236 km) tour taking in the best sights, download the map at *leluberonavelo.com* and away you go! The website also offers plenty of other Luberon itineraries, plus info on bicycle rental, accommodations, and other logistics. Of course, the rest of Provence offers sublime cycling as well. Check out *discoverfrance.com* for recommended guided tours, as well as *provence-a-velo.fr.*

Tour-d'Aigues has the remains of another Renaissance château, with an elegant 16th-century facade.

Roussillon

It's the town's vibrant red-ocher color against the dark green hills that's so striking, perched

figured out how to mix the pigment with rubber to thicken it (hence the red seals over jars, on bicycle tires, etc.)—and a whole new industry was born. Production dropped in the 1950s, and today only one company still operates.

Roussillon
 42 C2
Visitor Information
✉ Place de la Poste
☎ 04 90 05 60 25
roussillon-provence .com

Colorado Provençal, at its most beautiful at sunset

on the edge of a dramatically red canyon. This is the heart of one of the world's biggest ocher deposits, where 17 different shades of soil—violet, bloodred, orange, yellow, and everything in between—once were worked. The incredible beauty, alas, draws hordes of tourists in summer.

The spectacle is rooted in a 230-million-year-long history, when Provence was covered by the sea. Sands containing iron were deposited, later to be oxidized in brilliant tints of color—ocher. The Romans used the tinted earth for pottery glazes. In the 18th century, local Roussillonnais

You can visit the old ocher quarries via the 0.6-mile (1 km) **Sentier des Ocres** *($),* through a mini-canyon of fantastically shaped formations set against a pine backdrop (don't wear white to avoid staining). The village is worth a stroll as well: Tiny, steep streets wind past flowery facades painted in the local ochers, many filled with tourist shops.

Less than a mile (1 km) east of town on the D104, the **Conserva-toire des Ocres et de la Couleur** presents temporary exhibits linked to color; the *conservatoire* also offers one- to six-day classes on colorwash, whitewash, and patina.

Another old quarry, the **Colorado Provençal,** near Rustrel,

Conservatoire des Ocres et de la Couleur
⚑ 42 C2
✉ Usine Mathieu, D104
☎ 04 90 05 66 69
🕐 Closed Mon.– Tues. Nov.–Dec.
💲 $$
okhra.com

Colorado Provençal
⚑ 42 D2
✉ S of D22 toward Rustrel from Apt
💲 $

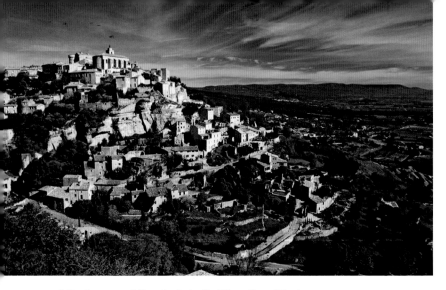

A Renaissance-era château dominates the hilltop village of Gordes.

Mines de Bruoux

✉ Rte. de Croagne, Gargas

☎ 04 90 06 22 59

⊕ Closed mid-Nov.–mid-March; guided tours only

💲 $$

minesdebruoux.fr

Gordes

🅰 42 C2

Visitor Information

✉ Le Château

☎ 04 90 72 02 75

gordes-village.com

Château de Gordes/Musée Pol Mara

✉ Place Genty Pantaly

☎ 04 90 72 02 75

💲 $

gordes-village.com

comprises an even larger site of rock formations. Seven walking trails wind past giant columns of red ocher. The **Sentier des Cheminées des Fées** and **Sentier du Satard,** both 0.6 mile (1 km) long, are the most dramatic; they start from the municipal parking lot in Bouvène, off the D22 south of Rustrel village.

One last ocher site to visit are the **Mines de Bruoux** in Gargas—a labyrinth of colorful galleries in an old ocher mine.

Gordes

Majestically spiraling up a white rock overlooking the Luberon's patches of farmland, the tiered village of Gordes is strikingly handsome—perhaps too much for its own good. It's the Luberon's No. 1 tourist site, overwhelmed with cars and visitors in summer. A springtime visit, when the cherry trees are in bloom, or fall, as the leaves turn golden, is a better bet.

The obviously strategic site has been occupied since prehistoric times. In the Roman period an *oppidum* was built here, and, in the Middle Ages, inhabitants living on the plain sought refuge in the fortified town. It was never taken, even during the Wars of Religion. What almost did Gordes in was attrition at the turn of the 20th century, as residents migrated to cities for factory jobs. Modern art came to the rescue. Cubist painter André Lhote discovered the village in 1938, drawing Chagall, Vasarely, and other modern artists to visit and summer here as well. Their painting bliss was cut short, however, when German troops in 1944 destroyed much of the village in retaliation for a Résistance attack. A monk from the nearby abbey of Sénanque intervened to avoid even further damage.

Though the town has been largely rebuilt, Gordes has managed to retain its old-world charm. A labyrinth of cobbled lanes harbors beautifully restored houses, many now occupied by shops selling the usual Provençal goods and cafés where well-heeled people sip regional muscat. Dominating the entire site is the **château,** dating from the Renaissance and constructed on the site of a medieval fortress. The 12th-century crenellated tower is all that remains from its earlier days, while three stories of Renaissance windows pierce the tall curtain walls. To visit, buy a ticket for the **Musée Pol Mara,** devoted to the contemporary Flemish master. Nearby, the **Église St.-Firmin** was constructed in the 18th century. Its murals are dedicated to the Virgin and a parade of saints, including St. Firmin. Continue down rue de l'Église, which brings you to **rue du Belvédère** and its glorious valley vista.

INSIDER TIP:

Get an early morning start to enjoy the ambience of the lively and colorful local markets in Coustellet, L'Isle-sur-la-Sorgue, Gordes, and many more.

—PENNY HEMERY
innkeeper, Bastide de Voulonne

Abbaye de Sénanque

Peace and quiet can be found at the nearby Cistercian abbey of Sénanque, one of Provence's three great Cistercian monasteries. It took a hundred years to build this austere ensemble of buildings, beginning in 1148. The community thrived in the 13th and 14th centuries, adding a mill, seven granges, and large areas of land throughout Provence. It was partially destroyed during the 16th-century religious wars and sold off during the revolution. A new community returned in 1854, only to be expelled due to new laws on religious consecrations in 1903. A new group of monks returned in 1988; they cultivate lavender and produce honey to help maintain the community.

Bountiful Bories

Throughout Provence's fields, you'll find scatterings of beehive-shaped *bories*, a kind of stone hut constructed with no mortar. Bronze Age Ligurians built the area's first examples, though their original purposes aren't known. Until the 18th century they were continuously used, repaired, and renovated for use as shelter and storage (with shepherds still using some in the Alpes-Maritimes). A borie village near Gordes *(beyond.fr)*, with 20 restored structures, including dwellings, an oven, sheep pen, and wine cistern, is a popular tourist stop. A less-touched-up village at Bonneiux *(enclos-des-bories.fr)* can also be visited.

Several guided visits—the only way to see the monastery—are offered throughout the day. They are in French, but a translated pamphlet helps explain some of what you see. The tour takes in the abbey's five 12th-century buildings: the abbatial church, the cloister, the dormitory, the chapter room, and the calefactory (heating room).

The abbey is one of Provence's most fabled lavender destinations, in spectacular bloom in late June and early July. ∎

Abbaye Notre-Dame-de-Sénanque

42 C2

1.9 miles (3 km) N of Gordes on D177

04 90 72 05 72

Closed Sun. a.m.

$$

www.senanque.fr

Lavender Country

Perhaps no other scent so readily defines Provence as the pungent, heady aroma of lavender, and no other scene than the fields and fields of the tiny purple buds growing in a profusion of mounds beneath a blue summer sky. Beloved for its scent, valued for its medicinal and soothing qualities, lavender has been used since Roman times—and the industry is still going strong.

Fields and fields of lavender explode into bloom in June and July.

In the Beginning

The ancient Romans used lavender flower heads to scent their clothes and public baths. In fact, the origin of the name comes from the Latin *lavare,* meaning "to wash." Lavender's antidotal qualities have also been known as long, with Mithridates, king of Pontus, inventing in the first century B.C. a famous remedy against insect bites called *Thériaque.* During the Middle Ages, when many believed that plague was spread by vapors in the air, lavender was sprinkled on floors and burned on streets and in disease-infested houses. It was also used to treat insomnia and drive away lice, moths, and bedbugs.

Lavender's popularity soared in the 16th-century royal courts, where the mode (at least according to Catherine de Médicis) demanded that gloves, handkerchiefs, and wigs be perfumed. Lavender production took off in Provence, but it was not until the 19th century that *lavanderaies* (lavender plantations) popped up throughout the countryside. Although lavender grows wild throughout Provence, at that point fields were planted for the express purpose of cultivation.

Lovely Lavender

Lavender belongs to the mint family, which also includes thyme, savory, oregano, and sage. While 70 species and subspecies of lavender have been identified worldwide, only three grow in Provence. True lavender *(lavande fine)* is found high up in dry, rocky soil. *Aspic,* which grows lower down, is similar to lavande fine except it has broader leaves and its branches hold a number of stems. And the less refined *lavandin* is a hybrid of lavande fine and aspic. For production purposes, *la lavande* is the most highly regarded by perfume makers for its sweet essential oil, though aspic and especially le lavandin are more productive and therefore more common—ending up in laundry and household products.

Lavender is planted in long, undulating rows in autumn or spring, with plants taking three or four years to mature. The first flowers appear in June, bursting forth in full glory by the end of the month in a hazy blue aura of beauty.

Harvesttime

Provence is the world's top lavender producer, producing more than 50 percent. The main growing areas are the Alpes-de-Haute-Provence (plateau de Valensole, Vallée de l'Asse), the Vaucluse (plateau des Claparèdes, plateau de Sault), the Drôme (Les Baronnies), and the Rhône River Valley. The harvest takes place from July to mid-August, when the scent overpowers the air.

During the three-week harvesting period, mechanized harvesters pick flowers all day, every day. Upon harvesting, the plants are left out to dry, then bundled and packed and sent to the distillery. Here, the essential oil is extracted: 120 pounds (55 kg) of flowers makes 1 pound (0.45 kg) of essential oil.

Best Lavender-Viewing Perches

Certain quintessential images of Provence have been immortalized on film and canvas, most of which have to do with lavender. Probably the most famous composition comes from **Abbaye de Sénanque** near Gordes (see p. 59); the best time to photograph this lovely Romanesque abbey is the early morning, when the lighting is perfect. **Simiane la Rotonde** near Sault is a gorgeous little hilltop village rising above fields of lavender. For wide-sweeping views of never ending fields of lavender, head to the **plateau de Sault** (see sidebar below) or the **plateau de Valensole** (see p. 197).

EXPERIENCE: Hit the Lavender Trail

A midsummer stroll through Provence's blooming lavender fields is one of those once-in-a-lifetime experiences. One of the prettiest areas is around Sault, where the 3-mile (5 km) **Chemin des Lavandes** (ventoux-sud.com), just south of town, wanders through fields of lavender to the delight of walkers and cyclists alike; interpretive panels provide production facts. If you prefer to drive, the **Association des Routes de la Lavande** (routes-lavande.com) has charted out scenic drives through lavender fields in the Sault area and elsewhere.

Most distilleries are open to the public, offering a firsthand look at the distillation process. **Distillerie des Agnels** in Apt *(rte. de Buoux, tel 04 90 04 77 00, les agnels.com)* offers year-round tours. Also highly recommended is **Arôma Plantes** *(rte. du Mont Ventoux, Sault, tel 04 90 64 14 73, closed Sun., distillerie-aromaplantes .com)*, a family farm and distillery on the slopes of Mont Ventoux.

Among several spas catering to lavender's relaxing side, the **Établissement Thermal de Dignes-Les-Bains** *(rte. des Thermes, Digne-les-Bains, tel 04 92 32 32 92, thermesdignelesbains.com)* offers lavender baths.

Finally, for an excellent overview, be sure to stop by the **Musée de la Lavande** in Coustellet (see p. 77; *rte. de Gordes, tel 04 90 76 91 23, $$*).

L'Isle-sur-la-Sorgue

Water appears at every turn in this compact medieval mill town, built on islands dotting five branches of the River Sorgue. Today, France's second largest antique market (after Paris) spreads out on weekends along the riverbanks, while a dozen antique malls exist around town.

Market Days
Thurs. & Sun.

L'Isle-sur-la-Sorgue
⚠ 42 C2
Visitor Information
✉ Office de Tourisme, place de la Liberté
☎ 04 90 38 04 78
oti-delasorgue.fr

Collégiale Notre-Dame-des-Anges
✉ Place de la Liberté
🕐 Closed Sun.

The region was swampland in the 12th century, when a handful of fishermen and their families built houses on stilts where the town now stands. Before long, the river was reined with waterwheels and canals, providing energy for burgeoning silk, wool, and papermaking industries, and L'Isle-sur-la-Sorgue became the most important town of the Comtat-Venaissin (now known as the Vaucluse). Several waterwheels still churn around town; the structures on rue du Dr. Jean-Roux and rue Jean-Théophile are especially picturesque.

The Sorgue meanders in and about the old town, its slow-moving green waters mirroring timeworn houses—many now containing tourist shops—and plane trees. In the heart of town,

the **Tour Boutin,** also called Tour d'Argent, is the oldest structure, dating from the Middle Ages, when the counts of Toulouse ruled. Its purpose remains a mystery.

Nearby, the **Notre-Dame-des-Anges,** with an Italianate belfry, dates from 1222 but received its Italian flair in the 17th century, making it one of Provence's most beautiful baroque examples. Note that the windows on the north side have been walled up (since 1666) in defense against the mistral winds. Inside, over the Carrara marble altar looms the 1630 painting by Reynaud Levieux, "Ascension of the Blessed Virgin," looked on by 22 statues by Jean-Baptiste Peru and 220 cherubs. ■

Antique Hunting

Parisian antique dealers know the secret: L'Isle-sur-la-Sorgue is *the* place to go for antiques. Indeed, on Sunday mornings, the largest *brocante* (flea market) and antique market outside Paris unfurls along the village's picturesque streets. The market gets going between 9 and 9:30 a.m., but get there earlier if you need parking.

The village also harbors a dozen antique villages occupying old mills and factories along avenue des Quatres

Otages, where more than 300 antique dealers exhibit on weekends. The tourism office has a list of shops, but the best approach is simply to wander and browse. For starters, **Le Village des Antiquaires de la Gare** (2 bis av. de l'Egalite, closed Tues.–Fri.), housed in an old weaving factory, is one of the largest, with 110 dealers.

Twice a year the town hosts major antique fairs, one over Easter weekend and the second in mid-August.

Don't forget to bring cash!

Fontaine-de-Vaucluse

Quiet jade waters reflect leafy plane trees in this peaceful medieval hamlet, tucked in a closed valley at the edge of the plateau de Vaucluse. Its intense beauty has been the inspiration of writers and poets through the ages, most famously the Italian Renaissance poet Petrarch.

You'll have to leave your car in a pay lot and walk to explore this unassuming little town; be forewarned that the place is a zoo in summer.

The River Sorgue is the town's centerpiece, colored emerald green by water parsnips. Restaurants, shops, and a handful of museums, mostly on the river's right bank, make for a pleasant stay. Overlooking all is a ruined château built to protect pilgrims visiting the tomb of the eighth-century hero St.-Véran, who, the story goes, saved villagers from a dragon.

INSIDER TIP:

Rent a kayak and take an exhilarating ride on the clear, shallow, swift-flowing waters of the River Sorgue.

—HEIDI ELLISON
National Geographic contributor

Follow the souvenir-shop-lined pathway up the River Sorgue to the base of a rocky cliff face, where a deep, emerald pool forms the **Fontaine-de-Vaucluse,** one of France's most extraordinary phenomena. The *fontaine* is the collapsed part of a cave system filled with water. Many divers and speleologists have tried in vain to determine the spring's depth, including the late Jacques Cousteau and, in 1985, a small submarine robot—and still no bottom has been found. The deepest explorations have reached 1,043 feet (318 m). What *is* known is that at its springtime peak, the spring produces 660,430,128 gallons (2,500 L), about the same amount that spills over Niagara Falls in 17 minutes. Learn more at **Le Monde Souterrain de Norbert Casteret** (Underground World of Norbert Casteret).

Probably the town's biggest surprise is the **Musée d'Histoire Jean Garcin: 1939–1945,** located on the busy path to the spring. Its thoughtful account of the French Résistance movement during World War II transports you to the dark world of war, with more than 10,000 objects and documents (*audio guide available in English*). It's named after native son and Résistance leader Jean Garcin (1917–2006).

The **Musée Pétrarque,** on the river's left bank, stands on the site where 14th-century Italian poet Francesco Petrarca (1304–1374) wrote *Canzoniere.* The small house museum features lithographs and watercolors of Petrarch and Laura, his unrequited love, as well as early editions of his books. ∎

Market Day
Sun.

Fontaine-de-Vaucluse
 42 C2
Visitor Information
✉ Office de Tourisme, Résidence Garcin, left bank of the Sorgue
☎ 04 90 20 32 22
oti-delasorgue.fr

Le Monde Souterrain de Norbert Casteret
✉ Chemin de la Fontaine
☎ 04 90 20 34 13
 $$

Musée d'Histoire Jean Garcin: 1939–1945
✉ Chemin de la Fontaine
☎ 04 90 20 24 00
🕐 Closed Tues. & Jan.–Feb.
$ $

Musée Pétrarque
✉ Left bank of the Sorgue
☎ 04 90 20 37 20
🕐 Closed Tues. & Nov.–March
$ $

Vaison-la-Romaine

Boasting ruins of a once wealthy Roman town and narrow medieval streets winding up to an ancient château, Vaison-la-Romaine has plenty of history to explore. But the picturesque little city offers much more, including Provence's largest market and a summer filled with theater and music and dance festivals.

Market Day
Tues.

Known for centuries simply as Vaison, the town didn't gain the second part of its name until the early 20th century, when Roman ruins were discovered beneath the streets of its Basse Ville (Lower Town). From beneath the ground emerged the vestiges of a splendid Roman city that once covered 148 to 173 acres (60–70 ha)—only 15 of which have been excavated (the rest of it remains under the modern city). What makes this site unique is the fact that it is made up of streets with shops and town houses, rather than individual landmarks (as at Arles and Orange), so you get a sense of the overall urban layout. Although little remains of the grand town that formerly flourished here, the literature provided helps re-create the Roman way of life. Comprising the largest archaeological site in France, two quarters can be visited: Puymin, adjacent to the Office de Tourisme; and La Villasse, across the

street and closer to the river.

Begin with the cypress- and pine-shaded **Quartier du Puymin,** where you can purchase one ticket for both sites. Immediately to your right as you enter is the enormous **House of the Laureled Apollo,** named for the head of Apollo in white marble found here. Up the hill, the **Musée Théo Desplans** displays sculptures, mosaics, and other objects found on the site. Be sure to see the "Maison au Dauphin" film that reconstructs one of the sumptuous dwellings in splendid 3-D.

The site's coup de grâce, however, is the **Théâtre Antique,** behind the museum, built in the first century A.D. It measured 315 feet (96 m) across, large enough to seat 6,000 spectators. The stage's front wall, complete with 12 hollows used to work the curtain, are all that remain of the stage area. At the wall's base, you can make out the location of three doors that actors would have taken. The theater has been used since the 1930s for summer concerts. There are also remains of a sanctuary, a craftsmen's district, and another villa to see.

The **Quartier de la Villasse** features the splendid rue des Boutiques, made from large limestone slabs on which horse-drawn chariots

Statues hint at Vaison's once grand Roman town.

could easily drive. Under the pavement is a huge sewer system, while an overhang on the street's west side protected pedestrians from inclement weather; look for the supporting column. The nearby **House of the Silver Bust,** covering 1.2 acres (0.5 ha), is the largest urban dwelling thus far unearthed in Vaison. The adjacent *thermae* and *palestra,* built in 20 to 10 B.C., is where Romans bathed and exercised.

Medieval Vaison

Cross the 2,000-year-old Roman bridge—which has survived many floods through the ages, including a devastating torrent in 1992—to Vaison's lovingly restored **Haute Ville** (Upper Town). During the tumultuous Middle Ages, Vaison's residents took to this towering hill for protection from raiding country-men under a rival lord, hiding behind ramparts and a defensive fortress. You enter through the fortified *porte* (gate), dating from the 14th century and featuring a belfry. Narrow cobbled lanes wander up the hill, past tiny fountain-graced squares and grand stone houses, many now occupied by shops and restaurants. Flowery gardens spill over the walks and gates, providing a very picturesque set-ting. If you take rue de l'Évêque to the left, you will eventually come to the ruins of the 1192 **château,** built by Raymond V, count of Toulouse. The only way to visit the castle is by guided tour through the tourist office. Magnificent views take in the

distant wine-carpeted Ouvèze valley and Mont Ventoux.

Back in the **Basse Ville,** there are two more medieval sights to visit. Once the heart of a medieval village that has long since disappeared, the **Cathé-drale Notre-Dame-de-Nazareth** *(from Quartier de la Villasse, head to the river; cathedral will be on right, on place de la Cathédrale)* is a fine example of Romanesque architec-

---

EXPERIENCE:
Villa Vacation

The French love to repair to countryside *gîtes* for a week or more to soak in the local landscape—shopping at farmers markets for *pique-niques* and dinner and visiting sights, then returning "home" to spend long hours at shaded tables to dine, drink, and take in the views *en plein air.* You can stay in *bastides* or *mas* (farmhouses)—your choice. Gîtes are generally fully furnished and equipped for self-catering. **Gîtes de France** *(gites-de-france.com)* is the largest, oldest, and most popular company offer-ing rentals. Others include: **HomeAway** *(homeaway.com);* **Airbnb** *(airbnb.com);* and **VRBO** *(vrbo.com);* or contact the local tourism offices.

---

ture with its lovely arches. It was built in the 11th century, using stones from preceding Roman buildings. Note the 11th-century white marble altar, decorated with carved grapes and leaves.

The little **cloister** behind is charming with its single olive tree and four galleries supported by columns with leaf-carved capitals dating from the 11th and 12th centuries. ∎

Vaison-la-Romaine

 42 C3

Visitor Information

✉ Place du Chanoine-Sautel

☎ 04 90 36 02 11

🕐 Closed Sun. Oct.–April

vaison-la-romaine .com

Quartiers du Puymin & La Villasse

✉ Entrance through Puymin site

🕐 Closed Dec.

💲 $$ to all historic sites within 48 hours; audio guide in English available

A Drive Around Les Dentelles

Circling Les Dentelles de Montmirail—the mountain ridges named for their resemblance to lace—this pastoral drive takes in quintessential Provence: hill towns, bucolic views, ancient vineyards, and plenty of opportunities to stop and sample the local wine.

Côtes du Rhône vineyards carpet the countryside surrounding Les Dentelles.

Leave the lower town of **Vaison-la-Romaine ❶** (see pp. 64–65) by crossing the Roman bridge and turning left on the D938. Just beyond the hamlet of Crestet, turn right on the D76 for 1.9 miles (3 km), winding up to the hill town of **Le Crestet ❷**. Park at the base of town and continue on foot. There's the 11th-century church of **St.-Sauveur** to peek in, as well as the ruins of a 12th-century castle atop the hill, the old residence of Vaison's bishops.

Continue on the D938 to Malaucène, where you take the D90 toward Suzette, 5.5 miles (9 km) away. Midway awaits the **Col de la Chaîne**, with its wide-sweeping vistas. Onward, the road cozies up to Les Dentelles, providing close-up looks at the finely chiseled limestone crests. The many signs for *sentiers* (trails) hint at the abundant hiking and mountain-biking opportunities.

You know you're approaching **Suzette ❸** by the signs for *caveau* and *dégustation*. The view

NOT TO BE MISSED:

View from Le Crestet
• **Gigondas** • **Séguret**

is the star in this hamlet, looking out over the mountains and Crête St.-Amand.

Still following the D90, pass through tiny Lafare and onward to **Beaumes-de-Venise ❹**. Beaumes is best known for its muscat wine, drunk cool as an apéritif, which you can taste in wine cellars along avenue Raspail. Or stop by the tasting room of the **Cave Balma Vénitia** (*Quartier Ravel, tel 04 90 12 41 00, beaumes-de-venise.com*), just outside town in the direction of Vacqueyras. Another site worth a mention is the blue-shuttered **Notre-Dame-d'Aubune**, down the street from Balma Vénitia. Built in the eighth century in gratitude for the French victories against the Saracens near Tours and

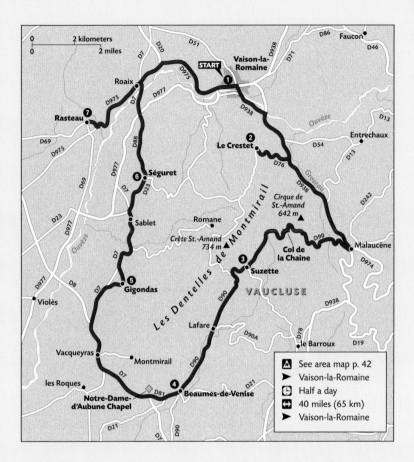

Map legend:
- See area map p. 42
- ► Vaison-la-Romaine
- Half a day
- ↔ 40 miles (65 km)
- ► Vaison-la-Romaine

Poitiers, the chapel's unusual tower was added in the 13th century.

The drive continues via the D81 and D7 through the flatlands, with wine-tasting opportunities at every turn. **Vacqueyras,** fortified in the 15th century, was the birthplace of troubadour Raimbaut de Vacqueyras. It's also home to robust and intense red wines. You soon come to the turnoff for sleepy **Gigondas ⑤,** celebrated worldwide for its powerful, robust wine. The shaded central **place Gabriel Andéol** has a few cafés and the ubiquitous wine-tasting cellars. Leave your car here to wander lanes that will bring you to **Ste.-Catherine's parish church,** with its lovely 14th-century facade.

The king of hill towns awaits down the road: **Séguret ⑥,** classified as one of France's most beautiful villages, a distinction it absolutely deserves. Steep, cobbled lanes wind past the Romanesque St.-Denis, a bubbling Renaissance fountain, and noble houses now containing restaurants, galleries, and wine-tasting shops.

Onward, a detour via the D88, D7, and D975 leads to **Rasteau ⑦,** where the **Musée du Vigneron** (rte. de Vaison-la-Romaine, tel 04 90 46 11 75, closed Tues. & Sun., & a.m. Sept.– June, $) features more than 2,500 winemaking tools. The adjacent **Domaine de Beaurenard** offers one last chance for wine-tasting before returning to Vaison-la-Romaine.

Orange

Europe's best preserved Roman theater looms over Orange's old town, a monumental reminder of the important Roman colony founded here in 35 B.C. A splendid triumphal arch, plus plenty of statuary, mosaics, and pottery, are other souvenirs of these early residents. While Orange today is a fairly large, busy city, its historic core is charming to explore.

On the edge of town, Orange's triumphal arch is adorned with military-themed sculptures.

Market Day
Thurs.

Orange
⚠ 42 B3
Visitor Information
✉ Office de Tourisme, 5 cours Aristide-Briand
☎ 04 90 34 70 88
🕐 Closed Sun. Oct.–March
otorange.fr

Théâtre Antique
✉ Place des Frères-Mounet
☎ 04 90 51 17 60
💲 $$ (combined ticket with museum)
theatre-antique.com

The idea was ingenious: The Romans headed by Augustus founded a colony in a land they had conquered (Provence) and used it as a veteran's retirement home, peopling it with soldiers from the Second Gallic Legion. The residents farmed the lands and henceforth enjoyed wealth in their later years. Called Colonia Firma Julia Secundanorum Arausio, the city had all the features of a civilized Roman town, including a forum, religious quarter, and theater. It was organized on a checkerboard layout based on the width of the theater's huge wall.

Théâtre Antique

Dominating the town center, the old Roman theater rises in its well-preserved state, a honey-colored stone edifice with a 338-foot-long (103 m) front wall, wings, passages for spectators, and storage rooms still standing—and used for performances to this day.

In the second century A.D., Roman citizens entered this very theater to enjoy the entertainment du jour—perhaps a mime show, or juggling act, or popular farce. Such diversions were used to propagate Roman culture and also to distract locals from political action and nationalistic claims. As the Roman Empire declined in the fourth century, the theater was officially closed and remained abandoned until it took on the role of defensive post in the Middle Ages and then a refuge by townspeople during the 16th-century Wars of Religion. Prosper Merimée, the director of Monuments Historiques in the 19th century, began extensive restoration work that brought the theater back to its former glory.

Begin your tour by watching the film (in French with translation), which, though grainy, provides a good run-through of the theater's history. Then, with an audio guide in hand, enter via stage right, at the base of the great stage. The seats at your back form a half circle that can hold 8,000 to 10,000 people. In Roman times, the massive stone wall in front was divided into several stories and, at its high point, was plaid with marble. Sound bounced off the facing hillside, providing perfect acoustics—a system that still works today. The wall is covered with columns, blocks, and statue niches. The only remaining authentic statue is the 13-foot-tall (4 m) statue of Augustus in the central niche, used to symbolize the emperor's universal presence. Other statues and columns are found in the Musée d'Art et d'Histoire d'Orange across the street. Note the new high-tech roof built to protect the stage wall.

The tour next takes you through dark, earthy arched galleries, with a special multimedia exhibit portraying the theater's greatest moments in four different

Les Indiennes

The bold, sun-drenched cottons gracing Provence's tables, windows, and beds are not indigenous to the region. Dutch and Portuguese traders introduced the fabric in the 1600s from India (hence their name, *les indiennes*). The fabric was highly popular throughout France, even at Louis XIV's Versailles. By the early 1770s, local manufacturers began making their own indiennes, incorporating French motifs into the design—cicadas, sunflowers, poppies. They were produced entirely by hand, including natural dyes derived from plants and minerals. Today, of course, the process is entirely mechanized, but the result is just as charming.

eras, from third century A.D. Greek comedy to a Rock of Ages musical extravaganza in the 1970s. From here, you have the option of climbing more stairs for a panoramic view over Orange as well as, on the theater's backside, visiting a temple and outbuildings whose uses have been difficult to determine.

Musée d'Art et d'Histoire d'Orange & More

Housed in the 17th-century *hôtel particulier* of a Dutch nobleman, the Art and History Museum of Orange traces the city's history. On the ground floor, a remarkable collection of Roman treasures from 25 B.C. to A.D. 10 includes famous friezes from the theater, mosaics, and objects of daily Roman life.

You'll also find exhibits focusing on Orange's later history, much of it spotlighting William I, count of Nassau. In 1544, Orange became a principality inherited by William I, who proceeded to

Musée d'Art et d'Histoire d'Orange

✉ Rue Madeleine Roch

☎ 04 90 51 17 60

$ $$ (includes theater)

theatre-antique.com

lead the Dutch revolt against Spanish rule. He became ancestor to both William III of England and the present-day royal Dutch family. One of the most interesting rooms, on the first floor, has five paintings once housed in Orange's Maison Wetter, dating from 1764. They depict the story of how *indiennes* fabrics were brought to Provence (see sidebar p. 69).

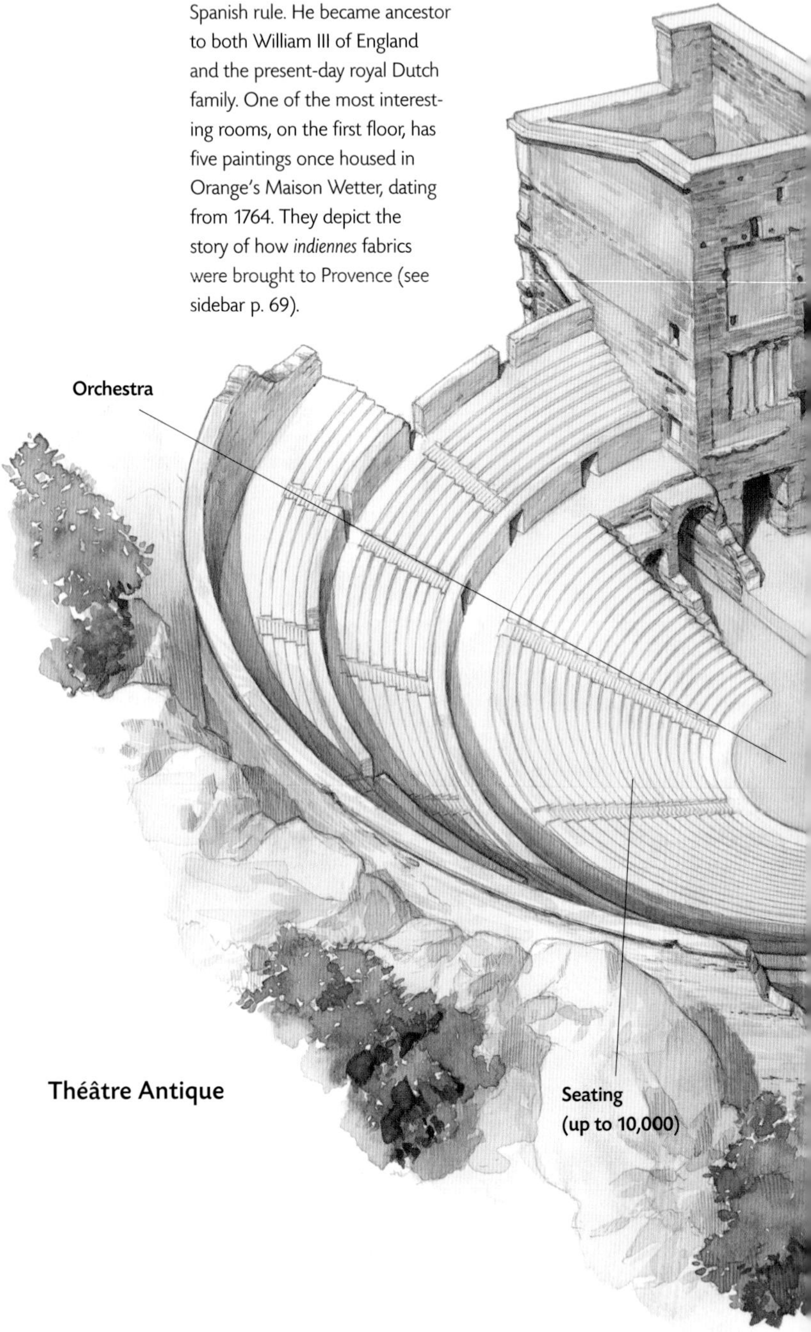

Orchestra

Théâtre Antique

Seating
(up to 10,000)

Be sure to walk up **St.-Eutrope Hill,** behind the theater, for a splendid view over town. Then stroll tiny pedestrian lanes in the old town (rue de la République, rue St.-Martin), with their ancient, pastel-colored town houses now holding restaurants, terrace cafés, and shops. Keep an eye out for the restored **Église Notre-Dame-de-Nazareth** *(18 rue du Renoyer),* consecrated in 519 and reconstructed in the 12th century in typical Romanesque style.

From here, follow signs to the **Arc de Triomphe,** built about 20 B.C. to celebrate the victories of the Second Gallic Legion. Unfortunately, the roads surrounding it are quite busy. ■

Statue of Augustus

Stage wall

Basilicae

Wooden stage

Roman Life & Culture

The Romans left vast ruins throughout Provence, hinting at a complex, intriguing way of life more than 2,000 years ago. What was their life like? Their cities? Their homes? Their clothes? Here are a few descriptions to help fill in some of the blanks.

Villas

Wealthy Romans' houses, which survived more often than less elaborate homes, consisted of a series of open and closed spaces with splashing fountains, statue-dotted pathways, and wall hangings to divide space. Porticoes and colonnades graced exteriors. Inside, rugs, hangings, furniture, and art objects richly decorated the rooms. The decor followed a simple rule of concentration: If something was hung on the wall, the floor was left bare; if there was nothing on the wall, inlaid marble or multihued mosaics covered the floor. The kitchen was often located on the north side, which was cooler and could better preserve foods. Sinks had water under pressure, connected to gutters that carried waste to outside sewers. Water inside a home was a luxury, so only the wealthiest Romans had it. The less fortunate had to fetch their water from fountains or wells.

Culinary Matters

Not every Roman was rich enough to feast. Breakfast (*ientaculum*) and lunch (*prandium*) were typically light and consisted mostly of bread and accompaniments, while dinner (*cena*) was the main meal, taking place in the late afternoon. A simple meal was mostly cold, including bread; salad of lettuce, beans, and lentils; olives; and cheeses. Hot dishes might include hams and pigs' heads, sausage in semolina, and bacon. Fancier dishes might have incorporated teats from a sow's udder or a lamb's womb stuffed with sausage. A recipe survives for a platter of small songbirds in asparagus sauce, carefully arranged with quail's

eggs. *Mulsum* (wine), flavored with honey or spices, was the usual drink of choice.

Bath Time

A daily public bath not only refreshed Romans from the hot Midi climate, but also served as a highly sociable affair. First the women would bathe, then the men. The first step was to toss off garments and perhaps work out in the exercise yards at the *palaestra* (open courtyard). Then came the plunge into the *natatio,* a great swimming pool of cool water. The *tepidarium* (warm room) was next, where bathers warmed themselves amid rich decoration. The floors were made of hollow tiles through which warm air was continuously forced from a great system of charcoal furnaces located in the substructures of the *thermae* (baths). The *caldaria* (hot baths) were next, followed by the *laconicum,* a marble-floored room filled with intense dry heat where the bathers perspired and then were scraped down with thin bronze strigils. Then they would go to the *frigidarium* (cold bath) to close their

pores. Afterward, they were rubbed down with towels and anointed with perfumed oils; the more elite partakers would finish with a massage.

Fashion à la Romaine

The clothing a Roman wore generally indicated his or her social standing. Slaves and workers wore plain tunics. Stripes on a tunic revealed an equestrian or senator. A uniform and cloak specified an army general, while an emperor wore a laurel wreath on his head. Only men who were Roman citizens could wear a toga, a semicircular piece of fabric draped around the body from the shoulders. A normal toga was always wool, usually of dull white. In the Republican days, men seeking election would often bleach their togas, hence their name—*candidati,* "extra-white" men. The man wearing a purple toga with golden embroidery could only be the emperor.

Women wore a tunic topped by a *stola,* an ample draping of cloth closed with ornate clasps and pins. Outdoors they donned a *palla* (shawl)—wealthy women owned palla in many colors.

Roman ruins at Glanum, near St.-Rémy-de-Provence

Châteauneuf-du-Pape

Striping 8,000 acres (3,237 ha) on the Rhône's east bank just north of Avignon, the Châteauneuf-du-Pape wine region is known worldwide for its majestic, full-bodied reds. The magical hilltop village at its heart is charming as can be, with its shuttered houses, narrow lanes, and *caveaux de dégustation* at every turn.

One of the town's many festivals that celebrate Provence's most famous wine

Market Day
Fri.

Châteauneuf-du-Pape
🅰 42 B3
Visitor Information
✉ Office de Tourisme, place du Portail
☎ 04 90 83 71 08
🕐 Closed Sun.
ot-chateauneuf-du-pape.mobi

Bishop Geoffroy of Avignon decided in 1157 to follow the ancient Roman tradition of making wine. Clément V planted vines in 1308. But the region's true winemaking tradition came with Pope John XXII, the "wine pope," who built his summer château here in 1317–1333 and planted vines on surrounding lands.

John XXII probably didn't realize that his lands possessed a happy geological coincidence for producing excellent wines. You'll not see fertile brown earth, but cream and rust-tinted river rocks deposited by Ice Age glaciers. The stones act as heat storers to absorb the Midi sun's warmth and reflect it back to the vines long after sunset. The result: full ripeness in the grapes yielding robust and full-bodied wines. The alluvial soil beneath, widely spaced vines, and the mistral winds also add to the wine's success.

Interestingly, Châteauneuf-du-Pape was the first wine region to have received its own Appellation d'Origine Contrôlée rating. Baron

Le Roy de Boiseaumarié, a distinguished local vintner, proposed specific geographical boundaries and minimum standards for wines to be given the Châteauneuf-du-Pape label. In 1933 area vintners won exclusive rights to market their wines under that label. From this came the government-controlled rating system used today (see sidebar p. 23).

The region covers 8,000 acres (3,237 ha), making it the Rhône's largest *cru* appellation. Yet it produces only two wines: red (representing 94 percent of the region's production) and white.

INSIDER TIP:

The ruined château is the amateur photographer's idyllic subject. Photos from inside or from afar will make for great stories back home.

—DAVID KENNEDY
National Geographic contributor

High in alcohol and easy to enjoy, the strong, full-bodied Châteauneuf red officially can be made using a mixture of 3, 7, or 13 varieties of grapes, though in practice only a few traditionalists use all 13. The predominant grape is Grenache, with Mourvèdre, Syrah, and/or Cinsault often added.

Visiting

The beautifully preserved medieval town has few shops or boutiques. Instead, the business

---

EXPERIENCE:
Savoring Côtes du Rhône

In the shadow of Châteauneuf-du-Pape's ruined castle, **Le Verger des Papes** *(verger despapes.com, English spoken)* doesn't look like much on the outside. But step inside and you enter a world 2,000 years old, with Gallo-Roman walls and stone wine vats that once held Roman wines. This is just one *cave* in Châteauneuf-du-Pape that gives you a back-to-the-roots experience of wine-tasting. The small **rue Joseph Ducos** in the medieval village is lined with different wine-tasting (and buying) opportunities. A good place to start is **Vinadea** *(8 rue Maréchal Foche, tel 04 90 83 72 21, www.vinadea.com),* the official Maison des Vins selling the wines of 100 Châteauneuf-du-Pape estates at cellar-door prices. Or stop by the **Musée du Vin Brotte** *(av. Pierre de Luxembourg, tel 04 90 83 59 44, brotte.com),* where an audio tour leads you through the region's wine story, topped with a sampling of several wines—all for free. To tour wineries, call ahead and make a reservation; the local tourism office offers a list of vineyard visits.

---

at hand is apparent in the many *caveaux de dégustation* offering tastings (see sidebar this page).

Narrow lanes lead up to the papal castle, **Château du Pape**—at least what's left of it, after being sacked in 1562 by Protestant troops during the Wars of Religion. It overlooks the sweeping vineyards first planted by the popes; on a clear day, you can make out the shadowy silhouette of Avignon's Palais des Papes in the distance. You can also drive to the château; go north out of town on the D68 to the first traffic circle (about half a mile/1 km), turn left then left again on the next road south. ■

More Places to Visit in Avignon & the Vaucluse

Market day in Carpentras

Carpentras

In bustling, crowded Carpentras, the quintessential medieval town center is lovely to wander. One interesting sight is the 14th-century **synagogue** *(place de l'Hôtel de Ville)*, France's oldest. It appears very plain on the outside, but is richly decorated inside; the prayer room, for instance, resembles a Louis XIV salon, with gold-painted paneling, jade green wood, and a sky blue ceiling full of gold stars. The synagogue has baths used in the monthly ritual purification of women as well as ovens where unleavened bread was baked. The former **Cathédrale St.-Siffrein** *(place St.-Siffrein)* is a pastiche of styles, from the 15th-century Provençal Gothic to an early 20th-century bell tower. St. Siffrein's feast day (Nov. 27) is Carpentras's largest fair and signals the start of truffle season. The market, one of Provence's largest, is held every Friday morning on place Aristide Briande; and the annual truffle market takes place on Fridays between late November and late March.

🄰 42 C3 **Visitor Information** *carpentras-ventoux.com* ✉ Office de Tourisme, 97 place du 25 Août 1944 ☎ 04 90 63 00 78

Cavaillon

This lively city is famous for its sweet cantaloupes, introduced during the Italian Wars by Charles VIII. Filling market stalls May to September, they are celebrated during the mid-July Fête du Melon. Roman artifacts found in the surrounding area are on display at the **archaeological museum** *(Hôtel Dieu Porte d'Avignon, tel 04 90 76 63 05, closed Nov.–April, $, combined ticket with Musée Juif-Comtadin)*. A Roman arch stands on place François Tourel *(in front of tourist office)*. Here, too, is the 12th-century **Cathédrale St.-Véran** and a beautiful synagogue (1772–1774) with its **Musée Juif-Comtadin** (Jewish Museum; *rue Hébraïque, tel 04 90 72 26 86, closed Tues., & Sun. Nov.–April, $, combined ticket with archaeological museum)*, exhibiting objects used for worship, books, and documents on the prayers.

🄰 42 C2 **Visitor Information** *cavaillon-luberon.com* ✉ Office de Tourisme, place du 25 Août 1944 ☎ 04 90 71 32 01

Mont Ventoux

Italian poet Francesco Petrarch (1304–1374) climbed Mont Ventoux in 1336 for no other reason than "a desire to see its conspicuous height"—thereby inventing the sport of mountain climbing. When he reached the top he "remained immobile, stupefied by the strange lightness of the air and the immensity of the spectacle." These days, there's a hairpin road that snakes to the top, crowded with cyclists in summertime (now and again the road is included in the Tour de France). The vegetation changes as you climb, from lavender fields and vineyards, through a forest of beeches and cedars, then pines. The lunar summit, at 6,263 feet (1,909 m), is a parched, bald semidesert, snowcapped at least half the year and nearly always blasted by winds up to 250 miles (402 km) an hour (Ventoux means the "windy one"). A great portion of the mountain was declared a UNESCO biosphere reserve in 1990. Hiking and skiing are popular seasonal pursuits. You can access the main summit route (D974) at **Malaucène**, a busy bourg with a fortified 14th-century church and fountain-filled historic heart. Or, take the quieter, prettier D19, which you can pick up south of Malaucène before Le Barroux. While in the region, be sure to taste the local specialty, *épeautre*, or wild barley (also known as "poor man's wheat"), washed down with a local Ventoux wine. 🅰 42 C3

Musée de la Lavande

Gleaming copper stills, flacons, and old-style labels take you through the story of lavender at this excellent museum in Coustellet. A bilingual video describes the cultivation process, then, audio guide in hand, you wander through a series of informative displays. The whole museum smells of lavender, and a shop at the end gives you the chance to bring home many forms of the herb. Lavender is distilled outside in season. *www.museedelalavande.com* ✉ 276 rte. de Gordes, Coustellet ☎ 04 90 74 92 40 🕐 Closed Jan. 💲 $$

Musée de la Lustrerie

This unique museum showcases a superb collection of chandeliers, dating from the 15th century to present day, proving that functionality can be artful as well. *mathieulustrerie.com* ✉ Hameau des Sauvans, Gargas ☎ 04 90 76 91 23

Pernes-les-Fontaines

Thirty-six fountains from the mid-18th century grace this quiet medieval town, a former capital of the Comtat-Venaissin. Near

Field Patterns

Provence's field patterns differ from those of northern France, part of the lingering influence of the ancient Romans. While fields in the north tend to be either large patchworks bounded by hedges or stone walls, or long and open spaces, Provençal fields are small, an artistic mingling of cultivated strips, vines, and fruit trees.

The Romans divided Provence into squares called "centuries," thereby creating a grid pattern for the rural landscape just as they created a town plan. Thanks to Roman inheritance laws, in which all sons were allocated equal shares of land, rather than just the eldest, field sizes were small.

Tools also influenced the region's field patterns. Since Roman times, southern fields have been tilled with the *araire*, a small, light tool that opens the earth without turning it over. It's conducive to sandy, stony limestone soil and can be drawn by a single animal—perfect for Provence's small, hilly plots. To prepare the ground for sowing, the farmer must plow each field twice, once up and down and once crosswise—hence the unique pattern.

There are no walls, in addition, in southern fields—another Roman touch. Physical barriers were not necessary to mark property lines, since everyone knew that enforcement of the legal code was taken seriously.

Finally, groves of trees are prominent features. The Romans planted clusters of olive and fruit trees in the middle of fields, providing a cool place to rest and store the water gourd while working in hot weather—an inspiration for artists for centuries to come.

Fort Saint-André, Villeneuve-lez-Avignon

the chapel of Notre-Dame-des-Grâces, incorporated into the old city walls, is the town's most striking fountain, the baroque **Fontaine du Cormoran,** with its majestic statue of an open-winged cormorant. If you drink from the **Fontaine de la Lune,** say locals, you will go crazy. The visitor center has a map for a fountain-themed walking tour.

🅰 42 C3 **Visitor Information** *tourisme-pernes.fr* ✉ Office de Tourisme, place Gabriel Moutte ☎ 04 90 61 31 04

Vénasque

This quiet little hill town, built on a rock spur in the heart of the Forêt de Vénasque, once reigned as the region's capital. During the barbarian invasions in the Middle Ages, the bishops of Carpentras retreated to this strategic spot, explaining the impressive collection of early Christian and medieval buildings. (In fact, the town gave its name to the Comtat-Venaissin.) As you stroll the pretty streets, seek out the **Église de Notre-Dame** *(at the spur's northern point),* whose well-preserved baptistery, built in the sixth century, is one of France's oldest religious buildings.

🅰 42 C3 **Visitor Information** *tourisme-venasque.com* ✉ Office de Tourisme, Grand'Rue ☎ 04 90 66 11 66

Villeneuve-lez-Avignon

In 1307 King Philippe le Bel built a castle across the Rhône from Avignon's papal palace, around which sprung up a "new town." As the popes' importance grew, so did the king's watchtower, the **Tour Philippe Le Bel** *(rue Montée de la Tour, tel 04 32 70 08 57, closed Mon. & Dec.–Feb., $),* which stands exactly where the Pont St.-Bénezet once joined the west bank. The tower still affords a marvelous view. In the town center, the 14th-century **Église de Notre-Dame** *(place du Chapître)* rises in medieval splendor—don't miss the peaceful cloister. Nearby, the **Musée Municipal Pierre de Luxembourg** *(rue de la République, tel 04 90 27 49 66, closed Mon. & Jan., $)* has among its four floors of artworks two masterpieces: the 14th-century "Madonna and Child," delicately carved of ivory; and the "Coronation of the Virgin" (1454) by Enguerrand Quarton, one of the Avignon school's leading lights. Down the street is the **Chartreuse du Val de Bénédiction** *(rue de la République, tel 04 90 15 24 24, $$),* once France's largest and most important Carthusian charterhouse. Established by Pope Innocent VI in 1352, much of it now lies in ruins. Nevertheless, the intimate cloisters and the monks' cells give a sense of yesteryear's spirit. The small chapel off Cloître du Cimetière has beautiful frescoes by Matteo Giovanetti. Overlooking the charterhouse is the **Fort Saint-André** *(montée du Fort, fort: tel 04 90 25 55 95, abbey: by appt., fort tower: $, fort-saint-andre.monuments-nationaux.fr, abbey: $$, closed Mon., abbayesaintandre.fr),* its 14th-century fortifications giving magnificent views over the Rhône to Avignon. Inside are the remains of the **Abbaye St.-André,** a tiny Romanesque chapel set amid a garden of roses, lavender, and wisteria.

🅰 42 B2 **Visitor Information** *villeneuvelesavignon.fr* ✉ Office de Tourisme, 1 place Charles David ☎ 04 90 25 61 33

The heart of the Provençal spirit, an agrarian realm of chalky peaks, beaches, medieval towns, and flamingo-dotted marshlands

South Along the Rhône

Van Gogh's chair

South Along the Rhône

South of Avignon, the River Rhône becomes sluggish and wide as it approaches the Mediterranean. The Romans flourished here, establishing cities at Nîmes, Arles, and St.-Rémy. But the region is probably most associated with Vincent van Gogh, who madly captured its sunflowers, starry nights, and olive trees in many of his best known works.

Roman Nîmes possesses some of the best preserved monuments from its toga-clad forebears, including Les Arènes, the world's finest example of a Roman amphitheater, and the Maison Carrée, a beautifully preserved temple. Today Nîmes is a lively city showcasing bullfights and flamenco music and lazy café afternoons. Nearby Pont du Gard, part of the Roman aqueduct that supplied water to ancient Nîmes, is one of Rome's most famous legacies.

Southward, the isolated realm of the

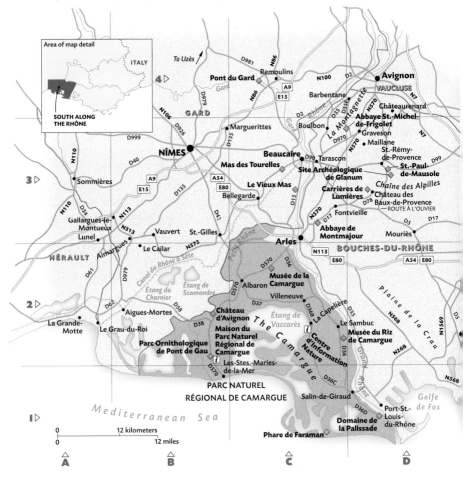

Nîmes is famed for its Roman-era monuments, with plenty of sunny cafés to take a time-out.

Camargue is the domain of the French *gardian* (cowboy), master of the indigenous white horse and wild black bull. Millions of birds gather here year-round (including flamingos!), luring bird-watchers by the hordes.

Nearby Arles is one of Provence's most charming towns, with medieval lanes and café-ringed squares. The Romans left behind the Arènes, a twin to the amphitheater in Nîmes, amid other monuments. North is Les Baux, former stronghold of the medieval warlords, whose lower town has been invaded by souvenir shops.

Lesser known, and much less touristy, La Montagnette—"little mountain"—to the north of Tarascon provides a scenic wander through forests sprinkled with medieval towns and a fascinating abbey.

On the nearby plains, van Gogh locked himself in the insane asylum at St.-Rémy, where he painted in a flurry of productivity. The Romans knew St.-Rémy long before, the remains of their town (called Glanum) providing a good primer on ancient Roman life. Today St.-Rémy is a pleasant market town with upscale shops installed in historic buildings. ■

NOT TO BE MISSED:

Nîmes's Roman amphitheater and Maison Carrée **83**

The amazing Pont du Gard, still standing after 2,000 years **85**

Horseback riding like a true Camargue *gardian* **89**

Van Gogh's Arles **95**

Medieval Les-Baux-de-Provence **98–99**

Market day in St.-Rémy-de-Provence **101**

Cavaillon
A7
Orgon
E714
Sénas
AVIGNON &
THE VAUCLUSE
p. 41
D569
N538
D23
Eyguières
D17
N7
N113
Salon-de-Provence
N569
D69
Pélissanne
St.-Cannat
A7
E80
Miramas
E714
N113
Coudoux
D10
A8
E80
St.-Chamas
D10
N7
Chaîne de Vitrolles
D543
Istres
Étang de Berre
Berre-l'Étang
Rognac
D21
St.-Mitre-les-Remparts
A7
E714
D9
D5
A51
Marignane
E712
Martigues
N568
N368
AIX, MARSEILLE, & THE VAR
p. 105
A55
N568
D49
D9
MARSEILLE
Carro
Carry-le-Rouet
E
F

Nîmes

Nîmes's historic core, bustling with chic boutiques and cafés, provides a taste of urban Provence, though most people come for its ancient history. The Romans established a colony here in 30 B.C., naming it after their river god, Nemausus. With the help of Caesar Augustus (27 B.C.–A.D. 14), the city flourished. Nîmes still has several monuments reflecting its past importance, including one of the world's best preserved Roman amphitheaters.

The Maison Carrée once stood among other important buildings on Nîmes's ancient Roman forum.

Market Days
Daily

Nîmes
🅼 80 B3
Visitor Information
✉ Office de
   Tourisme, 6 rue
   Auguste
☎ 04 66 58 38 00

ot-nimes.fr

DISCOUNT CARD:
The Nîmes Romaine combination ticket ($$) provides reduced admission to Les Arènes, La Maison Carrée, and Tour Magne.

Even though Nîmes belongs to the Languedoc-Roussillon province, its ambience is more Provençal, with its brightly colored café tables and languorous air—a touch of Spain added in to spice things up. Festivals of *corridas* (bullfights) are raucous affairs in the ancient amphitheater—the most important event being the Great Roman Games in spring, when the city transforms into a Roman city, with gladiators in the arena, a regal procession on the streets, and an emperor reigning over all.

The city can be difficult to negotiate by car. Essentially, the

historic district comprises a triangle bounded by boulevard Gambetta, boulevard Victor Hugo, and boulevard de la Libération/boulevard Amiral Courbet. Follow signs for the Arènes and park in the garage beneath. From here you can explore the old town by foot.

Roman Nîmes

A good first stop is the **Musée Archéologique,** which provides insight into the past with locally excavated statues, sarcophagi, coins, mosaics, and pottery. Note that in 2017 these collections are slated to move to the brand-new

Musée de la Romanité, facing the Roman amphitheater.

Otherwise, you will likely be drawn first to the magnificent, imposing **Arènes** lording over the historic center's southern edge. Built in the first century A.D., this is where gladiators and animals faced each other in bitter combat. The floor, or arena (which means "sand," used to soak up the blood), covered passages from which wild bears, bulls, and tigers were raised on an elevator to face the gladiator. The man rarely lost.

Built without mortar, Nîmes arena is in such good condition that it's still used for cultural, musical, and sporting events; bullfights are one of the main attractions—both the traditional Spanish corrida, where the bull is killed, and the Provençal *course Carmarguaise,* where it is not (see p. 89).

Two levels of 60 arches each compose the arena's facade, with an additional attic level, of which only traces remain. Romans were preoccupied with the concept of spectator flow pattern, and they perfected it here with a complicated system of corridors and stairs so that the entire place—23,000 to 24,000 people in 34 tiers of seats—could be emptied in minutes. In the Quartier des Gladiateurs, one room is dedicated to bullfights, another to gladiators, including costumes.

Another Roman monument stands a couple hundred yards away, at the end of the rue de l'Horloge: the elegant, restored **Maison Carrée** (Square House). Built from local stones between A.D. 3 and 5 and modeled after the Temple of Apollo near Rome, this Corinthian temple is the only entirely preserved building of the forum that once stood here. It's surrounded by columns, six on the short sides, 11 on the long (so it's actually a rectangle, not a square). Be sure to see the excellent 3-D film inside that puts the story of Nîmes in historical context.

While in the area, peek into the glass-and-aluminum **Carré d'Art,** a contemporary art museum designed by British architect Lord Norman Foster and often referred to as the Pompidou Center of southern France.

Jardins de la Fontaine

Just north of the Maison Carrée, a tree shaded *allée* wanders along a waterway to Jardins de la Fontaine (Fountain Gardens).

Jeans de Nîmes

Denim, the all-American fabric, originated in France—in Nîmes, to be precise; hence, its name: de Nîmes, "from Nîmes." It all started in the 18th century, when Nîmes's large Protestant middle class, banned from government posts, turned to trade and manufacturing. Among their products was a twilled silk and wool fabric called serge, popular among workers and fishermen for its sturdy, flexible quality. Serge made its way across the Atlantic, where it was used in slave clothing. When Bavarian immigrant Levi-Strauss opened up a dry goods store in San Francisco in the mid-1800s to supply gold miners, he and a pal came up with the idea of making work coveralls from the fabric from Nîmes that would endure the stress of mining. Thus was born a new fashion trend.

Musée Archéologique

✉ 13 bis blvd. Amiral Courbet
☎ 04 66 76 74 80
🕐 Closed Mon.

Les Arènes

✉ Place des Arènes
☎ 04 66 21 82 56
💲 $$

arenes-nimes.com

Maison Carrée

✉ Place de la Maison Carrée
☎ 04 66 21 82 56
💲 $

arenes-nimes.com

The old Roman Arènes is a common Nîmes backdrop.

**Carré d'Art—
Musée d'Art
Contemporain**
- ✉ Place de la
  Maison Carrée
- ☎ 04 66 76 35 70
- 🕐 Closed Mon.
- 💲 $$

carreartmusee.com

**Jardins de la
Fontaine**
- ✉ Corner of quai
  de la Fontaine &
  av. Jean-Jaurès
- ☎ 04 66 58 38 00

**Musée du
Vieux Nîmes**
- ✉ Place aux
  Herbes
- ☎ 04 66 76 73 70
- 🕐 Closed Mon.
  Guided visits
  3 p.m. Sat.
  (French only)

The Romans established their city around a sacred spring, where they built a sanctuary that included a temple, theater, and baths. Vestiges were discovered when the Jardins de la Fontaine were built in 1745. Today you can stroll among green pools surrounding fountains dotted with marble nymphs. At the garden's south end is the **Temple de Diane,** probably built in the second century A.D. On the north side towers the city's oldest Roman monument, the **Tour Magne** (*$*).

Other Roman remains include two gates from the ancient city wall: the **Porte de France,** the exit toward Spain along the Via Domitia; and the **Porte d'Auguste** (*blvd. Amiral Courbet*), where the Via Domitia entered town.

Old Town

The old quarter is a picturesque maze of pedestrian streets, cozy squares, fountains, and historic houses now holding cafés, restaurants, and boutiques. If you amble up Grande Rue you'll come to the **Cathédrale Notre-Dame et St.-Castor** (also called Cathédrale de Nîmes; *place aux Herbes*). Consecrated in 1096 by Pope Urban III, it is a composite of styles. During the 16th-century Wars of Religion, Protestants killed eight priests out front.

Next door is the small but interesting **Musée du Vieux Nîmes,** recounting the city's history since the Middle Ages.

INSIDER TIP:

While walking through the old town, stop at the fountain designed by M. Raysse representing a crocodile by a palm tree, both emblems of the city.

—MICHELINE PLACE
*National Geographic Expeditions
tour leader*

It's installed in the former Episcopal palace from the late 1600s, with a couple of period rooms reconstructing the interior of Nîmois houses. A surprise is the room devoted to the development of the famous blue-jean fabric—a local specialty (see sidebar p. 83).

Finally, the **Musée des Cultures Taurines** (*6 rue Alexandre Ducros, tel 04 66 36 83 77, open Tues.–Sun. mid-May–Oct. & first weekend Nov.– April*), behind the arena, celebrates regional and international bullfighting through works of art and everyday objects. ∎

Pont du Gard

Newly urbanized Nîmes did not have an adequate water source, so the Romans built a 31-mile-long (50 km) system of canals that brought fresh water from the springs at Uzès, 15 miles (25 km) away. One of the most amazing aspects of this complex system was the Pont du Gard. The Romans themselves considered the aqueduct the best testimony of their empire—what would they think if they knew their work would last 2,000 years in such majestic totality?

The 900-foot-long (275 m) Pont du Gard comprises three levels of arches: six crossing the River Gard; 11 in the middle tier; and 35 smaller arches carrying the water duct above. Imagine the work it took to hoist limestone blocks weighing up to 6 tons (5.4 tonnes) into place and fit them together—a thankless job accomplished by thousands of soldiers, craftsmen, and slaves during the reign of Emperor Claudius (R. A.D. 41–54).

The Pont du Gard carried 9.2 million gallons (34.8 million L) of water a day across the River Gard for Nîmes's ancient citizens.

Visiting

Both sides of the river provide access to the aqueduct. Your best bet is to park on the river's left bank, where you'll find an interpretive center and a fabulous museum offering films, models, maquettes, and a children's center. The quarry that supplied the pont's stone is also open.

From here, a short path leads to the aqueduct. You can walk across the structure's bottom tier, which has been used as a thoroughfare for centuries—in 1285 the bishop of Uzès ordered a toll be collected from all travelers crossing the bridge. And if you call ahead, you can take a guided tour across the top of the bridge, walking in the channel through which the water once coursed.

Trails lace the forested site. On hot days, swim in the river, or rent a kayak or canoe and skim across a reflection of the ancient aqueduct, towering 158 feet (48 m) above. ∎

Floods

The feisty River Gard has flooded through the centuries, the most recent devastation occurring in 2002—destroying the museum and cafeteria, as well as devastating the riverbank. The 2,000-year-old aqueduct, however, has remained standing every time.

Pont du Gard

🅰 80 C4

✉ Rte. du Pont du Gard, betw. Remoulins (RN 100) & Vers-Pont du Gard (D 81)

☎ 04 66 37 22 34

💲 Parking: $$

ot-pontdugard.com

The Camargue

Long-horned bulls and white horses with flowing manes run semifree throughout the Camargue, a marshland frontier south of the ancient city of Arles. The Camarguian *gardian* (cowboy) is alive and well, showing up at tourist events and *courses de taureaux* (bull games) when real work isn't going on. The Camargue is also a supreme bird preserve—home to more than 300 species, its most famous denizen being the greater flamingo. To watch these lanky pink birds gliding effortlessly in the pure blue sky, whole flocks of them, is one of Provence's most memorable sights.

Surrounded by lagoons and marshlands, the Phare (lighthouse) de Faraman, in the Camargue's southeast, was built in 1892.

The Camargue

🗺 80 B1–B2, C1–C2, D1

Visitor Information

✉ Office de Tourisme d'Arles, blvd. des Lices, Arles

☎ 04 90 18 41 20

arlestourisme.com

At Arles, the great River Rhône divides into two, its main arm, the Grand Rhône, taking a direct route to the Mediterranean, while the Petit Rhône meanders west. In between, in the rough shape of a triangle, is the Rhône River Delta—the Camargue—a marshy soup of wetlands, pastures, dunes, and salt flats, with the large Étang de Vaccarès (Vaccarès Lagoon) in the middle.

For centuries, humans have inhabited this land with a wary eye toward the sea and river, whose efforts to dominate are ceaseless. It was not until the 19th century that dikes and embankments were built, so that human domination was finally secured and farmlands could be extended to feed a growing population. A wildlife preserve was created in 1927 and the government established the Parc Naturel Régional de Camargue in 1970. The park preserves 328 square miles (85,000 ha) of this thriving ecosystem; its excellent trails and information stations make visiting easy.

The D570 traces the Petit Rhône's route from Arles to Les-Stes.-Maries-de-la-Mer, the Camargue's main town, while the D36 cuts down along the Grand Rhône to Salin-de-Giraud. In between, the bird-rich Étang de Vaccarès is accessible via smaller roads.

INSIDER TIP:

Get to know the Camargue by spending a few hours in a *manade* with *gardians*. They will share their passion for the bulls and horses as you enjoy traditional food and local music.

—MICHELINE PLACE
National Geographic Expeditions tour leader

Down to Les-Stes.-Maries-de-la-Mer

About 20 miles (32 km) south of Arles on the D570 is the award-winning **Musée de la Camargue** *(Mas du Pont de Rousty, Albaron, tel 04 90 97 10 28, closed Tues., $$, parc-camargue.fr),* which provides a thorough introduction to regional history and culture. The museum is housed in a *bergerie* (sheepfold) of the Mas du Pont de Rousty, built in 1812.

The imaginative exhibits skillfully translate the evolution of the relationship between man and the Camargue landscape—especially the constant fight against floods and the mistral to eke out a living. An interactive map of the Camargue helps put it all in perspective. Outside, a 2.2-mile (3.5 km) nature trail takes you into the heart of the Camargue.

The 18th-century **Château d'Avignon,** farther south off the D570, is furnished just as it was in the 1890s, when a wealthy Marseille merchant used it as a hunting lodge.

Farther south is the **Maison du Parc Naturel Régional de Camargue,** a favorite spot for bird-watchers. It's the park's main information center, with an exhibit of mounted birds helping to identify the live ones you can see outside the giant picture windows overlooking the Étang de Ginès (Ginès Marsh).

Next door awaits one of the area's major attractions, the **Parc Ornithologique de Pont de Gau,** where you'll probably get your closest look at the area's *flamants roses*—greater flamingos. This is the only site in Europe where flamingos breed regularly—on average between 10,000 and 13,000 pairs a year. A 2.8-mile (4.5 km) trail takes you through 148 acres (60 ha) of marshland. Other denizens: white storks, rollers, hoopoes, and Egyptian vultures (if you're lucky).

Next stop, **Les-Stes.-Maries-de-la-Mer,** full of Spanish charm with its tile roofs and devotion to *(continued on p. 90)*

(continued on p. 90)

Château d'Avignon

⚑ 80 B2

✉ Domaine du Château d'Avignon, rte. d'Arles

☎ 04 13 31 94 54

⏲ Closed Mon.–Tues. April–Oct., open Thurs–Fri. for group reservations rest of year

💲 $

chateaudavignon.fr

Maison du Parc Naturel Régional de Camargue

⚑ 80 B2

✉ Mas du Pont de Rousty/D570, Pont de Gau

☎ 04 90 97 10 82

parc-camargue.fr

Parc Ornithologique de Pont de Gau

⚑ 80 B2

✉ D570, 2.5 miles (4 km) N of Les-Stes.-Maries-de-la-Mer

☎ 04 90 97 82 62

💲 $$

parcornithologique .com

Les-Stes.-Maries-de-la-Mer

⚑ 80 B1

Visitor Information

✉ Office de Tourisme, 5 av. van Gogh

☎ 04 90 97 82 55

saintesmaries .com

Wild, Wild Camargue

On a summer Sunday in Les-Stes.-Maries-de-la-Mer, the main street suddenly clears. People crowd along its shoulders, craning to look down the empty road. Then a shout, and everyone cheers, as six men in black felt hats gallop by on white stallions with long billowing tails. Among them is the reason for this *abrivado:* a sextet of black bulls destined for the bull ring. People try to encourage the bulls to escape—the excitement has begun.

A Camargue tradition: the *roussataio*—the releasing of horses into city streets

With its vast, undeveloped marshlands, wild longhorn bulls, white stallions, and true-to-life cowboys—called *gardians* here—the Camargue is about as close to the Wild West as France gets. It's a tradition that goes back to the 16th century, when the first gardians established ranch houses—*manades*—to culti-vate the native cattle and horses. What has evolved is a singular way of life, one of hard work and independence and freedom.

The Camargue Horse

Small, nimble, known for their intelli-gence and agility, the horses descend from prehistoric animals. Indeed, they resemble the horses painted on the walls of Lascaux, dating back some 15,000 years. They roam the Camargue part of the year, grazing on stunted reed beds, and marsh and field grasses. Once a year, the gardians round them up. Instead of six-shooters in their holsters, these cowboys use three-forked prongs called *ficherouns* and horsehair lassos that, according to legend, were brought by Buffalo Bill himself. Inferior three-year-old males are removed and gelded. The others are broken and tamed for farm work and, these days, to give trail rides to visitors.

The Bulls

No one knows exactly where the wild bulls came from. Some say it's Attila the Hun who brought their ancestors from Asia Minor, which were then crossbred with the Spanish Navarre bull. Small in stature with lyre-shaped horns, spirited, cunning, and rebellious, these dark, rough-haired beasts

EXPERIENCE: Horseback Riding

Stocky yet agile, the Camargue's iconic white horses have long played an integral role in life on the *manade* (ranch or farm), with *gardians* using them to herd the black Camargue bulls. Experience these gorgeous beasts yourself at a number of manades throughout the Camargue, including **Mas Saint Germain** *(tel 04 90 97 00 60, massaintgermain.fr).* Here, you choose your horse among the many grazing in the field (or, more appropriately, it picks you), bring it to the barn to saddle up, jump astride, and off you go to explore the pastures and marshlands, oftentimes alongside true gardians. Along the way you'll spot some of the

Camargue's spectacular wildlife, including foxes, egrets, herons, and, with a bit of luck, flamingos.

Another recommended outfitter is **Le Palomino Le Boumian** *(rte. d'Arles, tel 04 90 97 93 12 or 06 09 31 89 98, palomino-leboumian.camargue.fr),* which offers promenades with lunch on the beach, as well as overnight camping excursions.

Visit *saintesmaries.com* for more horseback-riding possibilities. Many manades also offer lodging, horse shows, and other unique opportunities.

Whatever you do, be sure to bring plenty of mosquito repellent. The Camargue boasts some of France's most ferocious mosquitoes!

---

are not conducive to farm work. Instead, they roam the Camargue as they please until the bullfight season, when they are rounded up.

In spring, the *ferrada* takes place—the traditional branding of the cattle. In olden days (and still today), it's a time when families from far-off farms gathered and socialized. Year-old calves are branded with an iron stamped on their rump, their ears notched.

Bull Games

But the greatest events are the "bull games." Formerly, bulls were brought to farms, or to the village square, where they were released into an arena fashioned out of carts and barrels. There, young boys confronted them— the precursor of today's *courses Camarguaises.*

These bullfights vary greatly from their Spanish cousins. Most notably, the bull is never killed. He may become extremely angry and perturbed and grunt a lot, but most of the risk falls to the bullfighters, who face the bull on equal terms. Also, it's the bull—not the bullfighter—who is the star. People will travel from village to village to follow a champion

bull. One of the most famous was Le Sanglier, who has his own mausoleum in Le Cailar.

A *course* typically consists of six bulls from the same ranch—the strongest bulls kept for last, when the *raseteurs* (bullfighters) are most tired. At the sound of a trumpet, a bull is released into the ring, where await 20 young raseteurs dressed in white. Their goal: to unhook "attributes"—including strings and tassels—from the bull's horns with a finger-held rake. Points are awarded for retrieving different ones (and the bull receives points for avoiding them). It's a game of cat and mouse as the snorting bull charges and the boys spring to safety up and over low safety walls. The excitement comes when the boys take chances, egging on the bull, trying to make him charge. If the pursuing bull bangs the fence, the "Toreador" overture of *Carmen* is played. If the bull keeps his decorations for 15 minutes, he wins the crowd's respect and the "fight" is over.

The most prestigious bull games—the Cocarde d'Or—take place in Arles in July, where the best bulls and raseteurs compete for prizes. You can also see courses Camarguaises in Nîmes, Tarascon, and Les-Stes.-Maries-de-la-Mer.

**Domaine de
la Palissade**

🅰 80 D1

✉ BP5, Salin-de-
Giraud

☎ 04 42 86 81 28

💲 $

palissade.fr

bulls. The popular beach, board-walk, and souvenir shops give it a Coney Island feel as well. The tallest thing around for miles is the Romanesque **Église des Stes.-Maries** (place de l'Église), with its single, upright nave, built in the 9th and 12th centuries. Somber and cavelike, the interior has a crypt beneath the altar lit with hundreds of

INSIDER TIP:

If you are driving, an additional thrill is to take the Bac Sauvage, a ferry across the Petit Rhône that you might share with the horses.

—MICHELINE PLACE
*National Geographic Expeditions
tour leader*

Flamingo-Watching

On a warm May day, stroll in the Camargue wetlands and inevitably you'll come across a spectacle of nature: thousands of pink-and-red greater flamingos wading in the water, then suddenly taking off in a cloud of red and pink. The greater flamingo colony is typically most active during breeding season (Nov.–March), though it's possible to spot them year-round.

Some of the best places to watch these spectacular birds—as well as 400-plus other species—include the **Parc Naturel Régional de Camargue** and the neighboring **Parc Ornithologique** (see p. 87). The footpaths around **La Capelière** and the **Domaine de la Palissade** (see p. 91) also offer good viewing perches. Another option is to take a 4WD "safari"; check out *reserve-camargue.org*.

revered patron saint, is also preserved in the crypt, covered with a huge layer of dresses provided as offerings. On May 24 and 25, thousands of Gypsies pilgrimage here to worship the Marys and Sara. Be sure to climb the narrow spiral steps to the **Terrasse de l'Eglise** ($), the rooftop terrace surrounded by a parapet with battlements and machicolation—hinting at the church's onetime role as a fortress against Saracen, Arab, and pirate attacks.

If the loudspeakers are blaring near the beach, a *course de taureaux* is likely taking place at the Arènes, near the Office de Tourisme. Inquire at the tourist office for a schedule and ticket information.

To the Other Side of Étang de Vaccarès

From Les-Stes.-Maries-de-la-Mer, backtrack 14 miles (23 km) north to the turnoff for the D37, which brings you around the northern edge of Étang de Vaccarès.

Farther on at Villeneuve, the D36B sidles next to the water along the lagoon's east side, with observation towers along

Musée du Riz

✉ Rizerie du Petit
Manusclat

☎ 06 38 16 56 90

🕐 By appt. only

💲 $

museeduriz.fr

votives. Here are preserved the relics of the Sts. Mary—Mary Salomé, mother of the apostles James and John; and Mary Jacobé, the Virgin Mary's sister. Upon Jesus' crucifixion, they, along with Mary Magdalene, Lazarus, and other biblical figures, were shoved out to sea without sails or oars, finally washing ashore here. A statue of their Egyptian servant Sara, the Gypsies' highly

the way to bird-watch. The **Centre d'Information Nature,** in the hamlet of La Capelière, has exhibits on flora and fauna, plus trails to wander.

Follow signs to industrial **Salin-de-Giraud,** where the landscape changes dramatically. The enormous saltworks here have been in production since the 19th century. You'll see pyramids of the white stuff from an overlook just south of town on the D36D (there's a snack shop here, too).

A few miles farther south on the D36D is the **Domaine de la Palissade,** interesting in that it's only 2.5 miles (4 km) from the Great Rhône's mouth and the only area outside the dike system that protects the rest of the region from flooding. Four short paths help discover what the delta originally looked like.

North on the D36, the **Musée du Riz** (Museum of Rice) tells you everything about the Camargue's famed rice.

Aigues-Mortes

A gateway to the Camargue, located on the western edge and accessible via the D58, the medieval fortified town of Aigues-Mortes is most interesting for its history. In 1248 Louis IX (St.-Louis) and his 1,500 knight-filled ships left from here on the Seventh Crusade to the Holy Land. His successor, Philip III, added the walls to town, and by the 13th century, it was flourishing as France's only Mediterranean port (Marseille was then part of Provence). Victim of the delta's mercurial ways, the sea deserted Aigues-Mortes so that, despite attempts to dredge the harbor, it fell into decline after 1350. Today its narrow streets are filled with tourists who come to see the mile-long (1.6 km) walls; the **Tour de Constance** *(tel 04 66 53 61 55, $$),* the enormous defense tower; and the church from which St.-Louis left—but mostly to browse souvenir shops and to sit at sunny cafés. ◾

Aigues-Mortes

🗺 80 B2

Visitor Information

✉ Office de Tourisme, Porte de la Gardette

☎ 04 66 53 73 00

ot-aiguesmortes.fr

During the annual Gypsy pilgrimage to Les-Stes.-Maries-de-la-Mer, festivities include a procession down to the beach.

Arles

Arlesiens have long exalted in their panoply of Roman treasures—indeed, the amphitheater, arena, public baths, and *cryptoportiques* are some of the monuments still standing since Julius Caesar first granted Arles capital status for its help in defeating Marseille. Arles is just as famous for its connection to van Gogh—he painted many of his most famous paintings on Arles's streets, and this is where he chopped off his earlobe. Here, too, Provençal poet Frédéric Mistral built a museum memorializing his beloved Arlesiens. Everywhere you look, you come across relics of the town's past.

A Fête de Gardian—Cowboy Festival—in Arles

Market Days
Sat. (Blvd. des Lices
& Blvd. Clemenceau)
& Wed. (Blvd. Émile
Combes)

Arles
🅜 80 C3
Visitor Information
✉ Blvd. des Lices
☎ 04 90 18 41 20

arlestourisme.com

Accessed via different gates, Arles's historic core is encircled by a wall bounded by boulevard Émile Combes, boulevard des Lices, rue Gambetta, and the Grand Rhône.

A good place to begin a visit is outside the walls at the **Musée Départemental de l'Arles Antique,** a modern, airy museum built adjacent to the vestiges of a 1,476-foot-long (450 m) Roman chariot-race

track. Detailing Arles's classical past, its excellent exhibits provide a good preface for the ruins that you will see in town. Related artifacts—a rich assemblage of sculpture, mosaics, vases, jewelry, and inscriptions—complement them. Eleven detailed models of Roman and other landmarks—including the theater and amphitheater—help visualize what a great town Arles once was.

EXPERIENCE: Drinking Pastis

In the shade of a *terrasse,* order a pastis, an anise-flavored liqueur that's served ice cold, and take part in an age-old Provençal tradition. The story goes that a monk in pursuit of discovering the elixir of life invented the drink. (Others say it was a hermit who resided in the Luberon forest.) Whoever it was, the inventor stewed aromatic local herbs—thyme, star anise, fennel—in a giant pot, the resulting concoction that, it's said, protected the imbiber from the plague and quenched his thirst. In 1932 Paul Ricard commercialized the drink, and it's often referred to as Ricard. Its popularity may coincide with the fact that dangerous absinthe had been outlawed just years before, and this lesser evil was a suitable substitute.

You'll be served the liqueur in a tall glass, accompanied by a bottle of cool water and a bowl of ice. As you add water into the amber-colored pastis, the mixture turns milky. It's up to you to mix the amount of pastis and water, typically 1 to 5. Add the ice last. No matter what, it's the perfect refreshing drink on a hot, dusty afternoon. The French love it as an apéritif as well.

A discovery in 2004 added new gravitas to the already excellent collection—a virtually intact, 102-foot-long (31 m) Roman barge dating from the first century A.D. was lifted from the Rhône's muddy bottom and, at long last, is now on brilliant display in a new wing of the museum. The find also included a life-size bust of what's believed to be the oldest representation of Julius Caesar, along with Roman helmets, swords, a magnificent gilded lady, glass goblets, and hundreds of other treasures.

Here, too, you'll find a large display of mosaics that once adorned a dining room at Trinquetaille. The exhibits end with a walk through an alley of Roman Christian sarcophagi from Les Alyscamps (see p. 95), comprising one of the world's most famous collections.

Roman Arles

The most dramatic Roman landmark is **Les Arènes,** the arena built for gladiator standoffs.

Most of the walls remain of the two-level structure, each with 60 arches. It could seat 20,000 spectators, all of whom could disperse within minutes through 180 exits. The first bullfight took place here in 1830 to celebrate the taking of Algiers; bullfights are still hosted in early summer. For a good view, climb the three towers that remain from medieval times, when the amphitheater was turned into a fortress and houses invaded the perimeter.

Precious little remains of the nearby **Théâtre Antique,** the Roman theater—only twin Corinthian columns and a jumble of ruins. Built at the end of the first century B.C., it is one of the earliest freestanding theaters using radiating walls and galleries. Originally, the theater could seat 10,000 to 15,000 spectators. The exquisite Venus of Arles was found here in 1651, armless and broken into three pieces; it probably decorated the stage wall. The original is now in the Louvre.

DISCOUNT PASSES: Available at the sites and at the tourist office, the Pass Advantage covers entry to all sites for $$$. The Pass Liberté covers entry to five sites for $$.

Musée Départemental de l'Arles Antique

🖂 Presqu'Île du Cirque Romain/BP205

☎ 04 13 31 51 03

💲 $$

arles-antique.cg13.fr

NOTE: A free shuttle, the Navia A "Starlit," runs from the Clemenceau bus stop across the street from the tourism office to the museum.

Les Arènes

🅰 Map p. 97

🖂 Rond-point des Arènes

☎ 04 90 49 59 05

💲 $$

arenes-arles.com

Arles's Pont Van Gogh typifies the landscape that inspired some of van Gogh's greatest paintings.

Théâtre Antique
 Map p. 97

✉ Rue de la Calade

☎ 04 90 18 41 20

💲 $

Cryptoportiques
⚠ Map p. 97

✉ Access via Hôtel de Ville

☎ 04 90 49 59 05

💲 $

Thermes de Constantin
⚠ Map p. 97

✉ Rue du Grand Prieuré

☎ 04 90 49 36 74

💲 Included with entrance to Les Arènes

Nothing remains of the Roman forum, the typical monumental center of a Roman city, where people met, conducted business, and worshipped god, emperor, and notables. In Arles the forum was located where the **place du Forum** now stands. Since this forum was built to slope down to the river, a strong foundation was needed underground. The solution: dank, musty underground galleries called *cryptoportiques,* built at the end of the first century B.C. Later, during World War II, residents and Résistance leaders hid out here. You can access the galleries from inside the Hôtel de Ville.

Nearby, the **Thermes de Constantin**—the Roman public baths—remain in crumbling brick-marble-and-mortar glory. What you see represents only a small part of the once grand Palais Constantin, probably the largest baths in Provincia Romana, built in the fourth century. Note the underfloor heating system.

More Sights

For a better understanding of the region's Arlesian culture, the **Museon Arlaten** is a seemingly bottomless collection of all things Provençal: Nobel Prize–winning Provençal poet Frédéric Mistral (see sidebar p. 35) founded the museum in 1896 in an effort to revive his beloved culture and language. It's undergoing an enormous renovation, with plans to reopen in 2018.

On the east side of the place de la République, the former **Église St.-Trophime** is named for the third-century bishop of Arles. St.-Hilaire built the original church in the fifth century, but it was much altered in the 11th and 15th centuries in Provençal Romanesque style. It was here that St.-Augustine was consecrated the first bishop of Canterbury in the sixth century. Don't miss the outstanding sculpture group of the Last Judgment on the tympanum of the West Grand Portal, dating from the 12th century; the doorway was used as a comic strip of sorts to evangelize to anyone rushing past. The church's long, narrow nave features a series of chapels filled with treasures. In the **Chapelle des Reliques,** little boxes contain saint relics, including those of St.-Étienne, the first Christian martyr, and St.-Trophime. A paleo-Christian sarcophagus in the Chapelle St.-Genest shows the parting of the Red Sea.

To see the delightful cloisters, considered Provence's finest, exit the church and turn left, then left again at the sign **(Cloître St.-Trophime).** The masters of St.-Gilles carved this elaborate, two-tiered structure in both Gothic and Romanesque styles.

Nearby, the small **Musée Réattu** features a solid collection of fine art, including numerous paintings by Arlesian Jacques Réattu (1760–1833) himself.

There's a special emphasis on modern and contemporary artists, with the most significant works being 59 Picassos.

One last sight worth a peek is **Les Alyscamps** *(rue Pierre Renoudel at av. des Alyscamps, tel 04 90 49 36 74),* in the town's southeast corner. A necropolis founded by Romans, it gained fame when a Roman civil servant, beheaded for his Christian beliefs and made a saint, was buried here and miracles began to happen. Then everyone wanted to be buried here; by the tenth century, word had spread that even the heroes of Roncevaux—Roland and Olivier—were laid to rest here. Today, poplar-shaded **allée des Sarcophages** is a beautiful place to promenade past empty sarcophagi (the best have been removed to various churches and museums in Arles), a scene vividly depicted by Paul Gauguin and van Gogh. ∎

Museon Arlaten

Map p. 97

✉ 29 rue de la République

☎ 04 13 31 59 99

🕐 Closed for renovation until 2018

museoarlaten.fr

Église St.-Trophime

Map p. 97

✉ E side of place de la République

☎ 04 90 96 07 38

Cloître St.-Trophime

Map p. 97

✉ Place de la République

☎ 04 90 18 41 20

💲 $

Musée Réattu

Map p. 97

✉ 10 rue du Grand Prieuré

☎ 04 90 49 37 58

💲 $

museereattu.arles.fr

Van Gogh's Arles

Vincent van Gogh came to Arles in February 1888 during a snowstorm. After the streets cleared, he saw a shabby city confronting the new reality of the industrial age: river embankments that cut the city off from the Rhône, a new railroad line whose Belgian workers were housed in dilapidated dwellings. But van Gogh detected something special here. He took a room in a poor neighborhood by the station and painted his heart away. "Café de Nuit," "La Maison Jaune," and "Le Pont de Langlois" are just some of his most famous works created during this period.

Though van Gogh left an indelible print of Arles in his paintings, there are not many van Gogh sites left to see. The famous bridge, the yellow house, and the café were destroyed by American bombers during World War II, or after. Hôtel Dieu, one of van Gogh's subjects, has been converted to a media center and multimedia gallery, the Éspace Van Gogh (see p. 97). At Fondation Vincent Van Gogh (see p. 96; *fondation-vincentvangogh-arles.org*), recently moved to 35 rue du Dr. Fanton, special exhibits pay tribute to van Gogh.

The tourist bureau has placed a number of plaques depicting copies of paintings on the spots where van Gogh once stood with his easel; it also offers a walking tour of van Gogh sites.

A Walk Around Old Arles

This walk takes in the heart of Arles, its museums and monuments standing grandly amid bustling restaurants, boutiques, and souvenir shops.

Little Rome on the Rhône has gone about its business since the sixth century B.C.

NOT TO BE MISSED:

Les Arènes • Place du Forum
• Éspace Van Gogh

Begin at the classical **place de la République ❶,** centered around an obelisk that once graced Arles's Roman circus. On the western side stands **Ste.-Anne,** built in the Middle Ages and now housing modern temporary exhibitions. Across the way towers the grand **Église St.-Trophime** (see pp. 94–95), with the **Hôtel de Ville,** or City Hall, built in 1676. Enter the Hôtel de Ville where, to the left, you'll see the entrance to the Roman *cryptoportiques* (see p. 94).

Exiting the city hall the opposite way you entered, go right on narrow rue de la Calade. At the top of the hill you'll come to the

Théâtre Antique ❷ (see p. 93), rather forlorn with its stark two columns, essentially the only things left standing.

Go left on rue de la Bastille, then right on rue Diderot. This will bring you to the carnival atmosphere of the magnificent **Les Arènes ❸** (see p. 93)—shops, restaurants, peddlers all plying for your business. Visit the arena, then head into tiny, cobblestone rue des Arènes, taking you back to a different era. Turn right on rue de l'Hôtel de Ville, lined with chic shops. At place St.-Roche, continue straight on rue Dominique Maisto. You'll go past the Roman **Thermes de Constantin ❹** (see p. 94). Around the corner, on rue du Grand Prieuré, you'll see the entrance to **Musée Réattu** (see p. 95), home to 59 Picassos. Arles is famous for being van Gogh's home; the irony is that the town possesses no van Gogh paintings, but it does own these Picassos, presented by the artist himself to the city in gratitude for amusing him with bullfights.

Backtrack up rue Dominique Maisto (warning: Cars come barreling down this one-way street). Turn right on rue du Sauvage, passing the **Hôtel d'Arlatan** on the right, with Roman ruins visible below street-level windows. To see the **Fondation van Gogh ❺** (*35 rue du Dr. Fanton, tel 04 90 93 08 08, fondation-vincentvangogh-arles.org*), go right on rue du Dr. Fanton; the foundation's modern new complex hosts temporary exhibits with some connection to van Gogh—and always featuring at least one original van Gogh masterpiece.

Otherwise, proceed straight on rue du Sauvage to the lively **place du Forum** ⑥, buzzing with cafés (serving mediocre food). This square was once the site of the Roman forum, the central political, religious, and administrative meeting place. The **Grand Hôtel Nord-Pinus,** on the southern side, is one of Arles's finest places to rest your head (see Travelwise p. 212). A statue of **Frédéric Mistral** lords over the square, the Provençal poet leaning on a walking stick as if waiting for a train (as he himself complained when it was unveiled).

Straight on is the **Hôtel de Ville** that you've already visited. Turn right, alongside it, on rue Balze, then left on rue Frédéric Mistral and left at the T-intersection (rue de la République). The building you've just circled is the old Jesuit

college, today housing the **Museon Arlaten** ⑦ (see p. 94; *closed for renovation until 2018*).

From here, go down rue President Wilson. At place Felix Ray, turn right to the **Éspace Van Gogh** ⑧ (see sidebar p. 95), a former hospital known to van Gogh both as an artist (he painted the lovely garden space in the center) and patient; it was here where he was taken after his infamous altercation with Gauguin, when he cut off part of his own ear.

> ⓜ See area map p. 80
> ▶ Place de la République
> ⊕ 2 hours (more with stops)
> ⬌ 1 mile (1.6 km)
> ▶ Éspace Van Gogh

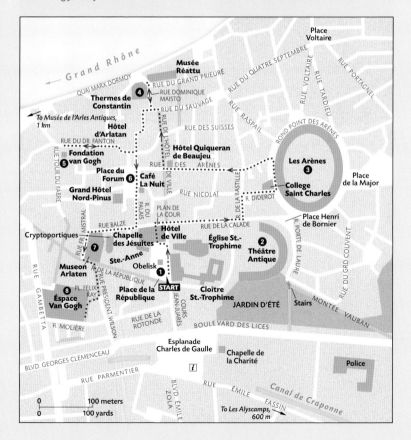

Les Baux-de-Provence

The setting is grimly medieval, the remains of an enormous stone citadel rising out of a shadowy, windswept massif high above the southern Alpilles. This is the ancient stronghold of the seigneurs of Les Baux, a rebel fiefdom that terrorized southern Provence. Today it is one of France's top tourist sights, attracting more than two million visitors a year—visit early or late in the day, or off-season.

Bloodthirsty warlords once terrorized from Les Baux, now a popular tourist draw.

Château des Baux-de-Provence

 80 D3

Visitor Information

✉ 18 miles (30 km) S of Avignon via the A7 & D27

☎ 04 90 54 34 39

chateau-baux -provence.com

The lords of Les Baux ruled in the Middle Ages, perhaps building their fortress as long ago as the ninth century. Claiming to be descended from Balthazar, one of the Three Kings, they did not acknowledge the French king, nor the emperors—they didn't have to, given their protective mountain setting. When Raymond de Turenne, a bloodthirsty distant relative, took over in 1372, he sent men throughout the land to kidnap people who, if their families couldn't pay the ransom, were forced to walk over the cliff's edge.

Les Baux was integrated into the county of Provence, then became a part of France, with Provence, in 1481. The population revolted, and Louis XIII responded by ordering the castle destroyed in 1632. It's thanks to Frédéric Mistral and other poets that the place was not forgotten.

The site comprises two parts: the "living city," a pedestrian-only village in the lower town, and the "dead city," or *ville morte*—the ruined castle complex.

Living City

The lower town has been painstakingly restored, its beautiful, ivy-clad Renaissance facades,

A simple yet ample *petit dejeuner* (breakfast) throughout Provence consists of a baguette, croissants, *confiture* (jam), *du beurre frais du fermier* (butter), and *café au lait* served in large, steamy bowls.

—ANNE RANDERSON
National Geographic contributor

churches, and *hôtels particuliers* now holding shops, shops, and more shops. Among the handful of sights is the **Musée des Santons,** displaying clay figurines from the 18th and 19th centuries. Up the street, beyond the ramparts, the **Porte d'Eyguières** was, until the 18th century, the city's only entrance. The **Église St.-Vincent,** on place de l'Église, encloses three chapels from the tenth century, with stained-glass windows presented by Prince Rainier of Monaco in 1960. On the same square, the **Musée**

Yves Brayer displays some of this well-known local painter's works—a sample of which you can see opposite, in the 17th-century **Chapelle des Pénitents Blancs.** Brayer decorated its walls in 1974 with colorful scenes of a shepherd's Noël.

Dead City

Windswept, rocky, with breathtaking views over the Alpilles, it's hard to believe that hundreds of years ago, 6,000 inhabitants resided on this plateau above the lower town. With audio guide in hand, follow the path through this dead city. At the entrance, the **Musée d'Histoire des Baux** provides a historical primer.

Reproductions of medieval weapons are on display, including a catapult and battering ram. The ruined château dominates the plateau, its fragments of towers and walls sticking out of the bare rock. The only intact part is the *donjon,* with views over the valley beyond.

Back toward the exit, the 12th-century **Chapelle St.-Blaise** has a film describing the Baux of the artists—van Gogh, Cézanne, and Gauguin. ■

Musée des Santons

✉ Inquire at tourism office

Musée Yves Brayer

✉ Hôtel des Porcelet, place de l'Église

☎ 04 90 54 36 99

🕐 Closed Tues. & Oct.–March

💲 $

yvesbrayer.com

Musée d'Histoire des Baux

✉ Château des Baux de Provence

☎ 04 90 54 55 56

💲 $$

chateau-baux -provence.com

Courtly Love

The House of Baux is certainly fabled for its bloody feuds, but courtly love reigned as well. For here, during the deepest, darkest days of medieval conflict, the realm's most famous troubadours— roaming musician-poets—flocked to sing ballads of love and chivalry to the court's beautiful ladies. Their lyrical poetry was written in Old Occitan, making it the first Romance language with a literary corpus.

Their flowery words precipitated a new age of creativity, ushering in a literary eroticism that hadn't been seen before.

Among the most famous troubadours at Les Baux, the great Provençal poet Fouquet of Marseille celebrated Adelasia, wife of Berald, Prince of Baux. After she died, thereby breaking his heart, he gave up his earthly pursuits, eventually becoming the archbishop of Toulouse.

La Montagnette

Scented with thyme and rosemary, a paradise for walkers and mushroom gatherers, this untraveled "little mountain" north of Tarascon and south of Avignon offers a cluster of delights—including an abbey, a château, and pastoral views all around.

La Montagnette
▲ 80 C3–D4

Visitor Information
✉ Office de Tourisme, av. de la République, Tarascon
☎ 04 90 91 03 52

tarascon.org

The remains of a 12th-century feudal castle dominates sleepy **Boulbon,** about 5 miles (8 km) north of Tarascon on the D35. Leaving place de la Mairie at the village's entrance, you will pass through the fortified **Porte Loriol** to **Grand'rue,** a street lined with flower-draped old houses. Near the château, **Église Ste.-Anne** was built in 1626.

About 4 miles (6.5 km) farther north on the D35 is the medieval village of **Barbentane,** overlooking market gardens along the Rhône. Its elegant, 17th-century **château,** the home of Barbentane marquesses since 1674, is built in classical style. Through the village's medieval gates, tiny lanes harbor ancient houses, including the **Maison des Chevaliers,** a seignorial house from the 12th century with 16th-century additions. Atop the hill is the medieval **Tour Anglica,** crowned by a round turret. Built in 1385 as the *donjon* of Barbentane's original castle, it was sung by Frédéric Mistral in the "Iscles d'Or."

Leaving the D35 via the D35E brings you up through sweet-scented forest to the neo-Gothic **Abbaye St.-Michel-de-Frigolet** (*tel 04 90 95 70 07, closed Tues.– Wed. Oct.–March, frigolet.com*), founded in 1133. Its name derives from the Provençal word for "place where thyme grows abundantly"—*ferigoulo* or *ferigoulet*. The thyme-related elixir produced here is celebrated for its curative powers. You are free to wander the peaceful grounds and peek into some of the buildings. The abbey restaurant (*tel 04 32 60 68 70*) offers meals, and the Hostellerie Abbaye de Frigolet (*tel 04 32 60 68 70*) has rooms overlooking the gardens. ■

Boulbon's *carreto ramado,* featuring horse-pulled chariots

St.-Rémy-de-Provence

Nestled at the foot of the Alpilles, surrounded by fields of wheat and red poppies, St.-Rémy is a peaceful market town of winding lanes behind vestiges of ancient walls. The Romans lived here. Nostradamus was born here in 1503, and in 1922 Gertrude Stein and Alice B. Toklas found St.-Rémy after "wandering around everywhere a bit." But St.-Rémy is most associated with Vincent van Gogh, who painted 150 canvases in 1888 after committing himself to an asylum here.

The Romans

Early on, the Romans built a city here on the Via Domitia, the road linking Italy and Spain. The ruins have been excavated and can be visited just south of St.-Rémy on the D5, at Glanum, one of Europe's most famous Roman sites. The **Site Archéologique de Glanum** comprises two parts: Les Antiques and, across the road, Glanum. Archaeologists believe that the excavated ruins represent only a sixth of the city's original size.

INSIDER TIP:

On Pentecost Monday, watch the Transhumance as hundreds of sheep walk through the town, passing by the mayor and other town officials.

—MICHELINE PLACE
*National Geographic Expeditions
tour leader*

At **Les Antiques,** the **Arc de Triomphe** dates from the reign of Augustus (63 B.C.–A.D. 14). Marking the entry road to the Roman city, it is decorated with reliefs illustrating Caesar's conquest of Gaul. The elegant, three-tiered **Mausolée des Jules** is the best preserved mausoleum of the Roman world, dating from 30 to 20 B.C. Raised by an important Roman family to honor their father and grandfather, its podium base is adorned on all sides with bas-reliefs depicting battle and hunting scenes.

Just up the road is the main sight of **Glanum.** The Romans used a layout characteristic of all their great cities—a low town with thermal baths and lavish villas; a middle town with a basilica and temples; and a narrow high town, with walls guarding the town entrance. Among the treasures are the houses along both sides of the rue des Thermes, abandoned in the third century; the remains of a fountain; thermal baths; a *palestra* (exercise yard); and a *piscina* (pool). There are also sewers, a forum, and a *nymphaeum.*

Van Gogh

Just down the road stands the church and chapel of **St.-Paul-de-Mausole,** lovely in its own right but best known for its association with van Gogh. The artist chose St.-Paul as a place of refuge between May 1889 and May 1890—after he cut off part of his ear. This year was his

Market Day
Wed.

St.Rémy-de-Provence
- 🗺 80 D3

Visitor Information
- ✉ Office de Tourisme, place Jean-Jaurès
- ☎ 04 90 92 05 22
- saintremy-de-provence.com

Site Archéologique de Glanum
- 🗺 80 D3
- ✉ Rte. des Baux-de-Provence
- ☎ 04 90 92 23 79
- 🕐 Closed Mon. Sept.–March
- 💲 Les Antiques: free. Glanum: $$
- glanum.monuments-nationaux.fr

St.-Paul-de-Mausole
- 🗺 80 D3
- ✉ Rte. des Baux-de-Provence/Av. Van Gogh
- ☎ 04 90 92 77 00
- 💲 $

Musée des Alpilles

✉ Hôtel Mistral de Mondragon, 1 place Favier

☎ 04 90 92 68 24

⏱ Closed Mon. & Sun.–Mon. Oct.–April

💲 $

musees-mediter ranee.org

most intense, and most prolific, during which time he produced some of his most famous works, including "Nuit Etoilée" ("Starry Night") and "Les Blés Jaunes" ("Cornfield and Cypress Trees"). His "Les Oliviers" and "Ciel Jaune et Soleil Resplendissant" were painted along the driveway leading to the complex.

EXPERIENCE:
Taste Liquid Gold

The picturesque lands south of St.-Rémy harbor some of Provence's best olive-growing orchards—and places to sample the unique green-fresh taste of the Alpilles terroir. From St.-Rémy, the D5 brings you into the region's heart, with farms and olive mills especially abundant along the D78F, D17, and D27; a visitor center on the D27 near Maillane has a map highlighting the **Route à l'Olivier**. Among the many olive mills (*moulins à olives*) to stop is **Moulin Castelas** (*D27, E of Les Baux, tel 04 90 54 50 86, castelas.com*), which offers intimate tours of the oilmaking process. Then sample some of the golden elixir yourself, including such aromatic-infused oils as thyme and Sicilian citron.

Founded in the 900s and much rebuilt in the 11th and 12th centuries, the St.-Paul site retains its Romanesque church and cloister. In 1810 the monastery buildings were purchased for use as a private hospital, and it remains an art therapy hospital, though van Gogh's room is open to the public.

You walk past the peaceful cloister and up stone steps to van Gogh's room, a tiny space with a green metal bed, a couple of chairs, a tiny wooden desk, and a view onto flower-dotted fields and a stone wall (a scene that also appears in many of van Gogh's paintings). This cell was later occupied by an interned German during World War I—Albert Schweitzer.

The tourist office has included in its tourist brochure a walking tour that takes in the world of van Gogh—starting from the entrance of Glanum and going to the heart of St.-Rémy, 21 panels portray reproductions of van Gogh's works on the precise spots he painted them.

Centre Ville

Surrounded by plane tree–shaded boulevards, the *centre ville* is filled with sophisticated boutiques, old fountains, and shady squares. Placques denote historical sites, including the birthplace of physician and astronomer Nostradamus (*rue Hoche*).

In the Hôtel Mistral de Mondragon, the **Musée des Alpilles** is a popular and rural art museum. It explains the natural and man-made landscapes of the Alpilles, including flora and fauna; centuries-old farming and trading traditions (including olive oil, sheep, and vines); and traditional costumes and celebrations.

Relating to van Gogh, the **Centre d'Art Présence Vincent Van Gogh** (*8 rue Lucien Estrine, tel 04 90 92 34 72, musee-estrine.fr*), located in the handsome Hôtel Estrine, features reproductions and slide shows on different themes related to the artist. Contemporary artists are featured on the upper floors. ∎

More Places to Visit South Along the Rhône

Beaucaire's harbor anchors a working city best known for the remains of its 11th-century castle.

Abbaye de Montmajour

Looming above marshlands on Mont Majour ("big mountain"), the stark medieval abbey is a shadow of its former thriving self. Founded in 948 by Benedictine monks, who lived here until 1790, it drew hordes of medieval pilgrims, and was even a papal retreat (circa 950). The abbey is vacant now, and the self-guided tour is a little hard to follow, even with the English-language pamphlet. Nonetheless, what you take away from this brooding monstrosity is a sense of peace and quietude. You nearly expect a monk to greet you around the next corner.
montmajour.monuments-nationaux.fr 80 C3 Rte. de Fontvieille 04 90 54 64 17 Closed Mon. Oct.–March $$

Carrières de Lumières

The world's most famous art and artists are celebrated in this multimedia extravaganza, in which 70 projectors are used to cover the 65-foot-high (20 m) walls and floors of a disused bauxite quarry, all set to sound. A new show is unveiled every year profiling the greatest names in the history of art. The unique space is also used for concerts, lectures, and other special events.
carrieres-lumieres.com 80 D3 Rte. de Maillane, Val d'Enfer (0.3 mile/0.5 km N of Les Baux) 04 90 54 47 37 $$

Fontvieille

This charming, low-key village is famous for the windmill that inspired French novelist Alphonse Daudet (1840–1897) to write his collection of lighthearted short stories, *Lettres de Mon Moulin (Letters from My Windmill)* in 1869. While **Le Moulin de Daudet** *(allée des Pins, tel 04 90 54 60 78, closed Jan., $)* was built to celebrate this great Provençal writer, it is not *the* windmill. To see that, you'll have to stroll along the 1.5-hour trail that circles past Moulin Ramet to the Moulin Tissot-Avon—voilà, Daudet's former haunt. The trail continues past the Château de Montauban, where Daudet resided with his cousins during his stay in town.

Just outside town, in the direction of Arles, you'll find along the roadside the remains of a Roman aqueduct and mill *(aqueducs-fontvieille -alpilles.com)* that once brought water from the Alpilles to the people of Arles.

fontvieille-provence.com 🅰 80 C3 **Visitor Information** ✉ Office de Tourisme, av. de Moulins ☎ 04 90 54 67 49

Call of the Cicada

As soon as the temperature reaches 72°F (22°C), Provence's *cigales* (cicadas) begin to sing continuously, announcing summer's arrival. They're hard to spot, but representations of this little insect are everywhere. Since the 19th century, models have been made from clay and hung near the entrance door or in the kitchen for good luck. You'll also find their images decorating fabrics and fashioned into all kinds of items, including soap and candles.

Maillane

Provençal poet Frédéric Mistral was born in a farmhouse on Maillane's outskirts in 1830. Upon his father's death, he and his mother moved into the small, pleasant town and, when marrying at the age of 46, he and his bride moved next door. Today, their home is the well-presented **Musée Frédéric Mistral,** with books, paintings, photos, and souvenirs the poet collected over the years. He is buried in the village cemetery.

✉ 80 D3 **Musée Frédéric Mistral** ✉ Av. Lamartine ☎ 04 90 95 84 19 🕐 Closed Mon. 🅂 $

Mas des Tourelles & Le Vieux Mas

At the reproduction of the ancient Mas des Tourelles winery, you learn how Romans produced wines. The intriguing visit takes in a film, exhibits, and the tasting of wines based on 2,000-year-old recipes. Various ingredients used for preservation included cinnamon, honey, and seawater. Nearby, Le Vieux Mas is the re-creation of a traditional working farm from the 1900s, showcasing farm animals and equipment. 🅰 80 C3

Mas des Tourelles *tourelles.com* ✉ 2.5 miles (4 km) SW of Beaucaire, on the D38 ☎ 04 66 59 19 72 🕐 Check website for opening times 🅂 $

Le Vieux Mas *vieux-mas.com* ✉ Rte. de Fourques (D15), 3.7 miles (6 km) S of Beaucaire ☎ 04 66 59 60 13 🕐 Check website for opening times 🅂 $$

Tarascon & Beaucaire Castles

Louis II built Tarascon Castle on the Rhône's east bank in the 15th century to defend the border. A storybook feudal fortress, complete with crenellations and a moat, the castle was actually quite luxurious inside thanks to Good King René, Louis II's son, who loved the good life. His last ten years were spent here in the company of poets and artists. Today, the structure is empty, save for ten 17th-century tapestries depicting the life of Scipio and some 18th-century pharmaceutical pots. Graffiti left by British sailors recall the castle's later use as a prison, between 1754 and 1778.

Across the river, Beaucaire Castle was a powerful citadel during the reign of St.-Louis and has dominated the town since the 11th century. Today it lies in ruins—only the round tower and chapel remain. The castle is open only for falconry displays, with falconers in Roman costume. 🅰 80 C3

Château de Tarascon ✉ Blvd. du Roi René, Tarascon ☎ 04 90 91 01 93 🕐 Closed Tues. Oct.–March 🅂 $$

Château de Beaucaire ✉ Place du Château, Beaucaire ☎ 04 66 59 26 72 🅂 $$

Poised between land and sea, a forested realm featuring dignified Aix, revitalizing Marseille, and dazzling St.-Tropez

Aix, Marseille, & the Var

The bounty of Aix's daily market at place Richelme

Aix, Marseille, & the Var

Set against a backdrop of a remote massif, Provence takes on a modern, sophisticated feel in this varied region centered around Aix-en-Provence, Marseille, and St.-Tropez.

Provence's ancient capital, Aix-en-Provence, gained its polished panache in the 17th and 18th centuries, when noble families funded a rash of *hôtel particulier* building. Cours Mirabeau shines as one of France's most elegant boulevards, with its giant elms, venerable cafés, and 18th-century fountains. Native son Paul Cézanne immortalized nearby Montagne Ste.-Victoire in more than a hundred paintings—thereby kick-starting cubism.

It's an exciting time for Marseille, only 15 miles (25 km) south, whose growth spurt is unprecedented since the Phoenicians first set foot here 2,600 years ago. Important, brand-new museums sparkle along the formerly gritty port, foremost among them the Musée des Civilisations de l'Europe et de la Méditerranée (MuCEM). But nothing beats sitting by the old port, sipping an authentic bowl of bouillabaisse at one of the outdoor cafés.

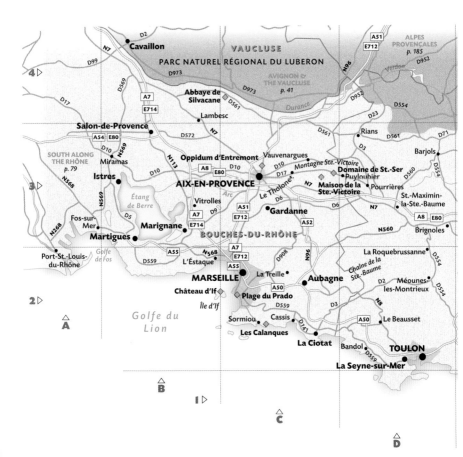

East of Marseille, *calanques*—limestone cliffs that plunge deep into azure waters—riffle the coast. A good base is the warm-hued fishing village of Cassis, famed for its crisp white wine. Nearby Hyères is an elegant, palm-shaded town, with the eucalyptus-scented Îles des Pourquerolles beckoning just offshore.

Farther east, St.-Tropez's reputation for its high life precedes it. Even if you're not rich and/or famous, you can admire the mega-yachts in the port, window-shop at chic bou-tiques along hilly, cobbled streets, and watch for incognito stars.

Inland, in the Vallée Intérieure, tiny lanes wind past vineyards, medieval towns, and one of Provence's trio of Cistercian abbeys. ∎

NOT TO BE MISSED:

Aix's colorful Saturday market **112**

Taking in Marseille's cultural metamorphosis, including the amazing MuCEM **116–123**

A hike (or dive) into the *calanques*, France's newest national park **124**

Sipping white wine in Cassis' charming little harbor **124**

Window-shopping in chi-chi St.-Tropez **126–127**

Exploring lesser known Provence in the Massif des Maures **128–129**

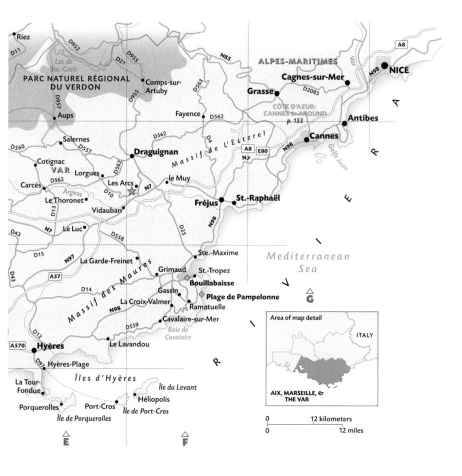

Aix-en-Provence

At dusk, a golden light warms the honey-hued buildings of this magical Midi town, as well-heeled Aixois sip apéritifs at one of dozens of plane tree–shaded squares, musical fountains playing a soft serenade. This is aristocratic, refined Aix, one of the most beautiful towns in the south of France. For what it lacks in major museums and historical sights, the old capital of Provence makes up in culture and ambience.

The small, cobbled place d'Albertas, planned in the 1710s

Market Days
Tues., Thurs., & Sat.

Aix-en-Provence
🅰 106 C3
Visitor Information
✉ Office de
Tourisme,
300 av.
Giuseppe Verdi
☎ 04 42 16 11 61

**aixenprovence
tourism.com**

More than 2,000 years ago, the war-waging Salyens, a Celto-Ligurian tribe, built their fortified town on the strategic plateau of Entremont (see p. 132), just north of Aix's present location. The Romans sacked the town in 123 B.C., and the Roman consul Sextius set up his own community around a thermal spring, calling it Aquae Sextiae, the waters of Sextius, thereby creating Gaul's first Roman settlement. As the Roman Empire fell in A.D. 476, Visigoths destroyed much of the city. Unlike many other Provençal towns, few traces of the Roman settlement remain; one of the principal gateways has been worked into the 16th-century **clock tower** in place de l'Hôtel de Ville, and excavated ruins can be seen under the glass floor of the lobby of **Spa Thermes Sextius** (Sextius Baths; *55 cours Sextius*), a luxury spa utilizing the same healing waters that the Romans adored.

In the Middle Ages, the counts of Provence took up residence in Aix, the most famous of whom was Bon Roi René (Good King René; 1409–1480). A royal patron of the arts, he founded many popular festivals and made Aix into a cultural center comparable to Avignon. In 1486 Provence was annexed to France, but until 1790 remained relatively autonomous. Aix was kept on as capital of Provence and became, beginning in 1501, the seat of the Supreme Court of Justice, otherwise known as the Parliament of Provence. Aix entered its golden age, with noble families building more than 160 *hôtels particuliers* in the Italian baroque style. It is these buildings above all that give Aix its dignified appearance. During the revolution, Aix's aristocrats fled, leaving the town to slumber until its recent revival as an arts town.

Along Cours Mirabeau

Elm-shaded cours Mirabeau is Aix's main artery, created in 1650 for carriages but soon after becoming the local promenade of choice. With its elegant hôtels particuliers lining either side and its procession of fountains, the *cours* is arguably the most beautiful street in the south of France. Café tables spill out onto the sidewalk, the most famous being **Les Deux Garçons** *(53 cours Mirabeau, tel 04 42 26 00 51, les2garcons.fr),* a former intellectual hangout with a spectacular interior dating from 1792.

When the plague contaminated city waters in 1720, lovely fountains were built to receive new sources of water—thereby earning Aix the moniker City of a Thousand Fountains. Four of the most beautiful grace the

cours, beginning with the most spectacular, the **Fontaine de la Rotonde** in place du Général de Gaulle. Designed by Napoléon III's chief civil engineer in 1860 at the former Porte Royale—for centuries the main entrance to the city—its three graceful marble statues represent Justice (facing Aix), the Arts (facing Avignon), and Agriculture (facing Marseille).

Christmas Santons

When the French Revolution of 1789 drove religion underground, the Provençaux took worship—as well as the traditional outdoor Christmas nativity scene—into their private homes. And thus was born the *crèche proven-çale*—mini-size cribs populated by brightly colored terra-cotta figures called *santons* that depicted not only the Holy Family, but all manner of ordinary life: bakers, musicians, card players, dancers. The tradition remains to this day, with several hundred workshops still making santons throughout Provence. See Travelwise pp. 225–226 for information on visiting santon workshops.

Resembling a mossy stump, the 17th-century **Fontaine des Neuf Canons** replaced a watering place where flocks of sheep came to drink during the transhumance. Farther up the cours, another mossy stump, the 17th-century **Fontaine Moussue,** is fed by hot water brought by underground channels and aqueducts from the **Fontaine des Bagniers** *(place des Chapeliers).* At the top of the cours stands the 19th-century **Fontaine du Roi René;** note the cluster of grapes in the statue's hand—above other pursuits, the king introduced the muscat grape to Provence.

DISCOUNT CARD: Receive discounts on sights and local transportation with the Aix Pays d'Aix Pass Card. The card is available from the tourist office and participating sights for €2.

Musée du Palais de l'Archevêché

🅰 Map p. 113

✉ Palais de l'Archevêché, 28 place des Martyrs de la Résistance

☎ 04 42 23 09 91

🕐 Closed Tues. & Jan.

💲 $

aixenprovence.fr

Musée Estienne de Saint-Jean

🅰 Map p. 113

✉ Hôtel Estienne de St.-Jean, 17 rue Gaston de Saporta

☎ 04 42 91 89 78

🕐 Closed Tues.

💲 $

aixenprovence.fr

Bourg St.-Sauveur

North of cours Mirabeau, the old town of St.-Sauveur runs between the old ramparts and the Tourreluque watchtower, the last vestiges of the medieval fortifications. In its heart rises the **Cathédrale St.-Sauveur** (place des Martyrs de la Résistance, tel 04 42 23 45 65), which comprises a curious hybrid of religious architectural styles both old and new: Roman foundations from the earliest days of the Christian era, a Merovingian baptistery from the fifth century, a Romanesque nave, and a Gothic nave. The intricately carved wooden doors of its western facade, carved by Toulon artist Jean Guiramand in 1508 to 1510 and normally behind shutters, are decorated with statues of the four great prophets and the 12 pagan sibyls. Inside you'll find several Provençal primitive works of art,

the most famous of which is "Le Buisson Ardent" ("Burning Bush"), a minutely observed triptych attributed to Nicolas Froment.

Nearby, on place des Martyrs de la Résistance, the small **Musée du Palais de l'Archevêché** is housed on the first floor of the Ancien Archevêché, the former archbishops' palace (1650–1730). The meager collection of Beauvais tapestries displayed here includes a series on the life of Don Quixote after cartoons by Natoire.

Down rue Gaston de Saporta, the small **Musée Estienne de Saint-Jean** is installed in the elegant, 17th-century Hôtel de St.-Jean. The museum is rich in local souvenirs from Aix's past, including objets d'art, *santons*, masks, and faïence.

The **Pavillon de Vendôme,** near the thermal baths, was built in 1665 by Pierre Pavillon for the duke of Vendôme, the scene of the latter's secret love affairs. The pavilion now houses a collection of Provençal furniture and paintings.

Quartier Mazarin

South of cours Mirabeau, this elegant quarter shelters a collection of aristocratic 17th-century town houses, built in a grid plan during the reign of Louis XIV. Among the prettiest streets are **rue Mazarin** and **place des Quatre Dauphins,** with its fountain of four dolphins. In this neighborhood you'll also find the **Caumont Centre d'Art,** which hosts important temporary exhibitions and showcases music and dance performances in a beautifully restored 18th-century mansion; don't miss the film

---

Portrait of an Artist

Paul Cézanne was born in Aix in 1839. He attended grammar school here (with fellow student Émile Zola) and returned to pursue his love of art after a brief Parisian stint. Many sights around town will be familiar to lovers of his paintings, including the Jas de Bouffan, his family home; Bibémus Quarries, where he studied shape and color; and, just north of town his studio, Atelier de Cézanne (9 av. Paul Cézanne, atelier-cezanne.com), which looks just as he left it, including his coat and beret hanging on the wall and, scattered about on tables and shelves, the little plaster cupid and other *objets* that show up in his still lifes. But the most prominent object related to this great artist rises just outside town, the domineering Montagne Ste.-Victoire, which he painted more than 60 times.

Along Aix's cours Mirabeau, said to be one of the most beautiful streets in France

about Cézanne's life in Aix. Also worth a peek is the nearby **Hôtel de Gallifet-Maison d'Art et d'Histoire** *(52 rue Cardinale, tel 09 53 84 37 61, closed Sun.–Mon., hoteldegallifet.com)*, which promotes local artists through temporary exhibits; the garden is ideal for sipping a glass of rosé.

The coup de grâce of all Aix museums, however, is the **Musée Granet,** an art and archaeological museum housed in a 17th-century priory of the Knights of Malta. Among the highlights are Italian school works from the 17th and 18th centuries (most notably, a *modello* by Guercino for his Exhumations of St. Petronilla in the Vatican collections); Flemish school works (including several Rubens); and excellent Dutch paintings (self-portrait by Rembrandt, circa 1665). Provençal painter François-Marius Granet (1775–1849), best known for his dark and atmospheric scenes of monastic

life, founded the museum in the 19th century. Despite the fact that an early director declared that this museum "would never be sullied by a Cézanne," the museum also owns eight of the local artist's paintings (none major).

An annex to the Granet is found in the **Chapelle des Pénitents Blancs** *(Granet XXe, place Jean-Boyer, at top of rue Maréchal Joffre, tel 04 42 52 88 32, $, museegranet-aixenprovence.fr)*, a chapel transformed into an airy museum space for Jean Planque's (1910–1993) outstanding collection of 300 Impressionist and Postimpressionist works. A painter and art collector, friends with the likes of Picasso and Dubonnet, Planque owned masterpieces ranging from Renoir to Picasso and including van Gogh, Bonnard, Dufy, and more. He wanted to share his collection upon his death, and we are all benefactors. A delight to visit. ■

Pavillon de Vendôme
- ✉ 32 rue Célony
- ☎ 04 42 91 88 75
- 🕐 Closed Tues. & a.m. Nov.–mid-April
- 💲 $

Caumont Centre d'Art
- 🅰 Map p. 113
- ✉ 3 rue Joseph Cabassol
- ☎ 04 42 20 70 01
- 💲 $$ (plus $ for special exhibitions)

caumont-centredart .com

Musée Granet
- 🅰 Map p. 113
- ✉ Place St.-Jean-de-Malte
- ☎ 04 42 52 88 32
- 🕐 Closed Mon. & a.m. Jan.–July
- 💲 $

museegranet -aixenprovence.fr

Exploring Old Aix

This delightful promenade takes in some of Aix's most charming—and historic—streets in the jumbled labyrinth of the old town of Bourg St.-Sauveur.

Cathédrale St.-Sauveur, a celebration of old and (relatively) new architectural styles

Begin at **La Rotonde ❶** (see p. 109), the fountain on the former site of the city's main gate, at the foot of elegant **cours Mirabeau.** Walk up the *cours,* admiring the cafés, *hôtels particuliers,* and fountains. Two of the largest town houses are No. 20, the 17th-century **Hôtel de Forbin,** and No. 28, the 18th-century **Hôtel du Chevalier Hancy.**

At **Fontaine des Neuf Canons ❷**, take a left at rue Nazareth and, at rue Espariat, go right, past rue Aude, to **place d'Albertas ❸**, full of Parisian elegance. Rococo facades front three sides of the secluded square, and the base of the lovely fountain dates from 1912. Open-air concerts are sometimes held here.

Backtrack to rue Aude and go right. At the junction, keep going straight, on rue Maréchal Foch. You'll pass by **place Richelme,** site of a daily fruit and vegetable market. Just beyond you come to **place de l'Hôtel de Ville ❹**, dominated by the **Tour de l'Horloge.** The

NOT TO BE MISSED:

Cours Mirabeau • Place de l'Hôtel de Ville • Cathédrale St.-Sauveur

clock tower has two clock faces: a typical one and, below that, an astronomical clock from 1661. On the latter, four statues, each representing a season, are shown in turn. The adjoining **Hôtel de Ville** (Town Hall), with its Italianate facade and sculptured wood doors, was built between 1655 and 1670 by Pierre Pavillon. On the square's south side, the **Ancienne Halle aux Grains** (former Wheat Exchange), built between 1759 and 1761, reflects the importance of wheat at the time. Topping the north facade, an allegorical pediment features the two important sources of water for farmers: the strong, steady Rhône, represented by a rough-looking man, and the temperamental, flood-prone Durance, symbolized by a woman half jumping out of the sculpture.

Pass through the clock tower and proceed up rue Gaston de Saporta. You'll pass by the **Musée Estienne de Saint-Jean** on the left (see p. 110) and, just beyond, also on the left, will be the **Hôtel de Châteaurenard ⑤**. A splendid town house built in the mid-1600s by Pierre Pavillon, it's a cultural center now. Peek inside to see the restored trompe l'oeil painted up the staircase, the 1660 work of Bruxellois Jean Daret, appointed king's painter by Louis XIV. The images rotate around the central figure of Minerva, on the ceiling above, who represents nobility.

Just up rue Gaston de Saporta, at the far eastern end of the place des Martyrs de la Résistance, is the **Palais de l'Archevêché**

(1650–1730), the former archbishops' residence, adorned with a Regency door. This is the headquarters for the International Festival of Lyric Art, which takes place on this square every July. Here, too, is the **Musée du Palais de l'Archevêché** (see p. 110), featuring a collection of Beauvais tapestries.

The walk ends farther up the street at the magnificent **Cathédrale St.-Sauveur ⑥** (see p. 110). Paul Cézanne's studio (see sidebar p. 110) is just a half a mile (0.8 km) farther up the road, via avenue Pasteur.

Ⓜ See area map p. 106
► La Rotonde
🕐 1 hour (more with stops)
↔ A half mile (0.8 km)
► Cathédrale St.-Sauveur

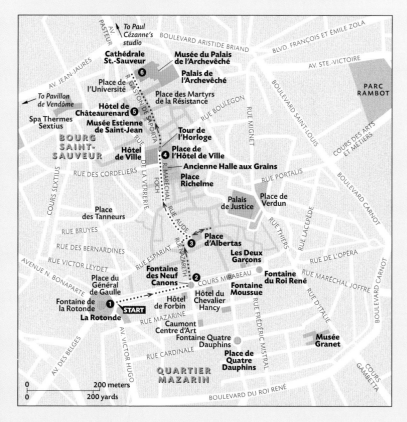

Route de Cézanne

Paul Cézanne, the forerunner of cubism with his blocky use of color, was fixated on painting Montagne Ste.-Victoire, determined to get it just right—its colors, its texture, the play of light. He painted it more than a hundred times. You can follow in the artist's footsteps on the Route de Cézanne, circling the mountain all around, pausing at places he knew so well. Along the way are pretty villages, vineyards and olive groves, and a famous château.

Montagne Ste.-Victoire

⚠ 106 C3–D3

Domaine de St.-Ser

⚠ 106 C3

✉ Mas de Bramefan/D17, Puyloubier

☎ 04 42 66 30 81

saint-ser.com

From Aix, the D17 heads east. You quickly enter a painter's paradise of woods and hills. Cézanne rented two rooms in **Le Tholonet** to store his materials. Between 1888 and 1904, he roamed the area in search of subjects that would conform to his vision of seeing in nature the cylinder, the sphere, and the cone; he found them in the **Château Noir**—visible from the D17—and in the **Bibémus Quarries** (marvellous-provence.com). The latter's red sandstone rocks set in a pine forest can only be visited by guided tour, but to get a glimpse (only outside tourist season), turn right on the chemin de Bibébus about 1.2 miles (2 km) outside Aix.

Onward, at St.-Antonin, the **Maison de la Ste.-Victoire** offers advice for hiking up the mountain.

Proceeding along the D17, you enter a fertile plain carpeted with vineyards and olive groves; stop by **Domaine de St.-Ser** for a tasting of fine Côtes de Provence.

Then take the D623 through **Pourrières,** a wine town whose name may be derived from campi putridi, a reference to the dead bodies of the Germanic tribes that lay here to rot following Marius's famous victory in 102 B.C.

Following the D23, D623,

and D10, you squiggle up through impossibly rocky terrain, eventually coming to the **Col des Portes,** with the mountain etched against the distant sky. Hiking trails meander off from here.

Proceed to the little town of **Vauvenargues.** The castle rising in the valley before you, built between the 14th and 17th centuries, has the best mountain view—Pablo Picasso, who greatly admired Cézanne, bought it in 1958 "to own the original." The Spanish artist is buried on the private grounds.

INSIDER TIP:

Bring a jacket if you plan to visit the peak of wind-whipped Montagne Ste.-Victoire; it's wintry cold on top even on a hot summer day.

—HEIDI ELLISON
National Geographic contributor

Beyond you'll find one of the easier hikes to the top of the mountain, along the **Sentier des Venturies.** Several parking areas—one in Vauvenargues, a couple others just beyond—lead to trailheads.

Modern Aix awaits just beyond. ■

EXPERIENCE: Finding Your Painting Muse

There's something about the purity of the Provençal light that has long lured artists. Van Gogh knew it, arriving in 1888 besotted by its vibrancy that he equated with that in Japan. Matisse was captivated as well, writing, "This is a place where light plays the first part. Color comes afterwards. First you have to feel the light, absorb it into yourself." You may find that you can't help but to put paint to canvas. Here's how to do it.

A Cézanne-esque still life at a Dominique Hordé workshop

There are many options for painting, whether it's a day-long workshop, weeklong class, or longer commitment; whether it's oil or watercolor or collage or some other medium. Whatever it is, you will find your muse in this loveliest of lovely lands.

Aix-en-Provence

Monique Faillard offers oil painting instruction to all levels and ages, with classes lasting five hours to five days or more. Contact her at **Ateliers du Soleil** (4 Traverse Notre Dame, Aix-en-Provence, ateliersdusoleil.free.fr).

Discover the beauty of Aix with artist **Catherine Moullé,** who gives both private and group sketching and painting lessons to beginners and experts alike; she focuses on carnets de voyage, travel sketchbooks. Check out her blog at quatrin aime.blogspot.fr or email her directly at quatrinaime@ gmail.com.

The Luberon

Mas des Amandiers (tel 04 90 06 29 60, mas-des-amand iers.com) is an 18th-century silk farm in Cavaillon owned by a famous portrait painter, Jean-Claude Lorber, who offers painting and drawing classes to beginners and

experts in a flower-graced setting especially glorious when the lavender blooms in July.

Dominique Hordé offers five-day workshops entitled "Couleurs en Luberon" (Colors in the Luberon; tel 06 80 27 29 62, dominiquehordé .com), experimenting with color to depict the breath-taking setting at Domaine La Molière.

For something unique, the **Conservatoire des Ocres et de la Couleur** in Roussillon (tel 04 90 05 66 69, okhra.com) offers art workshops throughout the year focusing on the region's richness of natural dyes and pigments.

Within easy reach of Bonnieux, Lacoste, and Gordes, **Arts in Provence** (tel 04 90 05 60 99, artsin provence.com) offers classes from a charming mas in the tiny hamlet of Les Bassacs. You have a whole roster to choose from, whether you're drawn to oil, water-color, or acrylic.

The Var

Painting in Provence (tel 04 94 76 78 69, painting-in -provence.com), based near the ancient village of Claviers, offers small classes to beginners and advanced painters alike. You can tackle landscapes, portraits, still lifes, and architecture.

Marseille

Once besieged by gangsters and smugglers, reputed for its grit and grime, this ancient port town has come alive since its induction as the European Capital of Culture in 2013. Boasting sparkling new museums, trendy restaurants and cafés, and a whole new attitude, Marseille buzzes as a veritable world-class city.

After centuries of grittiness, Marseille's Vieux Port (Old Port) sparkles with economic renewal.

Market Days
Fish market: daily a.m. General & flea markets: Tues.–Sun.

Marseille
🗺 106 C2

Visitor Information
✉ Office de Tourisme, 11 La Canebière
☎ 08 26 50 05 00

marseille-tourisme .com

DISCOUNT CARD:
Available at the tourism office, the City Pass covers one- to three-day ($$$$–$$$$$) admission to city museums, public transportation, guided city tours, and a boat trip to the Île d'If.

History

For 26 centuries, Marseille has been, in the words of Alexandre Dumas, the "meeting place of the world." Indeed, through the years the city's coffers have overflowed with the trade of exotic riches—cottons, silks, spices, perfumes, leather, and coffee—and a rich mix of immigrants from Greece, Italy, Spain, Armenia, West Africa, Southeast Asia, and North Africa have synthesized into the population, giving Marseille a mystique all its own.

The Phocaeans (Greeks from Asia Minor) came ashore in 600 B.C., setting up a trading post called Massalia on the site of today's Vieux Port (Old Port). After the Persians destroyed Phocaea in 540 B.C., the Athenian Greeks took over. The city flourished culturally and legally, the port reigning as a major trading center. After Rome conquered Provence in the late second century B.C., the Greeks retained Massalia as an independent republic, allied to Rome. All was fine, until the Greeks sided with the wrong Roman during the 49 B.C. civil war—backing Pompey rather than Caesar. A vengeful Caesar stripped Massalia of its treasures, and its fleet and trade were dispersed to Arles, Fréjus, and Narbonne. Nevertheless, it remained a free city, its excellent Greek university being the last place in the West where courses were taught in Greek. The city did not regain any major significance until the Crusades, when, as an independent republic, it supplied ships headed to the Middle East. It grew richer still under French rule, when its vast entrepôt of docks, shipyards, and warehouses processed raw goods from the far-flung colonies. During World War II, bombing destroyed much of the city.

That has all changed. With billions of euros being poured into its economy, Marseille has transformed into a booming business and cultural center, with more yet to come.

Vieux Port

Everything begins at Marseille's U-shaped Old Port in the city's heart, where ships have docked continually for 2,600 years. The commercial docks were transferred to La Joliette beyond the city's headland in the 1840s—the ancient port is more pleasure marina these days than working port, with yachts, small fishing boats, and sailboats filling more than 10,000 slips. Ferries chug across the harbor, transporting passengers from one side to the other, as well as to the nearby **Château d'If** (see p. 123).

The port's quays have been redesigned to be more pedestrian friendly, and shops and seafood restaurants (serving bouillabaisse!) bustle along its edges. At the head, the **quai des Belges** is the site of a daily morning fish market, with its makeshift trays stacked with squid, eel, sea urchins,

perhaps a squirming octopus or two. Supported by eight slender columns, Norman Foster's steel, seemingly paper-thin canopy, called **Ombrière,** reflects the goings-on beneath.

Along the revitalized quai du Port, on the port's north side, rises the impressive 17th-century **Hôtel de Ville** (Town Hall), with its statue of Louis XIV.

Musée des Docks Romains

- Map p. 119
- 4 place du Vivaux, 2e
- 04 91 55 36 00
- Closed Mon.
- $
- Métro: Vieux Port

musee-des-docks -romains.marseille.fr

Savon de Marseille

Sweet-smelling bars of soap in such seductive aromas as honey, lavender, and black cherry are one of Provence's mainstays. The soap tradition dates back to a 1688 law mandating that only bars made according to strict, ancient methods could be labeled as such. And this is what makes Marseille's soap so special: It's completely natural, made with at least 72 percent oil (olive, palm, or copra) and no artificial anything. Be sure you're buying the real deal: An official guarantee is always stamped into the *cube;* one side is marked *Extra Pur 72% d'Huile,* a second side has the cube's net weight in grams, and the maker's name and description are found on the last two sides.

For such a historic city, few vestiges remain from its earliest days. One exception is found nearby at the modest **Musée des Docks Romains.** Here a portion of the first century A.D. Roman quay—where oil- and wine-filled *dolia* (jugs) were stored—has been uncovered and left in its natural setting. Surrounding exhibits showcase items discovered in shipwrecks, mostly terra-cotta jars, amphorae, and coins, that help catalog the ancient importance of trade.

Musée d'Histoire de Marseille

- 🅰 Map p. 119
- ✉ 2 rue Henri-
  Barbusse, 1er
- ☎ 04 91 55 36 00
- 🕐 Closed Mon.
- 💲 $
- Ⓜ Métro: Vieux
  Port, Noailles;
  Tramway:
  Belsunce Alcazar

**musee-histoire-de
-marseille.marseille.fr**

Another exception are the Roman treasures of the **Musée d'Histoire de Marseille,** surprisingly located on the ground floor of a shopping center. (The ruins here were exposed during excavation for the mall, so the mall had first rights to stay.) But there they are, in their full glory, in a recently renovated and expanded space that comprises one of Europe's greatest history museums. Groupings of archaeological finds illuminate Marseille's long and revered history, beginning with Celto-Ligurian times and proceeding through the Greeks and medieval Marseille all the way to the rich Oriental trading days of the 17th and 18th centuries. Most intriguing are the amazingly preserved fragments of a Roman cargo boat from the third century and the hull of a fourth-century Greek boat. Your ticket also includes admission to the adjacent **Port Antique,** where excavations include a corner of the old Roman port.

The Revitalized Port Area

Two forts have guarded the port entrance for centuries, the 17th-century Fort St.-Nicolas on the south side and 12th-century Fort St.-Jean on the north. It's the latter where all eyes are focused these days, having been integrated beautifully into the new **Musée des Civilisations de l'Europe et de la Méditerranée** (Museum of European and Mediterranean Civilizations, aka MuCEM), the world's first museum to celebrate all Mediterranean cultures. The museum centers on a postmodernist, glass-and-black-metal structure by architect Rudy Ricciotti graced with an ever-so-lacy exterior that belies its construction of concrete. Suspended footbridges that are made for taking in the

Norman Foster's Ombrière provides modern shelter from the sun.

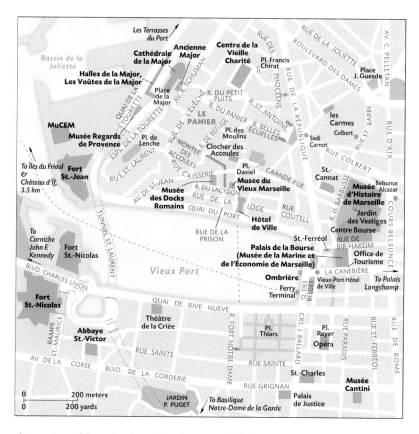

glorious views of the port and bay of Marseille connect it to the fort, making for a fascinating juxtaposition of old and new. The museum has temporary exhibits looking at the people and cultures of all countries bordering the Mediterranean, with history, battles, trade, colonialism, slavery, and arts all fair game. You have to pay for this part of the museum, but there's no charge to enjoy the views from the top of the MuCEM, sit at its café (well, you do have to pay for an espresso at the very least), stroll along the suspended walkways, and peek into the corners of St.-Jean—which includes a Mediterranean garden, sculptures, and a video on the fort's history. A definite must-do, if you do nothing else in the city.

From here, stroll along the beautifully renovated esplanade de la Tourette to the **Musée Regards de Provence,** a showcase for temporary modern Provençal art exhibits. It's housed in a *station sanitaire,* where once-upon-a-time international arrivals to the city went through a disinfection, screening, and vaccination process in an effort to fight the city's threat of epidemics.

MuCEM

 Map this page

✉ Three sites: Fort St.-Jean (*Quai du Port 210*), Panier (*Parvis de l'Église St.-Laurent*), & J4 (*Esplanade du J4 1, 2e*)

☎ 04 84 35 13 13

🕐 Closed Tues.

💲 $$

Ⓜ Métro: Vieux Port, Joliette; Tramway: République/ Dames or Joliette

mucem.org

Musée Regards de Provence

- Map p. 119
- 5 av. Vaudoyer
- 04 95 09 27 11
- $
- Métro: Vieux Port, Joliette; Tramway: République/ Dames, Joliette

museeregardsde provence.com

Nearby towers the dark-green-and-white-striped **Cathédrale de la Major,** constructed on the ruins of the Temple de Diane. The neo-Byzantine cathedral was built between 1852 and 1893—France's largest church raised since the Middle Ages (450 feet/ 137 m long, with the main dome rising almost 210 feet/ 64 m)—complete with domes and cupolas that look more Turkish than French. The large, airy nave

shops in the arched space beneath the cathedral that once served as the port's warehouses. Shop for picnic supplies at the neighboring **Halles de la Major** *(12 esplanade de la Tourette, leshallesdelamajor.com),* a super-trendy food hall with green-grocer, fishmonger, cheesemaker, and more.

If you continue strolling down the revitalized port area, you'll come to **Terrasses du Port** *(9 quai du Lazaret, tel 04 88 91 46 00,*

A religious procession at the Cathédrale de la Major

Cathédrale de la Major

- Map p. 119
- Place de la Major, 2e
- 04 91 90 52 87

is adorned with mosaic floors and red-and-white marble banners. Among the church's treasures is a graceful statue of St. Veronica wiping Christ's face on Calvary, by Auguste Carli.

From here, you can take in the port's more commercial side, with **Les Voûtes de la Major** *(esplanade de la Tourette, lesvoutes-marseille.fr)* offering chi-chi restaurants and

lesterrassesduport.com)—essentially a shopping mall, it offers exquisite harbor views from the rooftop.

Le Panier

Le Panier quarter—located north of the Old Port—is named after a popular 17th-century cabaret, though the quarter's cobbled, hilly lanes, snaking up from the quai du Port, date from the days of the Greeks. One of the city's oldest sections, Le Panier represents only a fraction of what existed before Hitler dynamited it during World War II to flush out the Jews and Résistance fighters hiding out there. Until the 1970s, it was a center for the purification of heroin that Marseille exported to Europe and the United States (hence the "French connection" depicted in the 1971 movie). Today, boutiques purvey paintings, pottery, and handcrafted soaps, while cafés buzz with life. The French know it as the setting for the enormously popular soap opera *Plus Belle La Vie*.

As you wander Le Panier, keep an eye out for a couple of sites: The old Greek *agora* (marketplace) stood at **place de Lenche,** while, at the summit of the old town, is ocher-washed **place des Moulins,** where 15 flour mills churned away in the 15th century.

Follow signs through the maze of picturesque streets to Le Panier's major draw—**Centre de la Vieille Charité,** housing two outstanding museums. Built between 1671 and 1745 as a poorhouse, the beautifully restored complex comprises a central courtyard surrounded on all four sides by arcaded buildings. Upon entering, you face the central chapel, a pure Roman baroque structure with an elliptical dome that now holds temporary exhibits. On the first floor of the surrounding buildings, hidden away in various rooms, is the highly touted **Musée d'Archéologie Méditerranéenne.** Its Egyptian collection, second in France only to the Louvre's, is beautifully presented in a tomblike ambience. It represents all aspects of ancient life on the Nile, from the ancient empire through to the Coptic period. Ancient artifacts include tiny bronze rings, mummified ibises used as offerings, and enormous sarcophagi. On the second floor, the **Musée d'Arts Africains, Amérindiens, et Océaniens** is the only French museum outside Paris devoted to tribal art. Artifacts range from

Centre de la Vieille Charité

 Map p. 119

✉ 2 rue de la Vieille Charité, 2e

☎ 04 91 14 58 80

🕐 Closed Mon.

🚇 Métro: Joliette; Tramway: Sadi-Carnot, République-Dames, Joliette

Musée d'Archéologie Méditerranéenne

☎ 04 91 14 58 59

🕐 Closed Mon.

💲 $

musee-archeologie-mediterraneenne.marseille.fr

Musée d'Arts Africains, Amérindiens, et Océaniens

☎ 04 91 14 58 38

🕐 Closed Mon.

💲 $

maaoa.marseille.fr

EXPERIENCE: Tasting (& Cooking) Bouillabaisse

Bouillabaisse is Marseille's supreme contribution to the culinary world. Originally it was a simple fishermen's dish, in which the best fish parts would be sorted out for sale, and the less desirable pieces kept aside to be prepared with a rouille sauce and bread rubbed with garlic. Today, there is the authentic dish, in which precise ingredients are used in a certain way, and plenty of second-rate *soupes des pecheurs* and *bouillabaisses à notre façon*. Restaurateurs concerned about protecting the authentic recipe drew up the Marseille Bouillabaisse Charter in 1980. To be sure you are sampling the real thing, make sure your chosen restaurant is a signatory of the charter. You can be guaranteed the authentic dish at **Le Miramar** (*12 quai du Port, tel 04 91 91 41 09, lemiramar.fr*), which also offers bouillabaisse-making classes every third Thursday. **Fonfon** (*140 Vallon des Auffes, tel 04 91 52 14 38, www.chez-fonfon.com*) in Vallon des Auffes is another winner.

Olympique de Marseille

More cult than sport, OM is France's most decorated football (American soccer) team. They play in the Stade Vélodome (*lenouveau stadevelodrome.com*), renovated and enlarged in 2014 in preparation for France's hosting of UEFA Euro 2016, including the addition of a roof and additional seating for a total capacity of 67,000. Don't miss a chance to take in the spectacle if OM is playing at home; tickets can be purchased online or at the stadium's ticket office. Guided stadium tours are offered Wednesday, Saturday, and Sunday (*resamarseille .com*). Visit om.net/en for more information.

Musée de la Marine et de l'Économie de Marseille

 Map p. 119

✉ Palais de la Bourse, 9 La Canebière, 1er

☎ 04 91 39 33 21

🚇 Metro: Vieux Port

Musée Cantini

🅰 Map p. 119

✉ 19 rue Grignan, 6e

☎ 04 91 54 77 75

🕐 Closed Mon.

🚇 Metro: Estrangin/ Préfecture

musee-cantini .marseille.fr

Abbaye St.-Victor

🅰 Map p. 119

✉ 3 rue de l'Abbaye, 7e

☎ 04 96 11 22 60

💲 $

🚇 Metro: Estrangin-Préfecture

vases and jewelry from the Near East; to Baoule statuettes from the Ivory Coast; to masks, papier-mâché objects, and *nierkas* (yarn paintings) from Mexico.

On & Off La Canebière

From the head of the Vieux Port, La Canebière—the city's main thoroughfare—was laid out in Louis XIV's expansion scheme of 1666 between the port and the ropemakers' quarter (the word *canèbe* is Provençal for "hemp"). The once grand promenade is slowly being given a face-lift, including a new tramway system.

Near the foot of the boulevard looms the glorious **Palais de la Bourse,** France's oldest stock exchange, built in 1860 by Napoléon III. On its ground floor the excellent **Musée de la Marine et de l'Économie de Marseille** offers a fascinating collection of ship models, engravings, and paintings that chart Marseille's growth as a port.

Farther up, La Canebière splits, with boulevard Longchamp extending to the lovely Palais Longchamp, a 19th-century pastiche of pools, fountains, and cascades. In the palace's north wing, the beautifully renovated **Musée des Beaux Arts** (*Palais Longchamp, tel 04 91 14 59 30, closed Mon., $, Metro: Cinq Avenue–Longchamp, Tramway: Longchamp, musee-des-beaux-arts.marseille.fr*) centers around art "acquired" by Napoléon's army. The south wing contains the **Musée d'Histoire Naturelle** (*Palais Longchamp, tel 04 91 14 59 50, closed Mon., $, musee-histoire .marseille.fr*), established in 1815 to classify more than 200,000 species.

On the other side of La Canebière, **Musée Cantini** is tucked away on the shop-filled rue Grignan. This fairly tiny space of modern and contemporary art shelters some big names—including Raoul Dufy ("Usine à Estaque," 1908), Paul Signac ("L'entrée du Port de Marseille," 1908), and one Picasso ("Tête de Femme Souriante," 1943). Many of the paintings depict local scenes.

West of here, the medieval **Abbaye St.-Victor** pokes up from the hillside, fortresslike in appearance with its crenellated towers and crudely peaked windows. Built on the site of an ancient necropolis, the original structure was destroyed by Saracens in the 11th century and rebuilt and fortified in the 14th century. The Saracens didn't get the crypts ($), however, which contain ancient sarcophagi, including that of martyr St.-Victor.

Farther Out

The **Basilique Notre-Dame de la Garde** overlooks nearly

every niche of Marseille from its 505-foot-high (154 m) perch atop Colline de la Garde. The domed neo-Byzantine-style structure was erected between 1853 and 1864 on the site of a 1214 chapel constructed by St.-Victor. It is topped by a 33-foot-high (10 m) gilded bronze statue of the Madonna, who watches out for the fishermen headed to sea (locals call her "Bonne Mère," or Good Mother). The interior is overwrought with gilded mosaics and murals, plus remarkable collections of

INSIDER TIP:

There are so many good specialties to try in Marseille ... but it would be a shame to leave without having an authentic bouillabaisse!

—CHRISTEL CHERQAOUI
National Geographic Books

ex-votos and other works of art, including an "Annunciation" by Lucca della Robbia. A new museum *(closed Mon., $$)* details the basilica's 800 years of history. Outside, a walkway extends around the entire building, providing a magical, 360-degree panorama overlooking Marseille and beyond.

Corniche John F. Kennedy shoots west from the Vieux Port, curving along the cliff-gouged, albeit built-up, coast, interspersed with beaches and centuries-old

villas. At the end awaits the **Plage du Prado,** a developed beach resort. Nearby, **Château Borély** *(137 av. Clot-Bey, tel 04 91 55 33 60, closed Mon., $$, musee-borely .marseille.fr),* surrounded by a park and botanical gardens, has exhibits on faïence and fashion in a magnificent 18th-century palace.

Out this way too is Le Corbusier's **Cité Radieuse.** Striving to create a city within a building, Le Corbusier designed 337 apartments in 23 different styles to provide the feel of living in a home; hallways are called "streets," and he included one street lined with shops, bar, restaurant, and hotel. It's still a living residence, but you can visit one apartment and public spaces by guided tour.

Just a little farther down the corniche, you'll hit the *calanques* head-on. A swath of it deemed a national park in 2012, this pastiche of white limestone cliffs plunging into azure blue waters is dramatic and wild—the easiest way to visit is by boat *(visite-des-calanques.com)* or, for the intrepid, hiking. Farther east, **Cassis** (see p. 124) is also a popular spot from which to visit.

Château d'If

Alexandre Dumas brought fame to this 16th-century prison-fortress, lording over a tiny island 2 miles (3.5 km) west of the Old Port. In his best-selling 1844 novel *Le Comte de Monte-Cristo,* his legendary fictional count of Monte-Cristo was incarcerated here as Edmond Dantès. Boats leave regularly from the quai des Belges. ∎

Basilique Notre-Dame de la Garde

- Map p. 119
- Place Colonel Edon, 6e
- 04 91 13 40 80
- Métro: Estrangin-Préfecture

notredamedela garde.com

Cité Radieuse

- 280 blvd. Michelet
- Tours by reservation only via tourism office; book online (marseille-tourisme.com or call 08 26 500 500)
- $

marseille -citeradieuse.org

Château d'If

- Marseille harbor
- 04 91 59 02 30
- Closed Sept.–March
- $$
- Boats leave from outside Groupement des Armateurs Côtiers Marseillais (GACM) office at Vieux Port (tel 04 91 55 50 09). Round-trip fare: $$$

if.monuments -nationaux.fr

Cassis & Les Calanques

Bijou-like Cassis, its pastel-washed houses tumbling down the steep hillside to the tiny port, has served as a coral-fishing harbor and, in the early 20th century, a favorite subject of the fauvists—including Raoul Dufy and Henri Matisse. But the seaside village is probably most famous for the *calanques*—stunning steep-walled coves—that surround it.

Market Days
Wed. & Fri.

Cassis
🅰 106 C2
Visitor Information
✉ Office Municipal de Tourisme, quai des Moulins, Oustau Calendal
☎ 04 92 39 01 03
ot-cassis.com

Parc National des Calanques
☎ 04 20 10 50 00
calanques
-parcnational.fr

NOTE: The *calanques* are sometimes closed July–mid-Sept. due to threat of forest fire, and the entire massif is off-limits when the wind blows more than 80 miles (129 km) an hour.

After perusing boutiques and dining in a portside seafood café, there's not much else to do in Cassis besides sunbathing and surf-splashing—nothing wrong with that! Of the town's five beaches, the largest is sandy **Plage de la Grande Mer,** on the breakwater's seaside. The **Plage du Bestouan** is sheltered at the port's western end. You can also try some wine-tasting at **Le Clos Ste.-Magdeleine** (*av. du Revestel, tel 04 42 01 70 28, clossaintemagdeleine.fr),* one of 12 Cassis vineyards.

And then there are the *calanques.* These absolutely stunning, indigo-water inlets edged with massive white-limestone shelter an extraordinary wealth of flora and fauna, including 900 plant species, of which 50 are classified as rare.

A 201-square-mile (520 sq km) swath was designated a national park in 2012, encompassing (part of) Port Miou, Port Pin, and En Vau. You can walk to all three from Cassis. **Port Miou** is the closest, about half an hour along the Sentier du Petit Prince. **Port Pin** is half an hour farther along the GR98 hiking trail, with **En Vau** being the farthest (and most difficult to reach), about an hour beyond Port Pin. You can also drive to En Vau along an unsigned dirt road off the D559; park at Parking de la Fontasse and walk on down.

But most calanques are accessible only by sea. Informal boat tours operate from Cassis' port; the little yellow kiosk there sells tickets for trips that take in 3, 5, 8, and 9 calanques (three is usually enough for most). ∎

EXPERIENCE: Diving the Calanques

Jacques Cousteau popularized diving along the Mediterranean coast more than half a century ago, and today there are many places to take the plunge. Among them: The regions of Hyères and Cavalaire—and, especially, the *calanques* between Cassis and Marseille. Here, the seabed falls away steeply, quickly offering plenty of chances to spot sea urchins, hermit crabs, barracuda, octopuses, morays, groupers, lobsters, John Dory, congers, and sea perch among the gorgonian coral and underwater rock formations.

Whether you're a beginner or expert, go with one of the dive operators in Cassis. **Cassis Calanques Plongée** (*cassis-calanques-plongee.com*) and **Narval Plongée** (*narval-plongee.fr*) are both good options. For other ideas, contact the Cassis tourism office (*ot-cassis.com*).

Hyères & Îles d'Hyères

Three golden islands hovering just offshore the palm-shaded city of Hyères offer a quick dip into the Mediterranean's exotic side. Legend states the isles were created from beautiful princesses who, chased by pirates, were turned into islands by gods. Whatever the case, each one has its own distinct personality.

Île de Port-Cros's picturesque port

The monks of Lérins colonized the islands in the fifth century. They were taken over by the Saracens in 1160 and later fortified by François I. For centuries the haunt of pirates and smugglers, only peace and calm await visitors today.

Measuring 4.5 miles long (7 km) and 1.9 miles wide (3 km), the largest and most developed island is **Île de Porquerolles.** It has two forts from the early days: Fort du Petit Langoustier and Fort Ste.-Agathe (with an underwater archaeological exhibition). Appreciate the island's beauty along several eucalyptus- and pine-shaded paths. For beachgoers, Plage d'Argent, to the west, and Plage de la Courtade, to the east, are each an easy 10- to 15-minute walk from the main village of Porquerolles.

Much of **Île de Port-Cros,** the hilliest and wildest of the three main islands, comprises France's smallest national park. A trail from the post office in the main village accesses an 18.6-mile (30 km) network of walking trails. From the beach at La Palud, on the island's north shore, snorkelers follow an underwater trail *(sentier sous-marin)* in a marine nature reserve to see sponges and octopuses.

Ninety percent of **Île du Levant,** the easternmost island, is a military camp, but its claim to fame is that a nudist colony has occupied its remaining space since the 1930s.

Hyères

In the 19th century, dignified and venerable Hyères was a favorite wintering place for such notables as Queen Victoria and Edith Wharton. Despite development of its coastal suburbs, the Côte d'Azur resort has retained its slightly faded charm. A profusion of palm trees and Moorish architecture imparts an exotic quality on the broad 19th-century boulevards. Through a medieval gatehouse you'll discover a quaint old town, offering lovely gardens and sea views. ■

Market Day
Sat.

Hyères
 107 E2

Visitor Information
✉ Office de Tourisme, av. de Belgique
☎ 04 94 01 84 50

hyerestourisme.com

FERRIES TO THE ISLANDS: Transports Maritimes et Terrestres du Littoral Varois *(tel 04 94 58 21 81, tlv-tvm.com)* has ferryboats that sail year-round from Gare Maritime de la Tour Fondue near Hyères to the Porquerolles. Round-trip ticket: $$$$. For the other two islands, TLV ferries depart from Port d'Hyères.

St.-Tropez

This 15th-century fishing village certainly was idyllic when the first artists arrived in the late 1800s, admiring its clear, beautiful light. Then Brigitte Bardot starred in the 1956 film *Et Dieu Créa la Femme (And God Created Woman)*, and St.-Tropez broke from obscurity, becoming an international symbol of the French high life. The favored getaway for Picasso and Armani, St.-Tropez has become synonymous with glitz and glamour. Even so, its medieval lanes, hidden plazas, and apricot-colored houses, all overlooking the azure Bay of St.-Tropez, remain as picturesque as ever.

Another pretty coastal town from afar, St.-Tropez shines with a star-filled reputation all its own.

Market Days
Tues. & Sat.

St.-Tropez
🗺 107 F2

Visitor Information
✉ Quai Jean-Jaurès, av. Général de Gaulle
☎ 08 92 68 48 28

sainttropeztourisme .com

History

Jutting out of the midst of the great Massif des Maures, St.-Tropez occupies one of the most rugged spots along the Côte d'Azur. Destroyed by Saracens in the Middle Ages, it became a tiny self-governing republic in the 15th century thanks to an offer made by a Genoese nobleman to repopulate the place. In 1637, the locals defeated a Spanish fleet that was threatening the

coastline. Worried by this display of military prowess, Louis XIV promptly removed all privileges. Nevertheless, the victory is still celebrated every June 15.

St.-Tropez remained forgotten until 1892, when Paul Signac arrived and built a villa that became a haven for artists—most notably Raoul Dufy, Henri Matisse, and others associated with fauvism.

You can see some of their efforts at the **Musée de**

l'Annonciade *(place Georges-Grammont, tel 04 94 17 84 10, closed Tues. & Nov., $).* Look for the superb views of St.-Tropez by Signac and Albert Marquet.

Visiting

While *le jet-set* of the 1960s is long gone, St.-Tropez's moneyed mystique is alive and well. For proof, stop by the **Vieux Port** (Old Port), crammed with shiny yachts—many chartered for more than $100,000 a week. As their captains and crews casually take in the sunset with a toast of Cristal, the "other side" sits steps away at the touristy cafés, sipping espresso and dreaming of being rich.

From the port, narrow streets crowded with fancy boutiques and swank bistros wind uphill to the 16th-century citadel. Here you'll find magnificent harbor views and the interactive **Musée d'Histoire Maritime,** which chronicles St.-Tropez's long history with the sea.

Despite its sparkling reputation, some corners of St.-Tropez remain unassuming and downright ordinary. In the heart of town, old-timers have played

pétanque at the plane tree–lined **place des Lices** for more than a century. This square is the site of the weekly markets, feasts of fruit, vegetables, honey, wine ... and, since nothing is too ordinary here, perhaps a movie star or two. Cafés surrounding the square include the notable **Le Café;** stars are said to still hide out in the restaurant at the rear.

INSIDER TIP:

Summer remains high season for celebrity-spotting along St.-Tropez's ever trendy Pampelonne beach.

—KRISTEN GUNDERSON
National Geographic researcher

St.-Tropez's closest beaches are **Bouillabaisse,** to the west; **Les Graniers** in Baie des Cannebiers, just past the citadel; and **Les Salins** on the cape, 3 miles (5 km) away. The most famous is **Plage de Pampelonne,** south of town, edged with cafés and restaurants, including the renowned Club 55. ∎

Musée d'Histoire Maritime

✉ Mont de la Citadelle

☎ 04 94 54 84 14

🕓 Closed Nov.

$ $

Le Café

✉ Place des Lices

☎ 04 94 97 44 69

🕓 Hours vary with season

Brigitte Bardot

In 1956, movie director Roger Vadim and a film crew burst into St.-Tropez to make a film starring his little-known actress wife. The film was *Et Dieu Créa la Femme (And God Created Woman),* the actress was Brigitte Bardot, and St.-Tropez never looked back.

The daughter of bourgeois Parisian parents, Bardot had been working as a model when she met Vadim at the age of 15. The nudity and love scenes in *And*

God Created Woman caused a scandal, and the film was a huge success. "B. B." shot to stardom, and her sun-kissed, barefoot, *femme-enfant* brand of sexuality made her an icon for a whole generation.

Bardot still lives in her villa outside St.-Tropez. But after three marriages and many love affairs, she has turned her attention to animals and devotes herself to animal rights causes.

St.-Tropez's Hinterlands

Vine-striped hillsides, far-off—and close-up—views of sparkling Golfe de St.-Tropez, a cluster of medieval hill towns: These are some of the more peaceful pursuits waiting just beyond St.-Tropez's buzz, in the remote Massif des Maures.

Enclosed by ramparts, toylike Ramatuelle dates back to the Middle Ages.

Gassin
🅰 107 F2
Visitor Information
✉ Golfe de St.-Tropez Tourisme, carrefour de la Foux
☎ 04 94 55 22 00
🕐 Closed Sun.

**golfe-saint-tropez
-information.com**

Ramatuelle
🅰 107 F2
Visitor Information
✉ Office de Tourisme, place de l'Ormeau
☎ 04 98 12 64 00

**ramatuelle
-tourisme.com**

Southwest of St.-Tropez, you come to the first of the hill towns, sleepy **Gassin** atop a rocky spur. Right away, you're treated to an amazing view, as far as the Golfe de St.-Tropez. The first mention of Gassin goes back to 1234, when the *castrum,* or castle, surrounded by ramparts, occupied today's rue de la Tasco. Follow **Leï Barre Promenade**—the medieval terrace marking the former rampart boundary—past a bevy of restaurants, each with prime vistas, including one aptly named Bello Visto. At the promenade's end, the panorama takes in the Baie de Cavalaire and the Îles d'Hyères (see p. 125).

Then wander the maze of atmospheric *ruelles,* with their bougainvillea-draped porticos and medieval gates. One street, tiny **l'Androuno,** is said to be the world's narrowest.

To the southeast, **Ramatuelle** is another medieval hill town. The central place d'Ormeau— Square of the Elm Tree (though the elm died and was replaced with an olive tree in 1983)—with its souvenir pottery and soap shops, is a touch touristy, but its ruelles with their ancient houses are charming as can be. The **Église Notre-Dame,** just off the square, dates from the 17th century, its bell tower a former lookout post. Inside, look for the bust of St.-André–Ramatu-elle's patron saint–carved from a fig-tree stump.

Just outside town, on the D89, the **Moulins de Paillas** are stone windmills used until the turn of the 20th century. The spot, 1,066 feet (325 m) above sea level, offers dizzying views over Baie de Cavalaire and the town of La Croix-Valmer on one side, Ramatuelle on the other.

Down at sea level, breezy, carefree **Cavalaire-sur-Mer** is a popular family resort, with a *pétanque* court in the middle of town and a pretty marina filled with yachts and working fishing boats. Every September, tuna fish-ermen set out from the marina, returning to sell their catch. On rue du Port, the **Casino du Golfe** is the St.-Tropez peninsula's only casino. Several beaches are worth a look, including the **Plage de Bonporteau,** at Cava-laire's west end. In August 1944, Allied forces landed on Cavalaire's shores to secure a southern beach-head in their effort to liberate Provence. Many memorials com-memorate the lives lost during the valiant struggle.

Cavalaire is a good place for water-oriented activities, including microlight flying, sailing, windsurf-ing, and, with its offshore wrecks and subsea flora and fauna, scuba diving. Regular ferry services leave for the Îles d'Hyères.

Heading back inland and far-ther north, you can see **Grimaud** for miles around, the remains of its feudal castle crowning a cluster of stone houses. The joy here is to wander the perfectly restored

lanes, admiring the porticos, stone stairways, bougainvillea-festooned facades, and blooming flowerpots. To visit, there are the castle ruins, abandoned after the French Revolution, as well as two mills, the restored **Moulin à Vent de Saint-Roch,** a flour mill built in the 17th century, and the remains of the 17th-century **Moulin à Huile de l'Hôpital,** the town's largest oil mill. Learn about the region at the **Musée des Arts et Traditions Populaires** (a folk museum). The picturesque **Chapelle des Pénitents Blancs** (1482) houses the shrines of St.-Théodore and St.-Lambert.

Côtes de Provence

The vines covering St.-Tropez's hinterlands are part of the Côtes de Provence appellation—producing mostly rosés. You'll see *domaines* (vineyards) adver-tised everywhere, most offering *dégustations* (tastings). Pick up information at the St.-Tropez tourism office or online. ■

Chestnut Country

In the Massif des Maures, the mountain-scape behind St.-Tropez, cork oak, maquis, and maritime pines thrive alongside the locally celebrated chestnut trees. So it's no surprise that you'll find all kinds of chestnut specialties here: chestnut flour (used even in pizza dough), *crème de marron* spread, can-died chestnuts, and, in autumn, *chastaign-ades* (grilled chestnuts). The leafy village of **Collobrières** has a small museum devoted to the mahogany-colored jewel and plenty of places to sample its various iterations; a chestnut festival takes place here every October (*collobrieres-tourisme.com*).

Cavalaire-sur Mer

🅰 107 F2

Visitor Information

✉ Office de Tourisme, Maison de la Mer

☎ 04 94 01 92 10

cavalairesurmer.fr

Grimaud

🅰 107 F2

Visitor Information

✉ Office de Tourisme, 679 rte. Nationale

☎ 04 94 55 43 83

grimaud-provence .com

Musée des Arts et Traditions Populaires

✉ 53 montée Hospice, Grimaud

☎ 04 94 55 43 83 (Office de Tourisme)

🕐 Closed Sun. & a.m.

Côtes de Provence Estate Crawl

An idyllic realm of medieval villages, pine and cork oak forests, vineyard-covered valleys, and plenty of opportunities to taste the local wine await on this bucolic drive in the Vallée Intérieure of the central Var—one of the Côtes de Provence's five discrete regions that have been given the *appellation d'origine contrôlée.*

Le Thoronet's cloister epitomizes the abbey's clean, elegant lines.

NOT TO BE MISSED:

Notre-Dame-du-Thoronet
• Tourtour

Begin in **Les Arcs ❶**, with its medieval core and Villeneuve castle (offering dining and rooms). Four-and-a-half miles (7.2 km) east of town, on the D91 toward La Motte, the **Château Ste.-Roseline ❷** *(tel 04 94 99 50 30, chapel closed Mon. & a.m., sainte -roseline.com)* is an offbeat castle in a vine-yard setting, where you can taste a *cru classé* wine produced since the 14th century. The adjacent chapel houses a 1975 mosaic by Marc Chagall, as well as the corpse of Ste.-Roseline herself (1263–1329) within a glass casket. Roseline cared for peasants during the Saracen invasions and, upon her death, her corpse is said not to have decomposed.

Just south of Les Arcs on the N7, you can taste (and buy) 16 different Côtes de Provence wines at the **Maison des Vins ❸** *(N7, tel 04 94 99 50 20, maison-des-vins.fr)*. Locals highly recommend the restaurant, La Vigne à Table. From here, continue on the N7 through

Vidauban, then head in the direction of Le Thoronet via the D84. Right away you'll see vineyards, then wind through woodsy hills interspersed with vines and hamlets. About 7.5 miles (12 km) on, turn right on the D17, continuing on the D79, which will bring you through Le Thoronet to the abbey of **Notre-Dame-du-Thoronet ❹** *(tel 04 94 60 43 90, $$)*, one of three Cistercian houses in Provence (Silvacane and Sénanque are the others). Largely built between 1160 and 1175 of vivid rose stone, it is one of Provence's purest examples of Roman-esque architecture. The church was constructed first, so the monks could pray as soon as possible. A self-guided tour visits the church, monks' dormitories, and cloisters.

From the abbey, follow the tiny D279 then D13 to the picturesque village of **Carcès,** perhaps stopping to taste at one of the *domaines* along the way. You can also taste in town. Charming **Cotignac ❺** lies 5 miles (8 km) away, via the D13, its medieval houses cozying against a hillside. Above, tufa cliffs hold caves once hollowed out for wine cellars and even residences. You can hike to them. From here, the D50 leads to **Entrecasteaux,** another picturesque medieval town.

Toward **Salernes ❻** via the D31, the scenery alternates between vineyards and piney hills. Near town, signs for *terres cuites* (baked earth) appear, as this village has been famous for its enamel tiles since the 18th century.

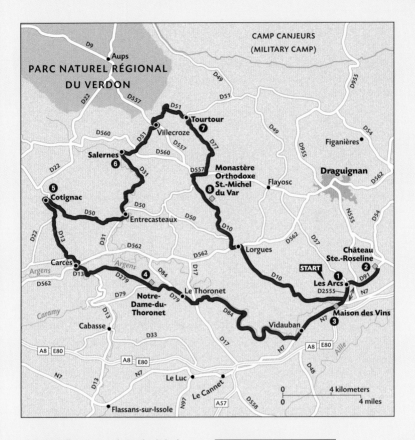

Pretty **Villecroze** is only 3 miles (5 km) away via the D51. Its *vieux village* harbors pastel-shuttered houses dripping with flowers. The town is set against tufa cliffs full of caves—*grottes troglodytes*—where a local lord lived in the 1500s. Tours are offered; they are reached through the town park *(next to the tennis courts)*.

Take the D51 to the D77, a twisty, high-to-the-sky road that explains the nickname of **Tourtour 7**, your destination—"village in the sky." Views atop this perch are stupendous, while the village, with its houses of pale, locally quarried stone, is charming as can be. The central square is lined with restaurants and cafés. There is a restored 17th-century *moulin à huile*, which presses olives after the harvest in mid-December and serves as an art gallery the rest of the year; the medieval **Tour Grimaldi** watchtower; and

> See area map p. 107
> Les Arcs
> A full day
> 60 miles (95 km)
> Les Arcs

two châteaus, one that now houses the *mairie* (town hall), the other an art gallery.

From here, drop back to Earth via the D77, through scrabbly ecru cliffs and pine trees. Take a right on the D557 toward Lorgues, then a left on the D10. Soon you pass the turnoff for the **Monastère Orthodoxe St.-Michel du Var 8** *(1909 rte. Lorgues, tel 04 94 73 75 75)*, a historic monastery that can be visited. The large town of **Lorgues** offers more chances for wine-tasting. Return to Les Arcs via the D10 and D2555/D57.

More Places to Visit in Aix, Marseille, & the Var

Aubagne

Filmmaker and writer Marcel Pagnol was born in this pretty town in 1895. While its outskirts have suffered a bit in the name of progress, its tree-shaded *vieille ville* remains much as Pagnol might have known it. The tourist office offers several Pagnol-themed tours, including a daylong, 5.6-mile (9 km) hike covering sites related to his life.

🅰 106 C2 **Visitor Information** *www.tourisme-paysdaubagne.fr* ✉ Maison du Tourisme, 8 cours Barthélémy ☎ 04 42 03 49 98

Brignoles

Get past the industrial outskirts to discover the charming historic core of this little town, once famous for sugar plums sent to the royal courts of Europe. Later, it became rich through bauxite mining. In **place Carami,** locals lounge at *terrasse* cafés beneath plane trees. The **Musée du Pays Brignolais** *(place des Comtes de Provence, tel 04 94 69 45 18, closed Mon.–Tues., $, museebrignolais.com)* has *santons,* paintings by the local Parrocel family, and a re-creation of a Provençal kitchen.

🅰 106 D3 **Visitor Information** *la-provence-verte.net* ✉ Maison du Tourisme, carrefour de l'Europe ☎ 04 94 72 04 21

Le Mistral

The dry, cold mistral wind rages down from the north up to 100 days a year. Some say it's the north's revenge on the south's otherwise idyllic weather. Its entrée is the Rhône River Valley, gusting up to 60 miles (97 km) an hour and brutalizing Avignon and Arles the worst but affecting most corners of the province. It's said to last in multiples of three—3, 6, or 9 days ... enough to drive you crazy. Indeed, an accusation of crime might very well be dropped if it is proven to have happened during the mistral.

La Ciotat

The world's first movie was premiered in this port city in September 1895, the work of the local Lumière brothers. They showed their *L'Entrée d'un Train en Gare de La Ciotat (The Arrival of a Train at La Ciotat Station)* at their father's theater, the **Théâtre Eden,** which still stands on boulevard Anatole France. Today, film history comes to life at the **Éspace Simon Lumière** *(20 rue du Marechal Foch, tel 04 42 71 61 70),* with photos, posters, and a film archive. Artists including Georges Braque (1882–1963) loved painting the **Vieux Port,** which still possesses some charm.

🅰 106 C2 **Visitor Information** *www.laciotat.info* ✉ Office de Tourisme, blvd. Anatole France ☎ 04 42 08 61 32

Oppidum d'Entremont

Perched on an aerie 1,200 feet (367 m) above the edge of a plateau, with a 656-foot-wide (200 m) valley view, Entremont was the capital of the advanced Celto-Ligurian tribe. They ruled between the third and second centuries B.C., when the Romans destroyed the city at the request of the Marseillais. Excavations have exposed a residential zone and traces of shops and warehouses. Of particular note are the number of decapitated statues that have also been uncovered, spearheading a debate: Were the heads of vanquished enemies removed by war chiefs as evidence of their bravery? Or did the tribe practice the ritualized preservation of the heads of the deceased for the creation of reliquaries? The current thought combines both theories. Many of the statues and objects found here are on display at the Musée Granet in Aix-en-Provence (see p. 111). *entremont.culture.gouv.fr* 🅰 106 C3 ✉ 1.8 miles (3 km) N of Aix-en-Provence via av. Solari (D14) ☎ 04 42 99 10 00 🕒 Closed Tues.

The fabled French Riviera, including celebrity-spangled Cannes, perfume-making Grasse, and contemporary art (starring Picasso)

Côte d'Azur: Cannes & Around

"To My Pretty": Arman's tribute to Picasso, at the Musée Picasso in Antibes

Côte d'Azur: Cannes & Around

Palm trees, body-squeezed beaches, languorous sea breezes, and a sparkling blue sea: This is the heart of the French Riviera, stretching from Cannes to Cagnes-sur-Mer and reaching inland to Grasse, Vence, and other hill towns. This realm also reveals major contributions to modern art (spearheaded by Pablo Picasso), perfume, and military architecture.

Cannes is all about strolling along La Croisette, its famed esplanade, taking in grandiose hotels, bather-packed beaches, and the star walk near the Palais des Festivals et des Congrès, site of the awards ceremony for the International Film Festival every May. Another world exists atop Le Suquet hill, the old quarter with a medieval castle overlooking the glistening bay. Offshore, on Île Ste.-Marguerite, the mysterious Man in the Iron Mask was locked up by King Louis XIV in the late 17th century. The eucalyptus-scented island, along with nearby Île St.-Honorat, is one of the Îles de Lérins, a tranquil escape from the coast's buzz.

After World War II, Picasso moved to the Côte d'Azur, where his works took on the joyful, colorful mood of the surrounding scenery. He helped revitalize the pottery industry in Vallauris, whose main street is now packed with pottery shops (of differing quality). Picasso at one point lived in the perfectly preserved hill town of Mougins, now most famous for its Moulin de Mougins restaurant.

Nearby Grasse has been the world's perfume capital since the 16th century, when Catherine de Médicis introduced the concept of scented leather gloves. Today, three perfumeries offer tours, and several museums in the town center provide further insight into the perfume business. You can even try your hand at creating your own scent.

Vence is a pleasant enough hill town, but most people pilgrimage here for one thing—the little white chapel designed by Henri Matisse in the 1950s. From the colorful stained-glass windows to the monochromatic Stations of the Cross to the priests' vestments, Matisse created it all, in what he considered to be his greatest lifetime achievement.

More modern art awaits in another hill town, nearby St.-Paul-de-Vence. The Maeghts built their art museum in the 1970s, a (then) state-of-the-art temple to house their extensive collection of 20th-century art. Giant sculptures by Miró, Calder, and de Staël dot the terraced grounds. Georges Braque, Marc Chagall, and Henri Matisse were some of the "unknown" artists who gathered at the town's Colombe d'Or, where they exchanged paintings for food and lodging. Owner Paul Roux built up one of the most important private collections of 20th-century art in the process. One can only

imagine what those struggling artists would think if they knew the price diners pay to view their works today (the only way to see them).

Picasso experienced some of his most prolific months in the moneyed town of Antibes, where he worked out of the ancient Grimaldi castle. The château now holds the Musée Picasso, one of the world's greatest collections of his art. Poised on the Mediterranean, Antibes has several more museums tucked away in its old quarter, including a small but interesting archaeological museum and a fort designed by the great military architect Vauban. The Summer Season was invented on nearby Cap d'Antibes, where F. Scott Fitzgerald, Ernest Hemingway, and their friends frolicked in the surf.

Two more hill towns worth a stop are tiny Biot, a major glassblowing center, and Cagnes-sur-Mer, featuring another Grimaldi castle, which now houses several eclectic art collections, and the last home of Pierre-Auguste Renoir, a house museum that appears just as if the Impressionist artist might return any moment. ∎

NOT TO BE MISSED:

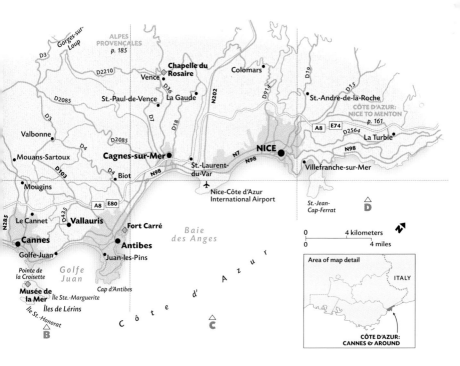

Cannes

Along the palm-shaded La Croisette, Cannes's famed seaside esplanade, camera-toting tourists intermingle with young bronzed couples sporting the latest trends, Chanel-chic ladies walking poodles, artists bent over their canvases, probably a movie star or two—you never know. The translucent blue sea shimmers on one side, lapping exclusive, parasol-dotted beaches, while on the other side tower exclusive hotels. There may not be many museums or monuments to visit, but who needs them, in this most glittery, sophisticated resort, where seeing and being seen is what it's all about? For ten days each May, this atmosphere culminates in the world-renowned International Film Festival.

Cannes's Vieux Port (Old Port), with the historic Le Suquet quarter rising beyond

Market Days
Tues.– Sun.

Cannes
🅰 135 B1
Visitor Information
✉ Palais des
Festivals, 1 blvd.
de la Croisette
☎ 04 92 99 84 22

cannes.fr

When Lord Brougham, lord chancellor of England, stopped in Cannes in 1834 to avoid a cholera outbreak, the tiny, tenth-century fishing hamlet's future changed forever. He built a Palladium-style villa in Le Suquet quarter. His mates followed, building their own glamorous villas, and ever since Cannes has been associated with luxury tourism. Palatial hotels were built in the 20th century, including the Carlton, the Martinez, and the Majestic.

Cannes got a true stamp of glitz and glamour in 1939, when it was selected to host the Festival International de Cinéma (see p. 40). Louis Lumière, inventor of cinema, was prepared to preside over the first festival, but World War II intervened. It was not until 1946 that Cannes had its day, when films such as Jean Cocteau's *La Belle et La Bête* and Alfred Hitchcock's *Notorious* had top billing at the old Palais des Festivals. Cocteau described the event as "a living comet that has touched down for a few days on La Croisette." Today, the red carpet unfurls at the **Palais des Festivals et des Congrès,**

INSIDER TIP:

To best appreciate the coastal scenery between Cannes and St.-Tropez, take a boat. The trips are popular, so reserve a few days ahead.

—TIM JEPSON
National Geographic author

a blocky structure built in 1982 on the headland between the Baie des Cannes and the Vieux Port. More than 50 festivals, congresses, and trade fairs take place here the rest of the year, and the building also contains a casino and nightclub. Outside, the handprints of stars and directors are immortalized in the sidewalk **allée des Étoiles du Cinéma**—Julie Andrews, Meryl Streep, and Sylvester Stallone are perennial favorites.

La Croisette

La Croisette, one of France's loveliest boulevards, runs east from the Palais des Festivals to the Pointe de la Croisette. Glamorous villas and clubs once lined its length, long since replaced by apartment blocks, grand hotels, and designer boutiques. Of the belle époque era, only the wedding-cake **InterContinental Carlton hotel** survives, a pompous neobaroque palace designed by Charles Dalmas. Shortly after the Carlton opened in 1912, it attracted Europe's haut monde, including royalty, to be followed later by screen stars.

Here, for instance, Elizabeth Taylor checked in, successively, as Mrs. Hilton, Mrs. Todd, and Mrs. Fisher. The ultimate in luxury, even its standard rooms boast marble-encrusted bathrooms, while the deluxe rooms guarantee exquisite views over the bay.

The **Centre d'Art La Malmaison** along La Croisette provides a cultural fix with temporary modern and contemporary art exhibits—especially those inspired by the Côte d'Azur—displayed in the former games room of the Grand Hotel.

Living the Life

Really, suntanning is what Cannes is all about. So it's been, ever since Coco Chanel (1883–1971) got

InterContinental Carlton

✉ 58 blvd. de la Croisette
☎ 04 93 06 40 06
intercontinental
-carlton-cannes.com

Centre d'Art La Malmaison

✉ 42 blvd. de la Croisette
☎ 04 97 06 44 90
🕐 Closed Mon. Oct.–April
$ $$
cannes.com

EXPERIENCE:
Star-Gazing

Since the Cannes Film Festival began in 1946, the glitterati have descended on the town to see and be seen. Here's how to put on your own best Marilyn Monroe.

• Hang out where the celebs hang out. You have good chances of "coincidentally" running into Hollywood's brightest at such über-luxe hotels as the **InterContinental Carlton** (*58 blvd. de la Croisette*), **Grand Hyatt Cannes Hôtel Martinez** (*73 blvd. de la Croisette*), and **Hôtel Majestic Barrière** (*10 blvd. de la Croisette*).

• Visit all the magical film sights in Cannes—including *the* red carpet—with the **Cannes & the Cinema tour** (*Fri. 2 p.m. in English; cannes-destination.com, $$*).

• Add your face to the *silhouettes de cinéma* (life-size, faceless cutouts of famous characters)—Charlie's Angels, Harry Potter, Shrek—standing up around town. The tourist office has a map.

The InterContinental Carlton hotel's two cupolas are said to have been inspired by the bosom of La Belle Otèro, the darling of American millionaires and Russian dukes alike.

Musée de la Castre
- ✉ Château de la Castre
- ☎ 04 93 38 55 26
- 🕐 Closed Mon.
- 💲 $

Îles de Lérins
- ✉ Ferries depart from quai Laubeu, Vieux Port
- ☎ 04 92 98 71 38
- 🕐 Check website for departure times
- 💲 $$$ (round-trip ferry)

cannes-destination.fr
cannes-ilesdelerins.com

too much sun here by accident in 1923 and returned to Paris, where the press and fashion world assumed the ultrafashionable woman had started a new trend. Gleaming, golden bodies in skimpy bathing suits continue the craze. Most of the best beaches are private, taken over by hotels across the street. If you don't have a key to one of those luxury rooms, you'll find two small public bathing areas at either end of La Croisette; more public beaches await along boulevard du Midi, farther west of La Croisette.

The Other Cannes

After a day in the sun, the thing to do is promenade. A favorite spot is **rue d'Antibes,** a few streets north of La Croisette, where chic boutiques tempt with their luxury wares. One street farther north, pedestrianized **rue Meynadier** is a bit more down-to-earth, with discount clothes, souvenir shops, and gourmet food stores in 18th-century facades. The iron-roofed **Marché Forville,** at the street's western end, is the town's primary fruit, flower, and vegetable market; it's open every day but Monday, when a *brocante* market (flea market) takes over.

At nearby **allée de la Liberté,** *pétanque* is played beneath shady plane trees. A flower market takes place here every day but Monday.

Tiny, restaurant-fringed **rue**

St.-Antoine winds up into the city's oldest quarter—**Le Suquet,** with its fabulous views over the city, the sea, and the Vieux Port. It's topped by the 17th-century **Église Notre-Dame d'Espérance,** the adjoining Cistercian **Chapelle de Ste.-Anne,** and a castle erected by Lérins monks in the 11th and 12th centuries. The **Musée de la Castre** here houses a collection of musical instruments and an exhibition on local history.

At the foot of Le Suquet, the **Vieux Port,** or Old Port, harbors a grand lineup of luxury yachts and pleasure boats. Seafood restaurants and sidewalk cafés edge the adjacent **quai St.-Pierre.**

Îles de Lérins

A 30-minute boat ride from the Vieux Port brings you to the peaceful oasis of **Île St.-Honorat,** one of the Îles de Lérins. In the fifth century, the monk St.-Honorat and seven of his disciples founded an abbey here. The **Abbaye de Lérins** became famous throughout the Western world, and pilgrims have visited its seven chapels since medieval times (the present abbey dates from the 19th century). A group of Cistercian monks lives here now. A tree-shaded trail circumscribes the tiny, vineyard-dotted isle, passing by monastic buildings. Take a stroll before lunch at open-air **La Tonnelle restaurant,** where wine made by the monks accompanies Mediterranean fare.

Honorat's sister established a convent on a neighboring island, today's **Île Ste.-Marguerite,** a 15-minute boat ride from the Vieux Port. It's most famous for its 17th-century prisoner, the Man in the Iron Mask (see sidebar this page). Fort Royal, where he was held, now contains the **Musée de la Mer,** which details the fort's history and shipwrecks. You can also visit his cell. ∎

NOTE: There is one boat for St.-Honorat and one boat for Ste.-Marguerite; no boat service connects the two islands.

Abbaye de Lérins

- ✉ Île St.-Honorat
- ☎ 04 92 99 54 00
- 🕐 Mass: 11 a.m. Sun. & 9:50 a.m. Mon.–Sat.

abbayedelerins.com

La Tonnelle

- ✉ Île St.-Honorat
- ☎ 04 92 99 54 08
- 🕐 Closed mid-Nov.–mid-Dec.

tonnelle-abbaye delerins.com

Musée de la Mer

- 🅰 135 B1
- ✉ Île Ste.-Marguerite
- ☎ 04 93 43 18 17
- 🕐 Closed Mon.
- 💲 $

The Mysterious Man in the Iron Mask

The Man in the Iron Mask arrived on Île Ste.-Marguerite in April 1687. Who was he? No one knows for sure. Voltaire, who spoke to the mystery man's former servants, believed he was the elder brother of Louis XIV—the inspiration for Alexandre Dumas's novel *Le Vicomte de Bragelonne,* written in 1848–1850. Others have surmised he was the illegitimate son of Anne of Austria (wife of Louis XIII), or of her and Cardinal Mazarin; the bastard son of the Duke of Beaufort (Louis XIV's brother); the bastard son of Charles II of England; or, perhaps, even Count Mattioli, imprisoned for selling to Spain the details of the negotiations between Louis XIV and Charles III of Mantua.

Whatever the case, the masked man was given preferential treatment, as if he were indeed a blue blood. Among the many legends is the one about the woman who came to visit and had a son by him. The child was sent to Corsica to be raised by a woman who was told to give the child the best possible attention, since he was of good breeding *(de buoné-parté).* His foster mother thereby named the boy Buonaparte ... the future Napoléon? The Man in the Iron Mask left the island for the Bastille in 1698, where he died in 1703, carrying the secret of his identity to the grave.

Mougins

A celebrity-favored *village perché* 4.3 miles (7 km) north of Cannes, once visited by the likes of Cocteau, Man Ray, Léger, and Picasso, dolled-up Mougins buzzes with boutiques, art galleries, and restaurants—the eminent Moulin de Mougins being the major draw. Here, too, an ingenious new museum mixes classical antiquities with choice pieces of modern art.

Mougins

🗺 135 B1

Visitor Information

✉ 39 place du Patriotes

☎ 04 92 92 14 00

mougins.fr

Chapelle Notre-Dame-de-Vie

✉ Chemin de la Chapelle, just SE of town

🕑 Daily July–Aug., weekends May–June & Sept., Sun. Oct–April

☎ 04 92 92 37 20

Musée d'Art Classique de Mougins

✉ 32 rue Commandeur

☎ 04 93 75 18 65

🕑 Closed Mon. Oct.–April

💲 $$

mouginsmusee.com

In the Middle Ages, Mougins was bigger than Cannes, rich from its harvest of olives, wine, jasmine, and roses. Pablo Picasso arrived in 1935 with surrealist photographer Man Ray (1890–1976), followed in time by Jean Cocteau and Paul Éluard.

Picasso lived just southeast of town across from **Chapelle Notre-Dame-de-Vie,** in a *mas* known as the Minotaur's Lair, on and off between 1961 and 1973. Fernand Léger, René Clair, Isadora Duncan, and Christian Dior are some of the other celebrities who have helped make Mougins a smart address.

The town is most known today, however, for the gastronomic wonders of **Le Moulin de Mougins** (see Travelwise p. 219)—a favorite spot among festival-going stars. Established

by celebrity chef Roger Vergé, its sun-drenched Mediterranean cuisine is immaculate. The white-plum-and-rose dining room, with its golden candelabras, occupies a 16th-century olive mill just outside town.

Visiting the Town

Park your car in the designated parking area outside the village walls and take your time strolling the medieval streets, ducking into shops, churches, and other sights along the way. The **Musée de la Photographie** *(tel 04 93 75 85 67, closed Jan.),* next to the 12th-century Porte Sarrazine, features a permanent collection of works by André Villers, best known for photographing Picasso (to whom the second floor is dedicated); Robert Doisneau; and fabulous Riviera photographer Jacques Henri Lartigue (1894–1986). ∎

Musée d'Art Classique de Mougins

In an utterly delightful juxtaposition of antique and modern, Mougins's latest addition to the art world takes you on a beautifully curated tour through the ancient worlds of Egypt, Greece, and Rome—with a modern twist. The tall and stately Arhenius sarcophagus, for example, is displayed near Jean Cocteau's whimsical drawing of "The Large Sphynx." A marble torso of Venus, dating from the early Roman Empire, is found next to Dalí's "Venus as a Giraffe," a white painted bronze from 1973. Throughout the museum you'll find ancient artifacts—funerary masks, pottery, silverware, armory—integrated with masterpieces by the likes of Rubens, Rodin, Warhol, and Picasso. The founder, British investment manager Christian Levett, hopes to demonstrate the pervasive influence of the ancient world in modern times—a point that he has proven loud and clear.

Vallauris

Pottery shops spill onto the sidewalks of Vallauris's main street, avenue Georges Clemenceau, the distant legacy of Pablo Picasso's discovery of painted ceramics here in 1948 that helped revitalize the ancient local art. Now the Musée National Picasso is among the town's draws.

Vallauris has been a pottery town since the Romans built potteries to exploit the local clay reserves. In the Middle Ages, the town was controlled by the abbots of Lérins, who built up a substantial market center that thrived until 14th-century marauders destroyed it. It wasn't until the early 16th century that the area became repopulated, with 400 Italians who reestablished the pottery industry.

Upon visiting in 1948, Picasso became infatuated with Vallauris's ceramic art. He met George and Suzanne Ramié, who owned the **Atelier Madoura** (madoura.com) and produced vessels to Picasso's specifications. Their studio, on avenue Suzanne Ramié, now run by their son, still produces Picasso's designs in signed limited editions.

The town's biggest sight is the **Musée National Picasso,** housed in the 12th-century chapel of the Château de Vallauris. Here, in 1952, Picasso covered the stone walls with his famous "La Guerre et La Paix"—"War and Peace," two panels that compose his last major political work. On the left, the horrors of "War" are depicted with a chariot and a figure bearing a bloody sword in one hand, a basket of the seeds of war, death, and destruction in the other. The figure confronts a peace fighter bearing a sword decorated with a dove—and an eerie transparency of his lover at the time, Françoise Gilot. "Peace," on the right-hand wall, shows a family enjoying a peaceful moment beneath a tree, while a child plows the sea, drawn by a winged horse.

INSIDER TIP:

Provence explodes with music and art festivals every summer. Check ahead to see what's going on.

—MICHELINE PLACE
*National Geographic Expeditions
tour leader*

Picasso's inspiration stemmed from Françoise's comment: "In peacetime, everything is possible; a child could plow the sea."

Your ticket will also get you into two other museums, both in the château: the **Musée Magnelli,** a collection of paintings, prints, and collages by Picasso contemporary and pioneer in abstract art, Italian artist Alberto Magnelli; and the **Musée de la Céramique,** displaying international ceramics.

Picasso presented the bronze statue of a man and sheep in the place de la Libération, in front of the castle-museum, to his adopted town in 1949. ■

Vallauris

 135 B1

Visitor Information

✉ Place du 8 mai 1945

☎ 04 93 63 82 58

🕐 Closed Sept.– June

vallauris-golfe-juan .com

Musée National Picasso, Musée Magnelli, Musée de la Céramique

✉ Château de Vallauris, place de la Libération

☎ 04 93 64 16 05

🕐 Closed Tues.

💲 $

Grasse

The fragrance of flowers permeates the cobbled lanes of Grasse's *vieille ville*, where perfume-making was born in the 1500s—and raised to high art. A visit to this charming village just north of Cannes, with its ancient houses, insightful museums, and several perfumeries, is not only pleasant but an education.

Historic Fragonard's exquisite display of perfumes

Grasse

🅰 134 B2

Visitor Information

✉ Office de Tourisme, place de la Buanderie

☎ 04 93 36 66 66

grasse.fr

Musée International de la Parfumerie

✉ 2 blvd. du Jeu de Ballon

☎ 04 97 05 58 00

🕐 Closed Tues. Oct.–March & Nov.; gardens closed Dec.–March

💲 $

museesdegrasse.com

Founded by Romans, Grasse was a bustling miniature republic in the Middle Ages, with tanning its most important industry. Then, in the 16th century, Catherine de Médicis, who disliked the smell of glove leather on her hands, saw the potential of the area's mild weather and fine soil to grow flowers—jasmine, roses, tuberose—for scented gloves. The glovemakers split from the tanneries, and when perfume became à la mode in the 18th century, they were poised for success. The industrial revolution of the 1800s redefined the perfume industry, as Grasse used new techniques of distillation, *enfleurage* (a process of extracting scents), and organic synthesis to

produce fine fragrances that took the world by storm. These days, much of the industry focuses on creating fragrances for household products, but fine fragrances for major perfumes remain part of Grasse's prestige and allure.

Vieille Ville

Wade through the traffic and crowded succession of traffic circles to the large *vieille ville*, at the top of town, where the main sights are found. You'll want to park your car, since the town's steep staircases and tiny, hilly roads are best explored on foot.

Begin your tour at the **Musée International de la Parfumerie.** The International Museum of Perfume traces the history of perfume and how it is made, from the harvesting and treatment of raw materials to the launching of the finished product. The third-floor greenhouse showcases irises, jasmine, and other plants chosen for their aromatic qualities.

The nearby **Musée Fragonard,** occupying the elegant Hôtel de Villeneuve, displays 15 paintings by the town's most famous resident, Grasse-born, Romantic-era artist Jean-Honoré Fragonard, along with works of two other town natives: Marguerite Gérard (1761–1837) and Jean-Baptiste Mallet

(1759–1835). Also nearby, the **Musée Provençal du Costume et du Bijou** (*2 rue Jean Ossola, tel 04 93 36 44 65, closed Sun. Nov.–Feb.*) displays Provençal costumes and jewelry dating from the 18th and 19th centuries. Each costume presents some aspect of Provençal culture, including a 1750 Louis XV–era beige-and-pink-flowered dress *à la française.*

Down the street, the **Musée d'Art et d'Histoire de Provence** is housed in one of Provence's most elegant buildings, dating from the late 1700s. Inside you'll find a rich collection of furniture,

paintings, and objets d'art charting high-class life in the 1800s, including Moustiers faïence, ceramics from Vallauris, and Provençal Nativity scenes.

Burrowed deep in the old town on place du Petit Puy Godeau, the Romanesque **Cathédrale Notre-Dame-du-Puy** (*9 Petit Puy Sq.*) dates from the 12th and 13th centuries, rebuilt in the 17th. Inside, to the altar's right, hang three

early Rubens (1601), including "Le Couronnement d'Épines" ("The Crown of the Thorns"). In the Chapelle du St.-Sacrement look for Jean-Honoré Fragonard's 1754 "Lavement des Pieds" ("Christ Washing the Feet of the Apostles").

On the other side of the Jardin Public, the **Villa-Musée Jean-Honoré Fragonard** is a small but special place. Fragonard, celebrated for his Romantic paintings and portraits, lived in this charming 17th-century villa in 1790 and 1791. A mix of original drawings and paintings and replicas hang on the walls. Nearby, the **Musée de la Marine** explores Grasse's military ties through the story of Admiral de Grasse, hero of the American Revolutionary War.

Fragrance Houses

Grasse has five major fragrance houses, three of which are open to the public: Fragonard, Galimard, and Molinard. The only one in the old town proper is **Fragonard** (*20 blvd. Fragonard, tel 04 93 36 44 65*), housed in the original perfume factory dating from 1782; it has a perfume museum, showcasing 3,000 years worth of bottles, perfume coffers, and beauty cases from around the world. Downstairs, join a guided tour through the small factory where perfume is made to this day.

Fragonard has another, more modern, factory just south of town (*Les 4 Chemins, rte. de Cannes, tel 04 93 77 94 30*). The two other perfumeries, **Galimard** and **Molinard,** offering free tours as well, are also south of town. ∎

Musée Fragonard
✉ Hôtel de Villeneuve, 14 rue Jean Ossola
☎ 04 93 36 44 65
🕐 Closed Sun. Nov.–Feb.
fragonard.com

Musée d'Art et d'Histoire de Provence
✉ 2 rue Mirabeau
☎ 04 93 36 80 20
🕐 Closed Tues. Oct.–March, & Nov.
💲 $
museesdegrasse.com

Villa-Musée Jean-Honoré Fragonard
✉ 23 blvd. Fragonard
☎ 04 93 36 52 98
🕐 Closed Tues. Oct.–March, & Nov.
museesdegrasse.com

Musée de la Marine
✉ 23 blvd. Fragonard
☎ 04 93 40 11 11
🕐 Closed Tues. Oct.–March, & Nov.
museesdegrasse.com

Parfumerie Galimard
✉ 73 rte. de Cannes
☎ 04 93 09 20 00
galimard.com

Parfums Molinard
✉ 60 blvd. Victor Hugo
☎ 04 92 42 33 24
molinard.com

The Art of the Perfumer

As beautiful as a symphony, a fine fragrance contains a complex combination of raw materials that harmonize to create the perfect composition. As a composer combines the notes of different instruments, the perfumer adds individual scents—fittingly called notes—to create the desired statement: luxury or passion or mystery or a day at the beach. It's a science that takes place in a lab, but one that requires the art of imagination and creativity and passion. Above all, however, the perfumer must have a good nose.

Fragrant jasmine—one of the costliest fragrances—grows in abundance in the hills around Grasse.

The Nose Knows

Everyone has the same number of olfactory receptors in their nose and upper palate—about five million. What separates the perfumer from everyone else is that he or she, through years of apprenticeship and an inherent talent to smell, can dissect a fragrance into various parts, taking smell to an incredible depth. A good "nose," as they are called in the industry, can identify more than 700 smells (most of us are lucky to remember 50). They must be able to recognize smells in minute concentrations,

some as little as two parts per million, and they must be able to retain them for weeks, months, even years. And that's just the start of it. These rare experts must then figure out how to blend the smells successfully.

There are more than 4,000 possible smells available to the perfumer—lemon and grapefruit are light and clean; balsam is woodsy yet delicate; lavender and basil are pungent and refreshing; vanilla is rich and exotic. They don't all have to be lovely scents. Cassis (black currant) smells like cat urine, but combined with certain other scents provides an underlying anchor. The ugly white ambergris root is what creates the silvery base of Chanel No. 19. There are also synthetic notes; the synthetic chemical aldehyde, for instance, which smells like starched laundry, is what gives Chanel No. 5 its sparkle.

To make it more complicated, fragrances go through many different phases once they come in contact with the skin. These are generally classified as top, middle, and base notes and must be perfectly blended to round out a perfume.

Impressions

Creating the fragrance's first impression, the "top note" is very light and evaporates quickly, lasting perhaps just a few minutes. Top notes are usually citrus and fruity, for instance cucumber or mint. As the top note fades, the "middle" or "heart note" forms the perfume's character and body, the one that is detectable after the fragrance has been on the skin a few minutes. It consists of heavier ingredients—geranium, lavender, pear, rose—that last a couple of hours and account for 60 to 70 percent of the blend. The "base" or "bottom note" emerges slowly, after several hours of wearing. It is richly scented—sandalwood, musk, patchouli—creating the lasting notes of the fragrance. It serves as the foundation upon which the perfume is based and evaporates slowly, lasting up to seven or eight hours.

Down to Business

In the olden days, the only way into the perfume business was to be born into it. These days, future perfumers can learn the art at various institutes and schools, where in endless drills they learn the raw materials, how to smell, and the proper fragrance vocabulary, as well as the chemistry of fragrances and how to put scents together.

After three years, students become technicians. The key to becoming a true perfumer, however, is to truly and passionately understand how to put a fragrance together—and this is where the artistic side comes in. Some people inherently have it. Some people can learn it through five, ten, fifteen years of hard work. And some people never get it.

There are 400 perfumers in the world, more than half of whom reside in the United States. Only 20 percent of perfumers focus on fine fragrances, where all the glitz and glamour is, while the others come up with the fragrances for household products such as detergents, cat litter, garbage bags—little niceties that, given the smelly alternative, are really a big deal.

EXPERIENCE: Channeling Chanel

Ready to test your nose? Make your own customized fragrance at a perfume workshop at Galimard's **Studio des Fragrances** (5 rte. de Pégomas, Grasse, tel 04 93 09 20 00, $$$$$, galimard.com). An expert perfumer will teach you all you need to know about a perfume's architecture. Then, with the expert's assistance, you'll test out the various combinations of scents, resulting in your very own personal fragrance. You'll name it and bottle it to take home.

And don't worry—all formulas are kept on file for reordering purposes. You can also create a layered line, including personalized body cream and shower gel. For true inspiration, accompany a master gardener through the flower fields of the nearby village of Gourdon.

Molinard's **Atelier des Parfums** (60 blvd. Victor Hugo, Grasse, tel 04 92 42 33 24, $$$$$, molinard.com) also offers a create-your-own-perfume workshop. Both houses require reservations.

Vence

A 12th-century troubadour called Vence *"le doux répaire"* ("sweet nest"), while Nostradamus in the 1500s wrote, "Garden of Vence, marvel of Provence." The town's tightly walled medieval heart remains a pretty, fountain-adorned village, but the main reason people come here sits about half a mile (0.8 km) north of town: Henri Matisse's endearing, light-filled Chapelle du Rosaire.

Matisse's Chapelle du Rosaire, a triumph of light, space, and deliberate use of color

Market Days
Tues.– Sun.

Vence
📍 135 C2

Visitor Information
✉ Place du Grand-Jardin
☎ 04 93 58 06 38
vence.fr

Strategically located 6 miles (10 km) from the sea, Vence was early on an important episcopal city. Its most famous bishops were fifth-century St.-Véran, who organized the town's defenses against Visigoth invaders, and 12th-century St.-Lambert, who defended the town's rights against its new baron, Romée de Villeneuve, igniting a rivalry between nobility and clergy that would last until the bishropic was dissolved after the revolution. Besieged by Huguenots during the Wars of Religion, the town did not fall, a fact commemorated each Easter with a festival.

The lovely setting did not miss the attention of artists—Matisse, Raoul Dufy, Jean Dubuffet, and D. H. Lawrence are some of the creative minds who showed up in the early 1900s. Russian artist Marc Chagall lived in Vence between 1950 and 1966. It's still a lively art town, with several galleries and summertime outdoor exhibits.

Medieval Vence

Through **Porte du Peyra,** the main 13th-century gate, you see the **Fontaine du Peyra,** built in 1822 to replace a 1578 version. Its clear mineral water comes from the River Foux just above the village; an old marble plaque lists the different amounts of minerals present. On the square's western edge stands the **Château de Villeneuve** and its 12th-century watchtower. Inside, the **Fondation Émile Hugues** features a permanent art collection and an annual series of exhibitions.

From here, turn right on shop-filled rue du Marché, then left on rue Alsace-Lorraine to **place Clemenceau.** The square is dominated by the *mairie* (town hall) and the Romanesque cathedral, built in the 11th century on the site of a Roman temple to Mars and restored in the baroque period. Be sure to peek at Chagall's mosaic of Moses in the bulrushes in its baptistery.

Chapelle du Rosaire

A 20-minute walk from the town center, across the River Foux and up avenue Henri Matisse, awaits this famous little chapel. Upon moving to Vence from Nice in 1941 to escape Allied bombings, Henri Matisse, then in his late 70s, fell ill and was nursed back to health by the town's Dominican sisters. In gratitude, he designed this chapel for them; it is still used by the Dominican nuns of the Rosary.

The chapel looks traditional on the outside—a whitewashed villa topped by a 43-foot-tall (13 m) wrought iron cross and bell tower. Two black-and-white ceramics by Matisse hint that this is no ordinary chapel, including the "Mary, Jesus, and St. Dominic" over the front door. In fact, Matisse claimed this chapel, built between 1948 and 1951, was his masterpiece, a "conclusive achievement of a whole life of labor and the flowering of a huge sincere and difficult striving."

The Village Fountain

Whether exquisitely designed and embellished with cartouches or plain and simple, fountains add a touch of romance to every Provençal village and town. The fact remains, however, that these beauties originated for their functionality rather than good looks. More than two millennia ago, the Romans had no choice but to build fountains throughout their *provincia*, and the rest of their colonies, to supply water to local communities. Without water, towns could not flourish. Fountains remained integral to community life throughout the Middle Ages and even into the 20th century. Today, of course, fountains serve merely a decorative purpose—though you can still drink from those that say *potable*.

The chapel's interior is a dazzling white space bathed in the subaqueous light of three stained-glass windows. Two feature yellow and blue leaves on a green background, while the chancel window has blue cacti and golden flowers.

Simple black-lined drawings on white ceramics—representing the colors of the Dominican habit—are the only other adornments. In the nave is a Nativity scene, and overlooking the altar a large St.-Dominic. The Stations of the Cross are line drawings jumbled together in one tableau, with each station hand-numbered accordingly.

Matisse designed every detail, down to the candlesticks, cross, priests' vestments, and the altar, constructed from a piece of a Roman stone bridge. In the adjoining hall, some of his colorful vestments are on display. ∎

Fondation Émile Hugues
- ✉ Château de Villeneuve, place de Frêne
- ☎ 04 93 58 15 78
- 🕑 Closed Mon.
- 💲 $$

Chapelle du Rosaire
- 🅰 135 C2
- ✉ 466 av. Henri Matisse
- ☎ 04 93 58 03 26
- 🕑 Closed Fri. & a.m. Mon., Wed., & Sat.
- 💲 $

St.-Paul-de-Vence

Walled within ancient ramparts, this immaculate medieval town north of Cagnes-sur-Mer, with its high-end boutiques and art galleries, caters to well-to-do tourists. It also offers one of Provence's most sublime 20th-century art museums—the Fondation Maeght.

St.-Paul-de-Vence's charm lured some of the 20th century's most famous artists.

St.-Paul-de-Vence

🗺 135 C2

Visitor Information

✉ Maison de la Tour, 2 rue Grande

☎ 04 93 32 86 95

saint-pauldevence .com

Sitting atop its hilltop aerie, St.-Paul-de-Vence was a flourishing medieval town, doing a fine business in wine, figs, olives, and orange trees. It took on its first note of importance in the 1500s, when François I enlarged the existing town with ramparts and fortifications to guard its strategic position overlooking France and the Savoy (Italy). Many of the ramparts exist to this day.

The town declined until after World War I, when leading artists from the Paris school began commuting by streetcar from nearby Cagnes. Picasso, Braque, Matisse, Renoir, Dufy, and Chagall (who's buried in the village cemetery) are among those who arrived with sketchbooks and paint boxes. Their destination: Café Robinson, the town's only inn at the time. It was run by Paul Roux, who accepted paintings in exchange for meals and lodging—eventually amassing a priceless art collection. Today, the inn is known as the fabled **Colombe d'Or** restaurant (see Travelwise p. 220), and some of those famous paintings are displayed on its walls—for the viewing of patrons only (alas, the price does not come cheap).

Medieval Village

Once occupied by the workshops of weavers, shoemakers, and saddlers, the old town's beautiful 16th- and 17th-century stone buildings—many still bearing the coats of arms placed by the original builders—are now filled with a madhouse of boutiques, souvenir shops, antique stores, and, above all, art galleries. Along rue Grande alone, the main street through town, you'll find more than half of the town's 64 galleries. The tourist office, located just beyond the Porte Nord de Vence (St.-Paul's North Gate), has a list of galleries, as well as a map highlighting the village's main historic points. Don't miss the lovely **Grande Fontaine** *(place de la Fontaine),* a fountain overlooked by beautiful old dwellings.

Of the sites to see, the most interesting is **Chapelle Folon,** located at the village's high point.

Originally the 17th-century White Penitent's Chapel, it's one of the Midi's most recent chapels to be decorated by an artist, Belgian Folon (1934–2005). You are lulled into the peaceful, surreal space by the magnificent, pastel-hued mosaic behind the altar, depicting St. Paul and the village of St.-Paul-de-Vence beneath the watchful eye of God. The altar in the shape of a welcoming hand, stained-glass windows, and murals add to the overall effect.

The adjacent Gothic **Église Collegiale** dates from the 12th century, though it went through many alterations until the 18th century; only the choir remains from the 12th-century building. The church is filled with art: Don't miss the painting of Ste.-Catherine-d'Alexendrie, attributed to Tintoretto, hanging to the left as you enter. The last altar on the right is St.-Clément's chapel, a masterpiece of baroque architecture from the 18th century, with a fantastic bas-relief of St.-Clément's martyrdom.

Chapelle Folon
- ✉ Place de l'Église
- ☎ 04 93 32 41 13
- 🕐 Closed Nov. Guided tour on request at tourist office ($$).
- 💲 $

Musée d'Histoire Locale
- ✉ Town center, opposite church
- ☎ 04 93 32 41 13
- 🕐 Closed Nov. & Sun. & Tues.
- 💲 $

EXPERIENCE: Playing Pétanque

In front of St.-Paul's Café de la Place, just outside the city walls, you'll spy groups of people tossing hollow metal balls down a tree-shaded court. They study the ball formations, confer among themselves, taking their time. You are witnessing the age-old game of *pétanque*—somewhat like English lawn bowling and Italian bocce ball—a scene that plays out in every Provençal town. At this particular pitch, movie star Yves Montand played every day, and Charlie Chaplin and Orson Welles were known to toss a *boule* or two as well.

Pétanque is rooted in the complicated game of La Longue (which itself is based on French *boules*), eliminating the fancy steps and leaps required before tossing the ball with *pès tancats* in Occitan (or planted feet, hence the name). The goal: Throw the balls as close as possible to a smaller ball called a *cochonnet* (piglet).

To play, hang around and ask to join in the next game. In St.-Paul, take a one-hour lesson offered by the tourism office *(saint-pauldevence.com, offered in French only, reservations required).*

The state-of-the-art Fondation Maeght showcases one of the world's greatest collections of 20th-century art.

Fondation Maeght

 Just outside village via La Colle, then up Montée des Trious

☎ 04 93 32 81 63

💲 $$$

www.fondation
-maeght.com

Across from the church, the **Musée d'Histoire Locale** is a tad hokey in its presentation of histori-cal wax-figure scenes, but it does give a good sense of the town's past, ranging from François I's visit in 1538 to assess the need for fortification, to Vauban's inspec-tion in 1701 of the newly built walls, to the mayor's success in 1870 in saving the ramparts from demolition. Finally, the **Musée de**

St.-Paul (*2 rue Grande, tel 04 93 32 86 95*) has special exhibits related to the town.

Fondation Maeght

Tucked away in pinewoods northwest of town, the Fonda-tion Maeght showcases an extraordinary collection of modern and contemporary art in a harmonious natural setting. Marguerite and Aimé Maeght were art dealers and publishers who collected, for starters, Picas-sos, Matisses, Légers, Chagalls, Calders, and Giacomettis. Only the most modern of build-ings could house this sublime art collection, so the Maeghts commissioned Catalan architect José Luis Sert to design their museum. The collaborative result is a low-slung, split-level structure with winglike expan-sions on the roof for circulation, set amid terraced gardens. Glass walls bring the indoors and out-doors together. Their museum, built "as a gift to the people," opened in 1964.

Inside, the works are regularly rotated, so you never know exactly what you're going to see—perhaps Bonnards, Kandinskys, Légers, Matisses, and/or Barbara Hep-worths. Whatever the case, you won't be disappointed. Temporary exhibitions are just as extraordinary.

Outside, gigantic sculptures are integrated into the building design and surrounding terraces and gardens. The biggest draw is undoubtedly Joan Miró's labyrinth, in which a maze of outdoor rooms feature whimsical ceramic sculp-tures and fountains. ■

Antibes

This old Mediterranean fishing town counts among its blessings Europe's largest yacht harbor (a thousand slips), sandy beaches, and a picturesque old town filled with boutiques, restaurants, and a bustling *marché Provençal*. But the main reason to visit is the Musée Picasso, an old castle overlooking the sea where, after World War II, a 65-year-old Pablo Picasso created masterpiece after joyful masterpiece, many of which are now showcased within its walls. Nearby, exclusive Cap d'Antibes is where the Summer Season was invented.

An active trading port since its earliest times, Antibes came into its own in the fifth century B.C. with the arrival of Greek traders, who called their fortified town Antipolis—meaning "city opposite," for its position across from Nice. The Romans took over in the first century B.C., renaming it Antiboul. For centuries Antibes remained the only metropolis between Marseille and Italy.

INSIDER TIP:

The Musée Picasso in Antibes is a must-stop, to see Picasso's works but also those by other 20th-century masters, notably Nicolas de Staël.

—HEIDI ELLISON
National Geographic contributor

After being besieged in the 16th century by Charles V of Spain, François I and his successors—realizing the city's strategic importance on the border of France and the Savoy (Italy)—began strengthening its fortifications. Overlooking the bay,

St.-Laurent Tower became Fort Carré. The stronghold was finished in 1710, with the completion of the ramparts entirely encircling the town. It was here that Napoléon Bonaparte was imprisoned for a week in 1794 after the fall of Robespierre. En route to his return to glory, Napoléon stepped ashore at Golfe-Juan in 1815.

Today, Antibes is a lively, active port town, with cultural sights to visit and buzzing restaurants and cafés. The residents include many English, Irish, and Aussies who help crew yachts (explaining the large number of English-speaking pubs).

Viel Antibes

Tucked behind the ancient seawall close to the sea, little cobblestone lanes crisscross Antibes's old town, where honey-hued houses contain shops full of Provençal wares and restaurants with inviting sidewalk seating. **Porte de France,** on rue de la République, is one of the last remaining vestiges of the city wall.

Keep walking down rue de la République (in the direction of the sea) and you will come to plane-shaded place Nationale and the charming **Musée Peynet et du Dessin Humoristique.** Popular

Market Days
Daily

Antibes
135 B1
Visitor Information
Office de Tourisme, 42 av. Robert Soleau
04 22 10 60 10
antibesjuanlespins.com

Musée Peynet et du Dessin Humoristique
Place Nationale
04 92 90 54 29
Closed Mon.
$

Master Builders

By the early 1500s, with the use of gunpowder in firearms that could knock down walls, the era of impregnable castles was over. A new kind of fortification was needed. Along came the citadel, or fortress, designed to perfection by Sébastien le Prestre de Vauban. Using a five-point star superimposed upon another and circumscribed within a ten-point star, he devised a means of extending the outerworks so far that no enemy could begin to attack at close range. He also incorporated stronger defense characteristics, such as building on a high point of land and using broad, low walls with bastions to enable soldiers to fire in any direction. Vauban's fortresses are sprinkled throughout Provence, including Fort Carré at Antibes and the citadels at Villefranche-sur-Mer, Sisteron, and Entrevaux.

Musée de la Tour

- ✉ Tour Gilli, cours Masséna
- ☎ 04 93 32 13 58
- 🕐 Open Wed.– Thurs., Sat., & p.m. Sun.; by appt. only
- 💲 $

Musée d'Histoire et d'Archéologie

- ✉ Bastion St-André, av. Amiral de Grasse
- ☎ 04 92 90 53 36
- 🕐 Closed Mon
- 💲 $

Fort Carré

- 🅰 135 B1
- ✉ Rte. du Bord de Mer (N98)
- ☎ 04 92 90 52 13 or 06 14 89 17 45
- 🕐 Guided tours every half hour 10 a.m.–4 p.m. Tues.–Sun.
- 💲 $

antibesjuanlespins.com

cartoonist Raymond Peynet, best known for his "Lovers" series—all the craze in postwar France—lived in Antibes. The museum displays more than 300 of his pictures, cartoons, and sculptures.

Following tiny rue Sade, you will come to the **marché Provençal** (*cours Masséna, open a.m. Tues.–Sun. June–Aug.*), a profusion of stalls beneath a 19th-century canopy stacked high with flowers, goat cheeses, olives, honey, and olive oil. Nearby, at the southern end of cours Masséna, is **Musée de la Tour,** part of the old town gates and now a local history museum.

Around the corner via rue du Bateau awaits the Musée Picasso (see below) and, down the far steps, the **Église de l'Immaculée Conception** (*rue St.-Esprit*), Antibes's former cathedral. Its colorful baroque facade belies the rather plain interior, though its treasures include a wooden crucifix from 1447 and a 15th-century altarpiece discovered in the walls in 1938, having been concealed during the revolution.

Follow the ramparts southward to the **Musée d'Histoire et d'Archéologie,** which offers a tiny yet interesting exhibition on the town's Roman heritage. Housed in the St.-André Bastion, built by Vauban at the end of the 17th century, the structure's brick-vaulted galleries still exude a military feel. The collections, however, take you back 2,000 years to the Romans: their sarcophagi, amphorae, and coins.

Star-shaped **Fort Carré** (Square Fort), dominating the approach to Antibes from Nice, appears foreboding atop its hilltop roost. Indeed, after Provence became French in 1481, and Nice remained Italian, this was the last stronghold between France and the states of the duke of Savoy (Italy). Under the auspices of Louis XIV, Vauban (see sidebar this page) improved on the 16th-century fortress, including larger firing holes for 18 cannon. There is not much to actually see, but guided tours (*tel 04 92 90 52 13*) illume its fascinating history.

Musée Picasso

After World War II, Pablo Picasso was offered space in the Grimaldi Castle, built in the 12th century (and revamped in the 16th). Thus begun a period of crazed activity—between mid-September and mid-November 1946—in which the Spanish artist created some of his most famous works. Newly in love with beautiful, young Françoise Gilot and seduced by the south's brilliant light, he experimented with not only painting, but pottery and sculpture, too. When Picasso left, he gave the museum all the work he had done—24 paintings, 80 ceramics, 44 drawings, 32 lithographs, 11 oils on paper, 2 sculptures, and 5 tapestries—composing one of the world's greatest Picasso collections.

You'll find Picasso's works on the second floor. Themes from Greek mythology, as well as the beauty and lighthearted nature of the Mediterranean coast, recur from one work to the next. Fauns, centaurs, sea urchins, and fish are common motifs. One room contains pencil sketches that show Picasso's working process; the honing of a theme in many different ways (notice the erasure marks). In another room, Michel Gima's black-and-white photos provide an intimate look at the artist at the château.

The works culminate in "La Joie de Vivre," a 4-by-8-foot (1.2 m x 2.4 m) tableau centered around a dancing woman-flower (said to be Françoise) who is bathed in light. Around her, a centaur plays a flute and fauns dance—seemingly capturing Picasso's own joy of life.

NOTE: It takes some work to visit the fort. Park at the Fort Carré parking area on av. du 11 Novembre, cross the street, and look for the green arrows that lead to the site. Be prepared for a hike. You can also walk from the port along the sea (it takes about 30 minutes), or take a shuttle.

Musée Picasso

✉ Château Grimaldi, place Mariejol

☎ 04 92 90 54 20

🕐 Closed Mon.

💲 $$

Vauban's Fort Carré has stood sentry over Antibes's harbor since the 17th century.

Hôtel du Cap-Eden-Roc

✉ Blvd. Kennedy, Cap d'Antibes

☎ 04 93 61 39 01

hotel-du-cap-eden -roc.com

Éspace de Littoral et du Milieu Marin

✉ Rampe de Graillon, blvd. Kennedy

☎ 04 93 61 45 32

antibesjuan lespins.com

Parc Thuret

✉ 62 blvd. du Cap, Cap d'Antibes

☎ 04 97 21 25 00

🕐 Closed Sat.–Sun.

Phare de la Garoupe

✉ Rte. Phare

Sanctuaire de la Garoupe

✉ Rte. Phare

On the ground floor, temporary exhibits showcase 20th-century trends. Don't miss the terrace, where a permanent collection of sculptures by local artist Germaine Richier are poised against the breathtaking backdrop of the Mediterranean; other artists represented here include Joan Miró ("Sea Goddess") and Anne and Patrick Poirier.

Cap d'Antibes

Grandiose villas set amid imported tropical flora confirm the cape's fabled reputation as a playground for the rich and famous. Indeed, you'll have to be rich and/or famous (or know someone who is) to get a peek beyond the peninsula's iron gates. At the very least, wander verdant lanes and admire from afar.

The legacy began just after World War I, when painter Gerald Murphy (1888–1964) and his wife, Sara, paid to have the Hôtel du Cap remain open after April (in those days, people *wintered* along the coast). Gerald invited close friend F. Scott Fitzgerald, and soon a whole line of fashionable New Yorkers followed, including Dorothy Parker and Ernest Hemingway. Soon, the trend of sunbathing, plus the parties and drinking that went along with it, took off, and other high-class hotels began opening in the summer months as well.

In the opening paragraph of *Tender is the Night*, Fitzgerald pictured the grand **Hôtel du Cap-Eden-Roc** (see Travelwise p. 218) as such: "On the pleasant shore of the French Riviera, about halfway between Marseille and the Italian

border, stands a large, proud, rose-colored hotel. Deferential palms cool its flushed facade, and before it stretches a short dazzling beach." The hotel is now pale yellow, but it still reigns as the doyenne of venerable hotels, drawing leading authors, film stars, politicians, and aristocrats. If you don't want to pay the price of a room, consider an apéritif at the **Pavillon Eden-Roc,** the hotel's restaurant, with its sweeping white terrace overlooking the sea.

On a rocky promontory at the end of Cap d'Antibes, the seaside oasis of **Éspace de Littoral et du**

INSIDER TIP:

With a loved one, find an isolated, rocky beach on Cap d'Antibes, sit under a parasol pine, pretend you are in an Eric Rohmer film, and talk, talk, talk, talk ...

—HEIDI ELLISON
National Geographic contributor

Milieu Marin surrounds a 19th-century stone tower; inside you'll find exhibits on marine life.

Also worth seeking out is **Parc Thuret,** in the center of the peninsula, a botanical garden begun in the mid-19th century; the **Phare de la Garoupe,** a lighthouse with a fabulous view; and the neighboring **Sanctuaire de la Garoupe,** a sailor's chapel containing votive offerings to Our Lady of the Sea. ■

EXPERIENCE: Beach Time

Some of the world's finest azure waters lap the sun-blessed shores of the Côte d'Azur, long a pilgrimage destination for sun worshippers from far and wide. Along its 100-some miles (160 km) of beach front, you'll find hidden coves and private, umbrella-dotted strands. There are family beaches, celebrity-studded beaches, topless beaches, even nudist beaches. Some beaches boast soft, golden sand, while others are famously pebbly. It pays to do a little research ahead of time to assure that you have the best beach experience possible.

Getting Oriented

As a general rule of thumb, the beaches from Menton to Antibes are pebbles, and Antibes west are sand. **Cannes** is famed for its gold-sand beaches full of glitz and glam (the town's luxury hotels own most of the beachfront, so you'll pay a price for sunning here), while **Nice** is just as beautiful but rocky—and almost entirely public (that is, free).

Ste.-Maxime's beaches boast fine sand and clear waters.

Winners

To really enjoy your own slice of paradise, go beyond the obvious. The 16-mile (25 km) stretch between Antibes and Juan-les-Pins is Mother Nature at her finest, showcasing natural sand (the other beaches truck in the sand); the best of the best here is probably serene **Plage Ponteil. Villefranche-sur-Mer,** between Nice and Monaco, is another good choice.

Small, pebbly **La Paloma Beach,** on the other side of St.-Jean-Cap-Ferrat, has both a private and public side. And in the little fishing village of **Théoule-sur-Mer,** the Esterel's red rocky outcrops overshadow sapphire blue waters, depicting a scene straight out of a 1960s French movie. For something even more hidden, try **Plage Notre-Dame** on the island of Porquerolles, designated a national park some 50 years ago; take a ferry from Toulon or Hyères.

Enjoying the Pebbles

To make the most of a pebbly beach, you need shoes—at least flip-flops—to walk on the hot stones. Also think about investing in a fold-up mattress. If this isn't for you, there are plenty of luxury private resorts that will rent you a sun bed and parasol.

Private for a Price

Some of the finer beaches charge for the privilege of lying on their sand (or rocks). For the price of €14 (or more), you can rent a lounge chair, umbrella, and other accoutrements. Beware that you may not be allowed to bring in your own food and be obliged to purchase from the beach restaurant—which isn't necessarily a bad thing; some menus are downright gourmand. Many hotels have their own beach property; you'll get a discount if you stay at the hotel.

Best Times to Go

Prime beach season is August, when the French escape their daily lives for the beach. So this might not be the best time if you're seeking solitude—and reasonable prices. The beaches are still fine in the fall and spring, though check ahead for crowd-potential events, such as the Cannes Film Festival in late May and Monaco's F1 Grand Prix in May as well.

More Information

For more information, visit *visitprovence.com* or *marvellous-provence.com*.

Napoléon in Provence

Every year, on the first weekend in March, the town of Antibes hosts a reenactment of one of history's most famous comebacks: the celebrated landfall of Napoléon Bonaparte from Elba, which marked the beginning of the emperor's dramatic return to power and subsequent final defeat at Waterloo.

A 19th-century Artaria print depicts Napoléon's landing at Golfe-Juan in 1815, the first step in his bid to return to power.

Europe's leaders thought they had rid themselves of the diminutive Corsican general for good when they exiled him in 1814. Napoléon had wreaked havoc on the continent the previous 20 years. He had fought Austria, Russia, Italy, Spain, Holland, Prussia, Malta, Turkey, Portugal, Egypt, Switzerland, and the British at every turn, using his superior military skills to lead France to an unprecedented period of European domination. At the peak of his strength, the empire and its associated allies stretched from the Atlantic Ocean to the Black Sea.

So when the 44-year-old French commander was defeated by a large coalition of forces in 1814 and banished into exile to Elba, a small Mediterranean island midway between the French island of Corsica and the Tuscan Italian coast, the continent beyond the Gallic borders breathed a collective sigh of relief.

A Leader in Exile

Not so fast. The terms of the Treaty of Fontainebleau were surprisingly generous to Napoléon. He was given the grandiose title of Imperial Emperor of Elba, making him more a head of state, albeit of a tiny realm, than a prisoner. Foreign dignitaries visited and were granted audiences with the island's new ruler. It was a far cry from the treatment you might expect of a hated, feared, and vanquished foe. He was even allowed to bring a retinue of nearly a thousand troops to attend to his needs in a style befitting an imperial emperor.

Return to Power

It was with these troops that, only nine months after his arrival, Napoléon sailed from Elba and headed unchecked toward the southern French coast, launching his audacious bid to return to power. Even though he knew he had previously won the hearts and minds of his army while waging his wars of conquest, Napoléon could not know how he would be received in his effort to overthrow King Louis XVIII, who had reestablished the prerevolutionary Bourbon dynastic line in France after Napoléon's demise.

On March 1, 1815, Napoléon and his troops reached the coast of Provence at Golfe-Juan, just outside Antibes, close to where he had ignominiously left France for exile the year before. He was at first greeted with ambivalence, as Provence had long been a stronghold of Bourbon support. No royalist forces initially helped their former commander, but neither did they confront him. Napoléon began a 240-mile (386 km) march north to Grenoble, through the towns of Grasse, Mougins, St.-Vallier-de-Thiey, Castellane, Digne-les-Bains, and others.

Along the road, popular sentiment started to turn, as loyalty to Napoléon, especially among peasants and the military, began to outweigh support for the king. On March 7, in a celebrated and pivotal incident outside Grenoble, a regiment of royalist troops sent by Louis confronted their former general at gunpoint. Napoléon stepped forward, opened his overcoat to offer himself as a target, and boldly challenged any soldier who wished to kill their emperor to do so then. En masse the troops rallied to Napoléon's side, adding to his growing tide of support. As Napoléon himself remarked, "Before I reached Grenoble they thought me a soldier of fortune. When I got there I became a prince."

Napoléon swept north through Grenoble and on toward the capital. Within two weeks, the king had fled, and Napoléon marched triumphantly into Paris to begin his famous Hundred Days, his short return to power that would end in total defeat at the Battle of Waterloo.

— by Larry Porges

EXPERIENCE: Retrace Napoléon's Footsteps

The course that Napoléon and his men took in 1815 on their northward march from Elba to Grenoble is today a lovely mountain realm of welcoming towns, wineries, perfumeries, cafés, and inns. Hop in the car and trace the general's steps, along the Route Napoléon.

The official driving route, inaugurated in 1932, begins in Grasse and travels for 202 miles (325 km) through the spectacular Alpes-Maritimes and the Alpes. It took Napoléon and his men a week to travel this route; you can drive it in about eight hours. Look for the brown eagle markers along the roadside—namely following the N85.

Stop at **St.-Vallier-de-Thiey** to picnic where the troops also stopped. Onward, enjoy an apéritif in sweet **Castellane,** where the troops ate lunch. You'll pass through **Malijal,** where Napoléon slept in the château (now the town hall and visitor center); **Sisteron,** with the Citadel Museum; and friendly **Gap.**

Visit *route-napoleon.com* for more information.

Biot

Bubble-dotted glassware, called *verre à bulles,* is the craft of choice in this picturesque medieval walled village perched inland a few miles from the sea—evident in the abundance of *verreries* in the surrounding area.

Market Day
Tues.

Biot
🔼 135 B2
Visitor Information
✉ 46 rue St.-
Sébastien
☎ 04 93 65 78 00
visit-biot.com

It wasn't always so. Before the 1950s, pottery was Biot's main industry, mostly thanks to its first-rate clay. Just before he died, painter Fernand Léger (1881–1955) bought a plot of land south of town, intending to set up a studio and produce ceramic sculptures. His widow, Nadia, organized the **Musée National Fernand Léger** (*chemin*

It's All in the Bubbles

The ancient art of glassblowing received a modern twist when Elol Monod, a Biot resident and ceramic engineer, used chemicals to produce air bubbles in the glass. The end result: solid, heavy glass in a spectrum of rich colors dotted throughout with light-catching air bubbles. Monod became so popular that he served as Biot's major in 1965–1974.

du Val du Pôme, tel 04 92 91 50 30, closed Tues., $, musees-nationaux -alpesmaritimes) in the space, covering most of the artist's career—from his early Impressionist efforts to his large, bold "machine art" canvases of the 1920s and '30s. In total, there are 348 original pieces, including mosaics, sculptures, oil paintings, and sketches. A bonsai arboretum nestles in the surrounding gardens, containing bonsai from around the world.

Glassmaking arrived in town in 1956, with the establishment of the **Verrerie de Biot** (*chemin des Combes, tel 04 93 65 03 00, verreriebiot.com*), below the old town. Eloi Monod, a potter and engineer who wanted to revive the craft of glassblowing in Provence, opened the factory with one blower and one glassmaker. Today, the complex—half factory, where you can watch men in shorts blow hot globs of glass into delicate shapes, half showroom, where you can buy the end product—has 70 workers. For a fee (*$*), you can take a guided tour that explores the history of glassmaking. Several other glassblowers have opened in the area as well.

Tourists flock to the medieval quarter of hilltop Biot, its main **rue St.-Sébastien** lined with glass shops. Of historical interest: The **Musée d'Histoire et de Céramique Biotoises** (*9 rue St.-Sébastien, tel 04 93 65 54 54, closed Mon., & Tues. Sept.–June, $*) has local costumes and artifacts, including domestic ceramics for which the town was originally known (most of which were donated by villagers).

On St.-Sébastien's far side, quiet **place des Arcades** is surrounded by Italian loggias, brought by Italians who settled here after the Black Death. Overlooking the square, the village church boasts altarpieces by Louis Bréa and Giovanni Canavesio. ∎

Cagnes-sur-Mer

Tucked amid the coast road sprawl between Antibes and Nice, Cagnes offers a few gems worth stopping for: the medieval Haut-de-Cagnes and its castle-museum, and the olive grove estate where the Impressionist artist Pierre-Auguste Renoir spent his later years.

There are three Cagnes: Cros-de-Cagnes, a seaside development; Cagnes-sur-Mer, an inland commercial area; and Haut-de-Cagnes, the medieval bourg. To visit the pedestrianized old village (the most interesting part), follow signs for Haut-de-Cagnes. You will have to leave your car at the bottom of the hill and walk up the steep, cobbled streets. With its fine Renaissance houses and the small **Église St.-Pierre,** there are plenty of reasons to stop and catch your breath.

At the top of the hill, the Grimaldis of Monaco built the Château Grimaldi—now the **Château Musée** (*place Grimaldi, tel 04 92 02 47 30, closed Tues., $)*—as a fortress-prison when they became lords of the area in 1309. In the early 1600s, Jean-Henri Grimaldi transformed the edifice into a palace. He commissioned Genoese artists to paint the interior; their efforts include the "Fall of Phaethon" in the main hall. The château today houses eclectic displays, including one room of portraits depicting 1930s chanteuse Susy Solidor—more than 40 works by the likes of Jean Cocteau and Raoul Dufy.

Pierre-Auguste Renoir moved to Cagnes in 1903 for relief from his arthritis. He bought an olive grove to the east of town, known as Les Collettes, where he built

The Château Musée—the Grimaldi family's home until the French Revolution—features a two-story courtyard.

a house and studio and worked until his death in 1919. Here he painted some of his most famous works, including "Washerwomen at Cagnes" and "The Farm at Les Collettes." The **Musée Renoir** (*19 chemin des Collettes, tel 04 93 20 61 07, closed Tues., $)* remains virtually as Renoir left it, including some of his paintings on the walls and everyday items lying about—among them his painter's coat and wheelchair. ∎

Cagnes-sur-Mer
🅐 135 C2
Visitor Information
✉ 6 blvd. Maréchal Juin
☎ 04 93 20 61 64
cagnes-tourisme.com

More Places to Visit in Cannes & Around

Tourrettes-sur-Loup, city of violets, charms with medieval ambience in its narrow streets.

Gorges-sur-Loup

In the lofty hinterlands of Grasse and St.-Paul-de-Vence, the rugged, waterfall-strewn Gorges-sur-Loup is a hiker's paradise. The D2210 delves into the heart of this cliff-shadowed region, passing a handful of villages along the way. In **Le-Bar-sur-Loup,** ancient houses surround the former château of the lords of Bar. The Gothic **Église St.-Jacques-le-Majeur** is lovely, but most people come to see the famous painting "Danse Macabre," the "Dance of Death," based on a 15th-century town legend about citizens who held a party during Lent and dropped dead. Nearby **Pont-du-Loup** is the home of **Confiserie Florian** (tel 04 93 59 32 91), the renowned sweets kitchen, with free samples offered at tour's end. The golden-stoned village of **Tourrettes-sur-Loup,** farther east, is famous for its violets, celebrated with the Fête des Violettes every March. 🅰 135 B2

Juan-les-Pins

To the west of Cap d'Antibes, Juan-les-Pins first came to life in the 1920s, when Americans brought the fun-loving way of life ... and jazz. When the Jazz Festival of

Juan-les-Pins was launched in 1960, all the big names were here: Louis Armstrong, Ella Fitzgerald, Duke Ellington, Sarah Vaughan, Ray Charles. The festival is still held every July. The rest of the time, Juan-les-Pins retains the hedonistic aura of its early days, coming alive at night, every night, all night long, with restaurants and nightclubs galore. 🅰 135 B1 **Visitor Information** antibesjuanlespins.com ✉ Office de Tourisme, 60 chemin des Sables ☎ 04 22 10 60 01

Musée Bonnard

One of the Nabi movement's principal contributors, Pierre Bonnard (1867–1947) bought a house in Le Cannet, just north of Cannes, in 1926, where he worked intermittently until his death. The villa has been modernized inside to become the world's only museum devoted to Bonnard. Ask for a map of the "footsteps of Bonnard" walk, which takes you to specific spots in the surrounding neighborhood where Bonnard painted some of his most memorable works. museebonnard.fr ✉ 16 blvd. Sadi Carnot, Le Cannet ☎ 04 93 94 06 06 🕐 Closed Mon. 💲 $

A sultry, sun-kissed niche with an Italian accent showcasing chic beaches, a prince's palace, and height-defying hill towns

Côte d'Azur: Nice to Menton

Changing of the guard at Monaco's palace

Côte d'Azur: Nice to Menton

In far southeastern Provence, the southern reaches of the Alps crowd down to the sea, creating a spectacular backdrop for Nice, Monaco, and Menton. Warm blue waters make for lazy days by the seashore, while a collection of world-class museums showcase Henri Matisse, Marc Chagall, Raoul Dufy, and other Postimpressionists who were seduced by the region's beauty. You will be, too.

France's fifth largest city, Nice is a pastel showcase of Italianate architecture. The promenade des Anglais—a beachfront esplanade dating from 19th-century British who enjoyed their daily constitutional with sea breezes—is now dominated by runners, bikers, and walkers. Mazelike streets crisscross Vieux Nice, ideal for an afternoon stroll, while several art museums feature a strong collection of naïf, Postimpressionist, and modern art. The Cathédrale Orthodoxe Russe St.-Nicolas is a surprise; the ornate, onion-domed church represents the large Russian population that flocked here before the Russian Revolution.

Eastward, three roads cutting across formidable limestone cliffs—called the three corniches—present different-level perspectives over the mountains and sea. The lower coast road accesses several beach resorts, including St.-Jean-Cap-Ferrat, where the Musée-Villa Ephrussi de Rothschild provides a glimpse into belle époque opulence. The medieval hilltop town of Èze, on the middle road, is perfectly preserved (and packed with tourists); the climb to the ruins of a hilltop château, now a cactus garden, promises magnificent sea views. The upper road, of course, provides the most glorious panoramas.

On the corniches' other side awaits Monaco, the royal residence of the Grimaldi family since the 13th century. You can visit the magnificent palace when Prince Albert is away, and, on a more

NOT TO BE MISSED:

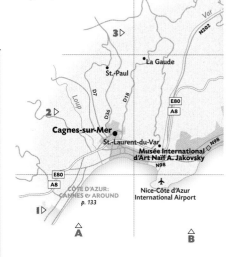

Var
N202
3 ▷
• La Gaude
St.-Paul
Loup
D7
D18
E80
A8
2 ▷
D36
Cagnes-sur-Mer •
St.-Laurent-du-Var •
Musée International
d'Art Naïf A. Jakovsky
N98
E80
A8
CÔTE D'AZUR:
CANNES & AROUND
p. 133
Nice-Côte d'Azur
International Airport
1 ▷
△
A
△
B

Surf's up in Nice, where beaches are pebbly and warm waters beckon

melancholic note, stop by the flower-strewn tombs of Princess Grace and Prince Rainier in the church where they were married. Monte-Carlo is the principality's glittery capital, with its world-famous casino dealing in millions of euros a day.

Languorous Menton is said to enjoy the sunniest weather of all Riviera resorts—316 days a year. It's famous for its gardens, lemons, and the artistic legacy of Jean Cocteau. Italy's proximity (just a mile/1.6 km away) is evident in the local accent, Italianate architecture, and especially in the tomato- and garlic-based cuisine.

In surrounding hills, vertiginous roads zigzag to ancient hill towns—Peille, Ste.-Agnès, Coaraze, Peillon, to name a few—virtually untouched by modern day and each one offering dizzying vistas. ■

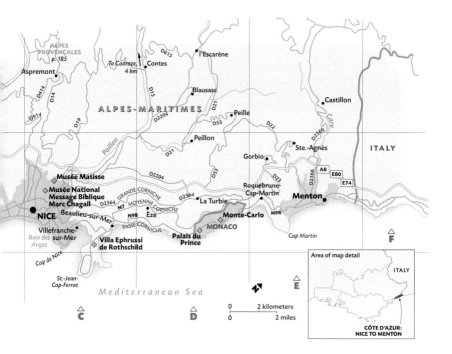

Nice

Beneath a brilliant Mediterranean sun, Nice basks in a long Italian heritage: fashionable and cosmopolitan yet relaxed. The translucent blue-green Baie des Anges washes its southern edge—the only downfall being pebbly beaches. But Nice is also France's fifth largest city, offering a lineup of world-class museums and other cultural sites. And that's the debate—go to the beach, or museums? Hopefully, you'll have time to do both.

Nice's grand old hotels edge the Baie des Anges.

Market Days

Daily: Cours Saleya (vegetables, fruit, & flowers Tues.–Sun., antiques Mon.)
Tues.–Sun.: Libération

Some Background

Nice became a part of France only in 1860, under the Treaty of Turin, heretofore falling under the reign of the counts of Savoy. The culture is sufficiently suffused with Italian influence—its architecture, cuisine (*pissaladière* and *pistou*, for instance), even language (a regional dialect called Nissart). But Nice's history also owes something to the British, who discovered the city as a warm winter wonderland in the late 1700s. In 1822 they subsidized a seafront esplanade, the beloved promenade des Anglais. Queen Victoria stayed in Nice later that century (in the Quartier Cimiez), initiating a long line of aristocrats who came and built elaborate villas. Among the masses who followed were writers and artists enraptured by the gorgeous setting: Dumas, Nietzsche, Apollinaire, Flaubert, Hugo, Georges

Sand, Stendhal, Matisse, and the list goes on.

In the not-so-distant past, Nice was plagued with a reputation for crime and corruption—largely due to the exploits of Jacques Médecin, the city's mayor from 1966 to 1990. Problems are still present, but an ongoing rejuvenation of several key places in the city, including avenue Jean Médecin, place Masséna, and place Garibaldi, as well as the addition of a tramway system, has given this charmer of a city a new gloss.

INSIDER TIP:

The best place for canines is Plage de Carras, where there's a special dog-friendly area called Site de la Lanterne.

—KELLY CARTER
Author of National Geographic's Dog Lover's Guide to Travel

Heart of Nice

Place Masséna, situated at the crossroads of avenue Jean Médecin and the old town (see pp. 166–167), benefited hugely from the recent construction of the new tramway system. The graceful, 17th-century arcades painted in quintessentially Mediterranean rose are now complemented with the modern touches of black-and-white pavement and Jaume Plensa's illuminated, color-changing Buddha statues suspended on poles high above; the pedestrian zone fans out from

here (aside from the trams), ideal for languorous strolling.

Place Masséna touches on the **promenade du Paillon,** a fabulous greenway right in the heart of Nice that begins at the **Jardin Albert Premier** and curves north for 0.7 mile (1.2 km), passing modern art, pocket gardens, statues, and fountains. At the promenade's northern tip, the ultramodern **Musée d'Art Moderne et d'Art Contemporain** (MAMAC) showcases European and American art from the 1960s on. The building comprises four marble-coated towers linked by steel walkways, all enclosed in glass. All the big names are here, including Andy Warhol and Roy Lichtenstein, with an entire section devoted to Nice-born Yves Klein (1928–1992). Nearby, the **Théâtre National de Nice,** under the new direction of Irina Brook, presents a program in French and English.

Even farther north, you'll enter the buzzing **Quartier Libération,** where you'll see nary a tourist at the local market *(closed Mon.).* Arlequin Gelati Italiani *(9 av. Malaussèna, tel 04 93 04 69 88, closed Mon.)* has to-die-for gelato. Also, duck into Galerie Eva Vautier *(2 rue Vernier, tel 09 80 84 96 73, closed Sun.–Mon. & a.m., eva-vautier .com),* one of the city's many contemporary art galleries.

Colline du Château

Overshadowing Vieux Nice, the only fortified remains you'll see at Castle Hill belong to the Tour Bellanda. The old castle grounds are now woodsy gardens that
(continued on p. 168)

Nice
⚲ 163 C2
Visitor Information
✉ 5 promenade des Anglais
☎ 08 92 70 74 07
nicetourisme.com

DISCOUNT CARD:
The French Riviera Pass *(nicetourisme.com/ frenchrivierapass)* offers 24- (€26), 48- (€38), and 72-hour (€56) all-inclusive passes for all participating sites and tours.

Musée d'Art Moderne et d'Art Contemporain (MAMAC)
⚲ Map p. 167
✉ Promenade des Arts
☎ 04 97 13 42 01
💲 $
mamac-nice.org

Théâtre National de Nice
✉ Promenade des Arts
☎ 04 93 13 90 90
tnn.fr

Exploring Vieux Nice by Foot

In the shade of Colline du Château (Castle Hill), Old Nice's tightly packed warren of pedestrian lanes harbors centuries-old Italianate houses, baroque churches, lively cafés, food stalls, and an energetic marketplace. This is where the seafaring Greeks first settled in 350 B.C., today the bustling Nice of the Niçois, a delightful mix of historic and trendy.

Begin at the revitalized **Place Masséna ❶** (see p. 165). At the base of the square, behind the fountain of Apollo, follow rue de l'Opéra to esplanade Georges Pompidou. You are clearly entering old town, a pedestrianized jumble of cafés and souvenir shops.

Turn left, and soon you see the neo-baroque **Opéra de Nice** *(4 rue St.-François-de-Paule, tel 04 92 17 40 00)* on the right, Nice's

NOT TO BE MISSED:

Place Masséna • Place Rossetti • Palais Lascaris

opera house rebuilt in the style of Paris's Opéra after a fire in 1881. Across the street, peek into **La Maison Auer** *(7 rue St.-François-de-Paule, closed Sun.–Mon., maison-auer.com)*, a primo chocolatier and confectioner purveying artisan chocolates and crystallized fruit in a flamboyantly rococo interior dating from 1820.

The road soon widens into **cours Saleya ❷**, a long plaza that fills with a flower market every morning but Monday, when antique vendors take over. After the market closes, the space crowds with café tables far into the evening hours.

Midway, place Pierre Gautier is overlooked by the huge **Palais des Ducs de Savoie** (Palace of the Dukes of Savoy), constructed beginning in 1571 for the sovereign family. The building is now known as the Ancienne Préfecture. Adjacent, the 1740 **Chapelle de la Miséricorde's ❸** baroque interior is said to be one of the world's most beautiful *(guided tours p.m. Tues.)*.

Heart of Old Town

Turn left on rue de la Poissonnerie where, at No. 8, you'll see the 1584 **Adam and Eve House,** named for the bas-relief on its facade. At the corner of rue de la Préfecture stands the **Église Notre-Dame de l'Annonciation,** dedicated to Ste.-Rita, the venerated patron saint of hopeless causes. Its staid exterior belies an exquisitely baroque interior—a mélange of columns, marbles, gilding, and

Old and new mingle in Nice's old town, a crowded neighborhood of historic buildings and lively cafés.

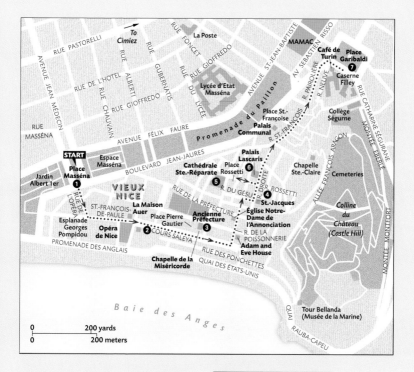

moldings. On the church's northern exterior wall you'll find a haphazard display of artifacts dating back to Roman times.

Continue straight to tiny rue du Gésu, turning right to place du Gésu and **St.-Jacques ④**. Constructed between 1640 and 1690, it was Nice's first example of baroque work. Gilded cherubs and frescoes fill the interior.

Facing the church, turn left and follow rue Droite to rue Rossetti, then turn left to café-filled **place Rossetti,** the old town's centerpiece. The baroque **Cathédrale Ste.-Réparate ⑤** lords above, built between 1650 and 1680. It's named for the 14-year-old martyr and patron saint of Nice, who died in the 14th century in the Holy Land and was said to have been brought here in a flower-bedecked boat by angels.

Backtrack on rue Rossetti and turn left on rue Droite. At No. 15, **Palais Lascaris ⑥** (tel 04 93 62 72 40, closed Tues.) provides a glimpse into aristocratic life. Designed in baroque-Genoese style, the edifice features rooms arranged

🖪	See area map p. 163
▶	Place Masséna
🕒	2 hours
↔	3 miles (4.8 km)
▶	Place Garibaldi

around two small inner courtyards adorned with statues and busts. A rare collection of musical instruments traces the history of music.

Proceed up rue Droite to rue St.-François. At place St.-François stands the former **Palais Communal** (Town Hall) from the 16th and 17th centuries. Follow the rue Pairolière to monumental **place Garibaldi ⑦**, surrounded by beautiful baroque buildings and sparkling with a face-lift in light of the tramway construction. The centerpiece statue commemorates native son Giuseppe Garibaldi, responsible for unifying Italy in the late 19th century. **Café de Turin** (5 place Garibaldi, cafedeturin.fr) is a great spot for seafood—as well as supreme people-watching.

Musée Masséna

65 rue de France

☎ 04 93 91 19 10

🕐 Closed Tues.

offer bay-and-city vistas, along with cafés, a waterfall, and two lovely old cemeteries. You can access the hill via several walkways leading up from old town, or take the *ascenseur* (elevator; *quai des États-Unis where the road makes dramatic curve at base of hill*).

Belle Époque Beauties

Wedding-cake mansions. Pastel-frosted villas. Garlanded palaces: The belle époque style flourished in Nice at the turn of the 20th century, when colossal classical buildings were smothered with profusions of carved garlands, flowers, and shields. Here are some of Nice's most beautiful examples:

• Hôtel Excelsior Régina *(71 av. Régina)*
• Hôtel Negresco *(37 promenade des Anglais)*
• L'Alhambra *(46 blvd. de Cimiez)*
• Musée des Beaux-Arts *(33 av. des Baumettes)*
• Villa Raphaeli-Surany *(35 blvd. de Cimiez)*

Musée International d'Art Naïf A. Jakovsky

🅰 162 B2

Château Ste. Hélène, av. de Fabron

☎ 04 93 71 78 33

🕐 Closed Tues.

💲 $

Musée des Beaux-Arts

33 av. des Baumettes

☎ 04 92 15 28 28

🕐 Closed Mon.

💲 $

Promenade des Anglais

Shaded by palms, the promenade des Anglais arcs along the seafront to the south of place Masséna, with belle époque villas and casinos on one side, the cobalt sea on the other. Once the place for afternoon constitutionals, the promenade is now taken over by runners and walkers, as well as bench sitters, who stare complacently out to sea.

Among the promenade's most famous landmarks is the **Hôtel Negresco** at No. 37, built between 1906 and 1912 for the Romanian Henri Negresco in belle époque style. The other famous building is the art deco **Palais de la Méditerranée** at No. 13–17, built by American millionaire Frank Jay Gould in 1929 and now a luxury hotel.

Nearly all the beaches stretch along the sweep of bay between Rauba Capeu and the airport; 15 or so are private, separated by public beaches in between (these get crowded—show up early. The **Plage Publique de Beau Rivage** is one of the better ones). You can walk along the bay's length (including the private beaches) if you stay close to the sea.

Nice's Cultural Side

Poised midway along the promenade des Anglais, you'll find the **Musée Masséna.** Housed in the 1898 Italian-style Palais Masséna, it showcases a locally accented collection of furniture and art, with highlights including works by Nice's primitive painters.

In the west of town, the **Musée International d'Art Naïf A. Jakovsky** presents an international collection of folk art in the lovely pink villa once belonging to *parfumier* Réné Coty. French artists on display include Pierre Bonnier, considered the French Grandma Moses.

Hidden away in an elegant neighborhood just east, the **Musée des Beaux-Arts** is housed in another sumptuous belle époque villa, built in 1878 for a Ukrainian princess. The collection, spanning the 15th to 20th centuries, began with the

The Hôtel Negresco is one of Nice's few remaining turn-of-the-20th-century grandes dames.

works given to Nice in 1860 by Napoléon III. The most celebrated classical paintings are by van Loo family members. The Impressionists, Postimpressionists, Nabis, and fauves are well represented, the most important of which are Raoul Dufy and Jules Chéret (1836–1932), the creator of modern poster art.

North, on the other side of the A7, you are transported to imperial Russia at the **Cathédrale Orthodoxe Russe St.-Nicolas.** Tsar Nicolas II built this ornate edifice between 1903 and 1912 in memory of a young tsarevitch who died in town in 1865. It served many exiled Russians who fled to Nice after the revolution.

East of the port, the **Musée Paleontologie Humaine de Terra Amata,** built over a site where mammoth hunters camped 400,000 years ago, gives a look at Europe's earliest inhabitants.

Matisse & Chagall

Jumping north of Vieux Nice, you'll come to the popular **Musée National Message Biblique Marc Chagall.** The small, modern museum centers on Chagall's Biblical Message Cycle, 17 enormous paintings of biblical inspiration. In the main gallery, 12 large paintings painted between 1954 and 1967 illustrate scenes from the Books of Genesis and Exodus. They are simply magical with their whimsical, colorful depictions of flowers, goats, and floating couples. A smaller room houses five paintings in the "Song of Songs" series, based on another Old Testament book. Graceful and lyrical in their composition, they are all done in shades of red that are somehow peaceful, not jarring.

Chagall's large mosaic depicting the prophet Elijah in his chariot of fire is displayed over a fountain, and preparatory sketches are also

Cathédrale Orthodoxe Russe St.-Nicolas

- ✉ Blvd. du Tzarevitch
- ☎ 04 93 96 88 02
- 💲 $

Musée Paleontologie Humaine de Terra Amata

- ✉ 25 blvd. Carnot
- ☎ 04 93 55 59 93
- 🕐 Closed Tues.
- 💲 $

musee-archeol ogique-nice.org

Musée National Message Biblique Marc Chagall

- 🅰 163 C2
- ✉ Av. du Dr. Ménard
- ☎ 04 93 53 87 20
- 🕐 Closed Tues.
- 💲 $$

musee-chagall.fr

Musée Archéologique

- ✉ 160 av. des Arènes de Cimiez
- ☎ 04 93 81 59 57
- 🕐 Museum & ruins: Closed Tues.
- 💲 $

musee-archeologique -nice.org

Musée Matisse

- 🗺 163 C2
- ✉ 164 av. des Arènes de Cimiez
- ☎ 04 93 81 08 08
- 🕐 Closed Tues.
- 💲 $

musee-matisse -nice.org

BOAT TOURS:
One-hour coastal boat tours depart from Nice's quai Lunel to round exquisite satellite bays of Cap de Nice, Villefranche-sur-Mer, and St.-Jean-Cap-Ferrat before cruising Nice's Baie des Anges (Trans Côte d'Azur, tel 04 92 00 42 30. trans-cote -azur.com).

on display. Poke your head into the auditorium, where the artist's stained-glass windows depict the creation of the world.

If you follow boulevard de Cimiez north into the Quartier Cimiez—the once fashionable hilltop neighborhood for British vacationers—you'll come to the **Musée Archéologique,** the ruins of the ancient Roman city of Cemenelum, dating from A.D. 69. Vases, sarcophagi, and glassware dug up at the site are found in the museum, while a short path outside winds through the amphitheater and public baths.

But the reason to make the trek this far north is the fabulous **Musée Matisse,** housed in a 17th-century, poppy red villa. Drawn by the scenery, as well as for health reasons and to be near his friends (Picasso, Renoir, and Bonnard lived nearby), Matisse began living in Nice year-round in 1921 and died here in 1954. The museum's collection of paintings, gouache cutouts, drawings, bronze sculptures, engravings, and illustrated books spans the artist's long career. The visit begins with his dark and somber still lifes, progressing through

INSIDER TIP:

From Nice, rent a car and explore the gorgeous hill towns in the backcountry, among them the stunning Èze and Haut-de-Cagnes.

—HEIDI ELLISON
National Geographic contributor

his Impressionist and fauvist attempts. Well-known pieces might include works painted in Nice, including "Tempête à Nice" (1919) and "Odalisque au Coffret Rouge" (1926). The visit then launches into his exuberant, colorful paper cutouts *(gouaches découpées),* a genre he began in 1950 at age 80. In the modern atrium downstairs is the pièce de résistance: the playful "Fleurs et Fruits" (1953), Matisse's largest masterpiece in France (13.5 by 28.5 feet/4.1 x 8.7 m) and his last work before his death. Here, too, is the latest addition, "The Swimming Pool," a monumental frieze with cutout, ultramarine swimmers, fish, sea stars, and a porpoise. ■

A City With Taste

Sitting prettily near the Italian border along the dazzling sea, Nice has a cuisine all its own. Based on the Mediterranean tradition with a special nod to Italy (which ruled over Nice until 1861), it is full of fresh fruit and vegetables, aromatic herbs, olive oil—and pasta. Among the specialties to look for: *pissaladière* (onion tart), *salade Niçoise,* ravioli, gnocchi,

stockfish (dried cod stew), ratatouille, *farcis Niçois* (tiny stuffed vegetables), *tourte de blette* (Swiss chard tart), and *pan bagnat* (salade Niçoise sandwich). Restaurateurs who offer Nice's authentic cuisine display the "Cuisine Nissarde" label in their windows—look for the smiling woman in traditional dress holding a basket full of fresh ingredients.

Nice's Hinterlands

The craggy peaks rising steeply behind Nice shelter a collection of lofty *villages perchés,* their foundations laid during Roman invasions in the second century B.C. The access roads may be tiny, twisty, and steep—at times even tortuous—but the dizzying views alone are worth the white knuckles.

Ste.-Agnès, the coast's loftiest village at 2,559 feet (780 m)

Clinging to a rock above the River Paillon de Contes, fortified **Contes,** 9.3 miles (15 km) northeast of Nice, was a medieval market for olives and ceramics. Olives have been crushed at the **Moulin à Huile de la Laouza** *(av. Raiberti, tel 08 99 03 47 17)* since the 13th century. The 16th-century **Église Ste.-Marie-Madeleine** boasts a retable by François Bréa.

North via the D15, remote **Coaraze** is one of the area's most untouched villages, its narrow streets winding up to a 14th-century church. Toward Monaco, off the D21, **Peillon** clutches its rocky promontory overlooking a valley of pine and olive trees. The view from the church, at the top of the main street, takes in the whole area. The **Chapelle-des-Pénitents-Blancs,** near the village entrance, has a group of frescoes of the Passion by Giovanni Canavesio, dating from 1489. The fact that boutiques have been banned may explain the lack of tourist hordes.

The road to sky-high **Peille** is breathtaking—for its narrow cliff-side engineering and tiny two-way tunnels as well as for its views. A quiet, undiscovered village is your reward. Some of the buildings date from the 14th through 16th centuries; place de la Colle has the finest ones. At the **Musée du Terroir,** a tiny local museum, descriptions are written in Pelhasc, a dialect specific to Peille. ■

Musée du Terroir

✉ Place de l'Armée, Peille

☎ 04 93 82 14 40

⊕ Closed Mon.–Tues.

Creating Paradise

Breeze-riffled palms and burgeoning lemon trees, curtains of bougainvillea and flocks of hibiscus, bloom-studded succulents and cacti, all set against a dazzling blue sea—this magical land could only be the Côte d'Azur, muse of artists and writers, antidote for cold northern winters. But it wasn't always so.

In the early 1800s, the arid countryside around Cannes harbored onions, chickpeas, and olives—not very attractive to the wealthy English who spent their winters here. Used to luxuriant gardens, they rushed to surround their opulent villas with exotic plants, from palms to cacti to avocados. As the Côte d'Azur became fashionable, a profusion of flora spread across its parched landscape, bit by bit transforming into the lavish paradise it is today. Glamorous and eclectic, the gardens they created are everywhere—from residential plots to city plantings to private collections, some of which can be visited by appointment. Indeed, there are few places in the world that possess such beautiful gardens as the Côte d'Azur. Here are some of the best.

Hyères's Gardens

Overlooking the red-tile-roofed old town, the **Jardin Provençal** unites two fabulous gardens. Packed with rare plants, brightly flowered **Parc Ste.-Claire** surrounds the 19th-century castle where American novelist Edith Wharton resided (and died) between 1927 and 1937. Cobbled paths wander up the hill to **Parc St.-Bernard**, specializing in Mediterranean plants (including 20 varieties of rosemary, 15 of phlomis, and 25 different cistus). At the top of the park, above montée de Noailles, is the **Villa Noailles** (tel 04 98 08 01 98, closed Mon.–Tues., villanoailles-hyeres.com), a cubist mansion enclosed within part of the old citadel. It was designed in 1923 by Robert Mallet-Stevens for the Vicomte Charles de Noailles, a patron of modern art. It's most famous for its concrete-and-glass cubist triangle garden by Gabriel Guevrekian. The villa

plays host to temporary contemporary art shows and design festivals. Be sure to walk to the west of the park and farther up the hill to the ivy-twisted castle remains, offering stunning views out to the Îles d'Hyères. **Office de Tourisme** hyeres-tourisme.com ✉ Av. de Belgique ☎ 04 94 01 84 50

Jardin Exotique, Èze

The Jardin Exotique's beautiful cactus garden crowns the picturesque old hilltop village of Èze (see p. 175), set among vestiges of the ancient castle. Sea views extend out over red-tiled roofs. ✉ Rue du Château ☎ 04 93 41 10 30 💲 $$

Menton's Gardens

Menton's splendid microclimate nurtures an abundance of subtropical Edens. The **Jardin Botanique Exotique du Val Rahmeh** (av. de St.-Jacques, Garavan, tel 04 93 35 86 72, closed Tues. Oct.–March, $$) was founded in the late 19th century by Lord Radcliffe, governor of Malta. A pebbly path takes you through a variety of tropical and subtropical plantings collected from as far away as the Himalaya and New Caledonia. Guided visits are offered. Nearby, the Valencia-style **Jardin Fontana Rosa** (tel 04 92 10 33 66, av. Blasco Ibañez, $$) is the 1920s creation of Spanish novelist Vicente Blasco Ibañez. It is full of roses, citrus trees, and water, as well as ceramic figures evoking great literary figures such as Cervantes and Victor Hugo. The **Jardin de Maria Serena** (promenade Reine Astrid, Garavan, tel 04 92 41 76 76, guided tours 10 a.m. Tues., $$) is famed for its palm trees. The garden surrounds the Second Empire–style Villa Maria Serena, designed by Charles Garnier in 1866.

Hardy cacti, such as this prickly crew at Monaco's Jardin Exotique, are staples of Riviera gardeners.

North of town, the **Jardins des Colombières** *(372 rte. de Super Garavan, tel 04 92 10 97 10, closed Sept.–June, $$),* designed between 1918 and 1927, is painter and garden-designer Ferdinand Bac's last and best known garden. It showcases a series of little gardens, each inspired by a personality of Greek mythology.

Villa Thuret, Cap d'Antibes

The famous botanical gardens of Villa Thuret is where, in 1865, G. Thuret established a botanical testing site with the aim of introducing more varied flora to the Riviera. Today, some 3,000 plant species representing the Riviera's extreme variety of microclimates and soil types flourish in this strolling wonderland, with 200 new species introduced every year. ✉ 62 blvd. du Cap, Cap d'Antibes ☎ 04 97 21 25 00 🕐 Closed Sat.–Sun. See also Monaco's Jardin Exotique (see p. 179) and Villa Ephrussi de Rothschild (see p. 184).

The Three Corniches

A giant wall of limestone cliffs towers above the blue sea between Nice and Menton, making access between the two towns historically difficult. Over the centuries, three different roads— each higher than the next and not necessarily accessible one to the other—have been cut into the rock to transport people back and forth: the Basse Corniche along the coastline; the Moyenne (Middle) Corniche; and the topmost Grande Corniche. Each one offers glorious sights—and views.

La Turbie's Trophée des Alpes

Villefranche-sur-Mer

🅰 163 C2

Visitor Information

✉ Place François Binon

☎ 04 93 01 73 68

villefranche-sur-mer.fr

Chapelle de St.-Pierre-des-Pêcheurs

✉ Place Pollonais, Villefranche-sur-Mer

☎ 04 93 76 90 70

🕐 Closed Tues. & mid-Nov.–mid-Dec.

💲 $

Basse Corniche (N98)

Built in the 1860s to bring gamblers to the new Monte-Carlo casino, the Basse Corniche opened up once isolated fishing villages that have since blossomed into seaside resorts (explaining the common lines of traffic along the way). Leaving Nice on the N98, you almost immediately come to **Villefranche-sur-Mer,** an immaculately maintained village stacked up the hillside. It's always been a hardworking fishing town, though these days you'll see everything from yachts to battleships in its deepwater harbor. In town, seek out the **Chapelle de St.-Pierre-des-Pêcheurs** on the waterfront, a tiny chapel whose thick walls and barrel vaults were decorated in 1957 by Jean Cocteau (see side-bar p. 183). The poet, novelist, playwright, filmmaker, and painter spent part of his childhood in Villefranche, and he dedicated this work to the fishermen. Clean, free-flowing black lines, accented with pastel washes, depict, to the left, "Homage to the Women of Villefranche" and, on the right, "Homage to the Gypsies" (of Les

Stes.-Maries-de-la-Mer). The remaining images, in the nave and apse, represent scenes from St. Peter's life. In 1560 the dukes of Savoy built the **Citadelle St.- Elme** on the hill overlooking the harbor. Today the fort houses the **Musée Volti,** which displays sculpture and modern art.

Just beyond Villefranche is **St.-Jean-Cap-Ferrat,** a flowery peninsula studded with belle époque estates hidden behind shrubbery and fences. One of them you can visit (for a price)— the sumptuous **Villa Ephrussi de Rothschild** (see p. 184).

In the neighboring resort town of Beaulieu-sur-Mer, the **Villa Kéry- los** *(impasse Gustave Eiffel, tel 04 93 01 01 44, $$, villa-kerylos.com)* offers an unexpected peek into the life- style of ancient well-to-do Greeks. German archaeologist Théodore Reinach built this circa-second- century-B.C. estate in 1902–1908 according to specific historical refer- ences. An audio guide takes you through every room.

Beyond Beaulieu, you are treated to spectacular vistas before easing into **Monaco** (see pp. 176–180).

Moyenne Corniche (N7)

This spectacular drive is reward enough, with its balcony views over cliff and sea. Midpoint you come to the medieval hilltop vil- lage of **Èze.** Its nickname, Eagle's Nest, accurately describes its diz- zying roost 1,550 feet (472 m) directly above the sea. With such altitude, it's hard to believe that Èze was historically a fishing vil- lage, whose poor fishermen had

quite a trek after a day's work. Though today's town is mostly about its galleries and souvenir shops, the small church of Èze, rebuilt with a classical facade and two-story tower between 1764 and 1771, is worth a stop. Steep, shop-filled lanes climb up to the **Jardin Exotique,** a cactus-and- succulent garden planted among the old castle ruins.

Grande Corniche (D2564)

The stunning Grande Corniche, capping the cliff tops 1,600 feet (487 m) above the sea, originally was the Romans' Via Aurelia, used to conquer the west. In the town of **La Turbie,** you can't miss the **Trophée des Alpes** (Trophy of the Alps; *18 av. Albert 1er, tel 04 93 41 21 15, closed Mon., $$),* the domineering monument denoting Augustus' victory in 13 B.C. over 44 Ligurian tribes. Built in 6 and 5 B.C., it was restored between 1929 and 1933 and now has a new museum. ■

Musée Volti

✉ Citadelle, av. Sadi Carnot, Villefranche-sur- Mer

☎ 04 93 76 33 27

⏱ Closed Tues.

Èze

✉ 163 D2

Visitor Information

✉ Office de Tourisme, place Général de Gaulle

☎ 04 93 41 26 00

eze-tourisme.com

Jardin Exotique

✉ Rue du Château, Èze

☎ 04 93 41 10 30

💲 $$

Stop to Breathe the Air

Driving the corniches is fine, but getting out of the car and breathing in the fresh sea air is even better. There are more than 9.5 miles (15 km) of marked trails on the small peninsula of St.-Jean-Cap-Ferrat, winding behind millionaires' villas and offering spec- tacular coastal views. Among three separate routes, the Sentier Littoral is the longest, running the full length of the cape, with singular vistas across the Riviera coastline. The Sentier Touristique de la Pointe St.- Hospice is shorter, a one-hour round-trip from Paloma Beach. Ask for a map at the tourist office in St.-Jean Cap-Ferrat *(5 av. Denis Semeria, www.saintjeancapferrat.fr).*

Monaco & Monte-Carlo

Ebullient with legendary glamour and glitz, Monaco delivers with a fairy-tale castle perched high atop Le Rocher—the Rock. But Monaco is also a 21st-century, forward-thinking place, thanks to the late Prince Rainier III who, during his reign from 1949 to 2005, fashioned his principality into a dynamic, glittering, high-rise-filled enclave. Its belle époque Monte-Carlo Casino is the fabled venue where fortunes are won and lost.

The dreamy principality of Monaco is also a very real economic enclave.

Monaco

🅰 163 D2

Visitor Information

✉ 2a blvd. des Moulins, Monte-Carlo

☎ 93 15 98 98

visitmonaco.com

NOTE: When calling Monaco, the international prefix 00 377 must be dialed, followed by the 8-digit number.

Some Background

On Jan. 8, 1297, Francesco Grimaldi, dressed as a monk, overpowered the guards of the Genoan fortress built on the Rock of Monaco. He was the first Grimaldi to reign over Monaco, the beginning of the world's oldest ruling monarchy. Charles VIII, king of France, first recognized Monégasque independence in 1489. During the French Revolution, the royal family was arrested and imprisoned, but later released.

The Grimaldi family returned to the throne under the 1814 Treaty of Paris.

Monaco's absolute monarchy was replaced in 1911 by a constitution, which was reformed by Prince Rainier in 1962. Francesco's descendant, Prince Rainier expanded the size of the municipality by 20 percent. Upon his death in 2005, his son, Albert II, ascended to the throne as the new sovereign.

Banking and industry are important in Monaco, but

tourism has been the most obvious source of foreign revenue since the 1800s, when a railway from Nice first brought people to the newly built casino, opera house, and expensive villas that have turned the state into a playland for the rich.

Philadelphian film star Grace Kelly came to Monaco in 1954 to film *To Catch a Thief* and ended up capturing Prince Rainier's heart. Their storybook romance ended tragically in 1982 with her death in a car accident.

Monaco is tiny—less than a mile (2 km) square (smaller than New York's Central Park). Only 5,000 of its 30,000 residents are Monégasque citizens, with the rest being French, Italians, and others who have come for fun, sun, and tax breaks.

INSIDER TIP:

Take your dog for a romp in the green space on avenue de Grande Bretagne, opposite the Trocadéro; there are even waste disposal bags available.

—KELLY CARTER

author of National Geographic's Dog Lover's Guide to Travel

Built around the steep sides of the yacht-filled Port de Monaco, Monaco is divided into three main *quartiers:* Monaco-Ville, the ancient quarter atop the 197-foot-high (60 m) cliff along the port's south side, where most of the sights are found; Monte-Carlo, with its casino and annual Grand Prix, on the port's north side; and Fontvieille, the residential and commercial area southwest of Monaco-Ville.

Visiting Monaco

Monaco-Ville possesses a mix of royal glamour and medieval charm. You enter via the steep **Rampe Major,** approaching the palace square past the statue of Francesco Grimaldi, furtive and mysterious in his cloak. Beyond looms the **Palais du Prince,** Prince Albert's royal residence (Princesses Caroline and Stéphanie live down the street). Built on the site of a 13th-century Genoese fortress, the palace has been refined over the centuries, metamorphosing from a skeletal fortress into an elegant residence with a Renaissance facade. Out front a *carabineer*—palace guard—stands frozen in his immaculate red-and-white uniform; changing of the guard takes place daily at 11:55 a.m.

Your ticket permits entrance into 15 rooms of **Les Grands Appartements** (State Apartments), with an audio guide narrating detailed historical information on the principality and the royal family and highlighting various objets d'art and Grimaldi portraits. First stop is the **Cours d'Honneur,** in Italian Renaissance style. The horseshoe staircase, its balustrades decorated with three million stones of Carrara marble in geometric patterns, is where the head of state addresses Monégasques during important state matters. You are taken

Palais du Prince

🅰 163 D2

✉ Place du Palais

☎ 93 25 18 31

🕐 Open only when the prince is not home, usually March–mid-Oct.

💲 $$

palais.mc

**Musée Océano-
graphique de
Monaco**

✉ Av. St.-Martin

☎ 93 15 36 40

💲 $$$

oceano.mc

**Musée des
Timbres et des
Monnaies**

✉ Terrasses de
Fontvieille

☎ 93 15 98 98

💲 $

**Collections
des Voitures
Anciennes**

✉ Terrasses de
Fontvieille

☎ 92 05 28 56

💲 $$

palais.mc

through the **Gallery of Mirrors,** used as an antechamber for guests awaiting reception by the royal family. The gold-and-white hallway, adorned with crystal-drop chandeliers and marble floor mosaics, is filled with Ming vases, Japanese cups, busts of Prince Charles III, and other treasures.

The palace's highlight is the **Throne Room,** the setting for official Monégasque court events since the 1500s. This is also the room where, in 1956, the civil marriage between Prince Rainier III and Grace Patricia Kelly was celebrated by the prime minister. Looking quintessentially regal with its red-damask walls alternating with gilt wood panels, its centerpiece is the lacquered gilt throne in Empire style, crowned by a canopy of Vienna velvet, on which the prince rests his crown. In one corner you can't ignore the 1982 portrait of the glowing royal family dressed in casual clothes and broad

smiles, painted just months before Princess Grace's fatal car crash.

From the palace, signs lead to the **cathedral** *(4 rue Colonel, Bellando de Castro, tel 93 30 87 70)*, rebuilt in 1878 using white stone from La Turbie. Centuries of Grimaldis are buried here, including Prince Rainier and Princess Grace (her flower-strewn tomb is marked plainly with the words "Gratia Patricia, MCMLXXXII"). Of particular interest are the circa 1500 retable to the right of the transept, painted by Louis Bréa, and the episcopal throne in white Carrara marble.

The world-renowned **Musée Océanographique de Monaco,** its grandiose facade rising from a towering cliff, was founded in 1910 by Prince Albert I and run by underwater-explorer Jacques Cousteau for years. The rarest fish of the seven seas swim in 90 tanks; don't miss the display of living coral.

EXPERIENCE: Taking in Monaco's Grand Prix

Every May since 1929, the sleekest, fastest automobiles have zipped around the streets of Monaco in the Grand Prix de Monaco, one of the world's foremost car races. The course is narrow, hilly, dangerous—and exceedingly exciting to watch. Organized by the Automobile Club de Monaco, the race kicks off with a practice session on the Thursday before the real deal.

On the day of the race, you can watch from grandstand seating (from $3,000 for platinum VIP seating to $200 for a variety of options including basic grandstand seating), from a private balcony (if

you know someone), or from the restaurants of the Hôtel de Paris (for a price). Popular viewing spots include **Casino Square,** in front of the fabled casino; **Tabac corner;** and **Piscine** (swimming pool), all with breathtaking harbor views as well as of cars whizzing past. For tighter purses, Rocher general admission (less than $100) offers partial views of the harbor and restricted viewing—a great deal if you arrive early enough for the best spot.

Visit *monaco-grand-prix.com* for additional information and to purchase tickets.

The ever regal Hôtel de Paris, perhaps most famous for its ornate Café de Paris

Fontvieille

In Fontvieille, the neighborhood southwest of Le Rocher, three museums are found on one level of the Centre Commercial (a shopping center): the **Musée des Timbres et des Monnaies** (Museum of Stamps and Coins), covering four centuries of Monégasque minting; **Collections des Voitures Anciennes** (Collection of Antique Cars), Prince Rainier's antique car collection, including the 1956 Rolls-Royce Silver Cloud that carried the prince and princess on their wedding day; and the **Musée Naval** (Naval Museum), Prince Rainier's scale models of famous boats and ships.

Some 7,000 varieties of cacti and succulents are found at the **Jardin Exotique,** built into the side of a rock farther up the hill. Your ticket also gets you into a cave complex, full of stalagmites and stalactites, and the **Musée d'Anthropologie Préhistorique** (Museum of Prehistoric

Anthropology). The latter looks at the history of the human race, including the inhabitants that settled in the Monaco area some million years ago.

Nearby, the **Nouveau Musée National de Monaco,** housed in the belle époque Villa Paloma, is dedicated to art and performance (more temporary exhibits are displayed in another villa, Villa Sauber, in Monte-Carlo).

Monte-Carlo

Its reputation for flamboyant glamour and opulence preceding it, Europe's most fabled casino needs no introduction. It's named for Prince Charles III, who opened the casino in 1865 to raise much needed revenue for the principality. His plan worked—"Mount Charles" was so successful that five years after the opening, taxation was abolished (and still is).

The first gaming tables were housed in various venues until 1878, when architect Charles

Musée Naval

✉ Terrasses de Fontvieille
☎ 92 05 28 48
$ $

Jardin Exotique
✉ Blvd. du Jardin Exotique
☎ 93 15 29 80
$ $$ (includes anthropological museum)

jardin-exotique.mc

Musée d'Anthropologie Préhistorique
✉ 56 bis blvd. du Jardin Exotique
☎ 93 98 80 06
$ $$ (includes Jardin Exotique)

Nouveau Musée National de Monaco
✉ 56 blvd. du Jardin Exotique
☎ 98 98 48 60
$ $$

nmnm.mc

Casino de Monte-Carlo

✉ Place du Casino

☎ 98 06 21 21

🕐 Salons Européens: noon–late daily, slot machines 2 p.m.–late daily; Salons Privés: 4 p.m.–late daily; Club Anglais: 10 p.m.–late daily

💲 Entrance to Salons Européens: $$$ Entrance to Salons Privés & Club Anglais: $$$$$

casinomontecarlo .com

NOTE: A dress code is required to enter the gaming halls (a tie and jacket can be rented at bag check). A passport is required for entry.

Garnier designed the present belle époque beauty, with its green copper cupolas, rococo turrets, and gold chandeliers. The sumptuous opera house was part of his plan as well.

The casino's facade appears imposing, but anyone can wander its ornate entrance hall. To the right as you enter are public slot machines. Ahead is the candelabra-lit two-story atrium entrance hall, paved in marble and ringed with a forest of ionic columns.

One door leads into the **Salle Garnier,** the opera house, with its luxurious red-and-gold decor accented with bas-reliefs, frescoes, and sculptures. Designed by Charles Garnier, who was also responsible for the Opéra Garnier in Paris, the interiors retain their extravagant belle époque glamour. Top-notch international performances of opera, ballet, and concerts have been staged here for more than a century.

The gaming halls are just as opulent, containing a succession of rococo rooms with mirrors, frescoes, bas-reliefs, and gilded mahogany. Even if you're not a high roller, it's worth paying the fee just to take a look at these fabled rooms. Or take a guided tour *(tel 98 06 14 90, $$$$$).* Roulette, *trente et quarante,* and slots are played in the **Salons Européens** (European Rooms), while European and English roulette, *trente et quarante,* chemin de fer, blackjack, and craps are the games of choice in the **Salons Privés** (Private Rooms).

The casino sits on an urban hilltop surrounded by fancy hotels (including the **Hôtel de Paris,** *place du Casino, tel 98 06 30 00),* special-occasion restaurants, and the world's most expensive boutiques (Hermès, Cartier, Chrstian Dior). ∎

The Casino de Monte-Carlo, known as the "cathedral of hell" in its 19th-century heyday

EXPERIENCE: Quintessential Provençal Markets

You'll discover the secret to Provence's glorious, sun-kissed cuisine in the early morning bustle of the region's fabled farmers markets. Throughout the realm on at least one day a week, any village or city worth its mustard—or basil or tarragon—hosts a *marché* where vendors purvey the province's finest produce. Do like the locals and wander the aisles, filling your basket for a *pique-nique*, dinner, or gifts to bring home.

Market Tips

Markets are largest in summer, though some take place year-round. They typically begin at 8 a.m. and continue until noon or 1 p.m. Remember not to touch the merchandise—that's a French *non-non*. Point to the item you want and let the vendor serve you.

When you're done strolling and buying, take advantage of some of the local goings-on. Listen to musicians or grab lunch at one of the nearby cafés. Watch a soccer game or round of *pétanque*.

And finally, don't be in a hurry. Market day is the time for locals to socialize, to catch up with the latest news. It's quintessential Provence at its best.

Seasonal Delights

Look for asparagus beginning in March. Spring brings strawberries, cherries, and almonds. Throughout summer you'll find tomatoes, eggplant, zucchini, peppers (and lavender and sunflowers!). Fall is for game birds, mushrooms, and the grape and olive harvests. Black truffles arrive after November.

Weekly Markets

Market days for all villages

Fresh from the farm at Aix-en-Provence's early morning market

have been noted throughout the guide, but here are some of the best.

Apt: One of the biggest, taking place for nine centuries throughout the entire town center. *Tues. & Sat. a.m.*

Arles: This famous market has more than 1.5 miles (2.5 km) of stalls. *Wed. a.m. & Sat. a.m.*

Forcalquier: Dating back to antiquity, it's the most important market in Alpes-de-Haute-Provence. *Mon. a.m. & Thurs. p.m.*

L'Isle-sur-la-Sorgue: Hundreds of stalls set up along the banks of the River Sorgue in this pretty Vaucluse town, famed for its antiques. *Sun. a.m.*

St.-Rémy: Stalls cram streets throughout the old town vending local goat cheese, olive oil soap, and more. *Wed.*

Uzès: One of the most romantic settings around, with stalls set up in the arcades of medieval place aux Herbes. *Wed. & Sat. a.m.*

Daily Markets

Avignon Les Halles on place Pie is a bustling covered food market where you'll find all kinds of local products. Those in the know come at 11 a.m. on Saturdays, when a leading regional chef gives a free cooking class to onlookers. A recipe is provided, with details on which stalls sell which ingredients. *Closed Mon.*

Nice The long plaza of cours Saleya fills with a flower market every day but Monday, when antique vendors take over.

More Information

Visit *avignon-et-provence.com* and *marvellous-provence.com*.

Menton

In this enchanting town near Italy's border, you'll find one of the Côte d'Azur's most stunning tableaus: Beneath a bright blue sky, apricot-hued houses march up the hillside toward Alpine peaks, the turquoise sea lapping at their base. This beautiful geography ensures that Menton is the Riviera's warmest resort, with winter temps rarely dropping below 50°F (10°C) and tropical foliage blooming year-round. No wonder people compare it to the Garden of Eden. Two museums devoted to artist Jean Cocteau, baroque churches, and beaches are just some of its lures.

Jean Cocteau covered the walls of the Salle de Mariages, in Menton's Hôtel de Ville, with esoteric wedding scenes.

Market Days
Daily

Menton
🅜 163 E2

Visitor Information
✉ Office de Tourisme, Palais de l'Europe, 8 av. Boyer

☎ 04 92 41 76 76

tourisme-menton.fr

The Romans called the area Sinus Pacis (Gulf of Peace) and set up the garrison of Lumone on Cap Martin, but no colony. With little outside interaction, the Gulf of Peace remained virtually undeveloped until the 19th century. Lord Brougham, an eccentric Englishman, discovered the place around 1830 while seeking a warm winter haven. Since then, Menton has grown into a well-moneyed, genteel resort with an Italian flair—the border is only a mile (1.6 km) away.

The **promenade du Soleil** winds along the seashore from the boat-filled harbor in the town center, past beaches, restaurants, and apartment houses built in the 1930s for well-to-do Parisians. It leads to **Cap Martin** a mile (1.6 km) away, where palm trees shade beautiful old villas.

Along the way, housed in a tiny-turreted, 17th-century bastion standing sentinel over the harbor, you'll find the **Musée du Bastion.** Conceived by onetime Menton resident/artist extraordinaire Jean Cocteau (see sidebar opposite), the works here are his key pieces: pebble mosaics, his first tapestry, as well as several pastels from his "Inamorati" ("Lovers") series. Cocteau is buried outside, his tombstone reading "Je reste avec vous" ("I stay with you").

Nearby the dazzlingly new **Musée Jean Cocteau—Collection Séverin Wunderman** is housed in a striking modern building by French architect Rudy Ricciotti. The museum, funded by collector Séverin Wunderman, centers on a collection of Cocteau's graphic works. This site is not to be missed.

Across the street stands the **Halles Municipales** (Town Market), its stalls overflowing with fresh lobsters, crayfish, almond-and-marzipan tarts, big red tomatoes, and lemons, lemons,

lemons. Menton is famous for its lemons—celebrated in February with the Fête des Citrons. Seek out that *délice* Mentonnais—a lemon butter crust covered with lemon crème brûlée and red fruits.

From the market, stroll through the place aux Herbes to **rue St.-Michel,** bustling with shops, restaurants, and cafés. On the next street over, rue de la République, you'll find the **Hôtel de Ville** *(17 rue de la République, tel 04 92 10 50 00, Salle des Mariages closed Sat.–Sun., $).* Cocteau transformed the walls of its **Salle de Mariages** in the 1950s with marriage-related scenes: In front, a Niçoise lemon picker marries a local fisherman, while on the right-hand wall, a wedding scene features people in Maghreb costumes, perhaps referring to the Saracen roots of many Mentonnais. The opposite wall contains one of Cocteau's favorite subjects, Orpheus in the scene where the mythic poet discovers that his beloved is dying.

The earliest known visitor to Menton—the Nouvel Homme de Menton—arrived 30,000 years ago. See his skull, and learn about the region's prehistory, at the nearby **Musée de Préhistoire Régional** *(rue Loredan-Larchey, tel 04 93 35 84 64, closed Tues.).*

Vieux Menton

The Italianate houses of the *vieille ville* step up the hillside along twisty medieval streets. To explore it, follow rue St.-Michel east to place du Cap, where rue des Logettes accesses narrow rue des Écoles Pie, which switchbacks up the hill. Finally you come to place de la Conception, home to the 1762 **Chapelle des Pénitents Blancs** *(tel 04 92 41 76 76, open 3–5 p.m. Mon.),* with its magnificent baroque facade.

The prize awaits in the parvis St.-Michel just below, the **Basilica St.-Michel-Archange,** said to be southern France's largest baroque church. Built between 1619 and 1653, its gilded marble interior features a high altar surmounted by a statue of an armor-clad St. Michael. The chapel to the altar's right, dedicated to Ste.-Devote, belonged to the Grimaldi family. In the saint's picture above the altar, you can make out in the background a view of Monaco Le Rocher.

On the town's west end, the tired-looking **Musée des Beaux-Arts** houses a collection of European paintings spanning the Middle Ages to modern times. ∎

Renaissance Man

Eminently associated with the Côte d'Azur, surrealist filmmaker, playwright, writer, actor, set designer, and artist Jean Cocteau (1889–1963) shone for his versatility and brilliance. He wrote volumes of poems *(La Lampe d'Aladdin),* criticism ("Le Rappel à l'Ordre"), psychological novels *(Thomas l'Imposter, Les Enfants Terribles),* plays *(La Voix Humaine),* and films *(Le Sang d'un Poète, La Belle et la Bête, Orphée, Le Testament d'Orphée).* He created pebble mosaics, tapestries, pastel drawings, and, in his 70s, he painted frescoes in the town hall of Menton and in the chapel of St.-Pierre at Villefranche-sur-Mer. Cocteau insisted that he was primarily a poet and that all his work was poetry—indeed, it is.

Musée Jean Cocteau– Collection Séverin Wunderman

✉ 2 quai de Monléon

☎ 04 89 81 52 50

🕐 Closed Tues.

$ $$ (includes adm. to Musée du Bastion)

museecocteau menton.fr

Musée des Beaux-Arts

✉ Av. de la Madone

☎ 04 93 35 49 71

🕐 Closed Tues.

More Places to Visit Nice to Menton

Castillon

An earthquake in 1887 destroyed Castillon, 7.4 miles (12 km) north of Menton via the precarious D2566 en route to Sospel, then it was bombed in 1944. The Provençal-style village you see today, dating from 1951, is considered a model of modern rural planning. It is a self-proclaimed artisan village, with several shops purveying stained-glass windows, artwork, clothing, even a microbrewery. The **Syndicat d'Initiative** *(rue de la République, tel 04 93 04 32 00, castillon06.com)* has expositions of local art. 🅰 163 E3

Musée Villa Ephrussi de Rothschild

Though Rothschild baroness Béatrice Ephrussi already owned a Monaco mansion, she couldn't give up the opportunity of owning another on St.-Jean-Cap-Ferrat, on land that King Leopold II had planned to carve out for himself. Her vision became this pink-confection, Venice-style villa overlooking the sea. The villa is full of paintings, furniture, and objets d'art, including a Savonnerie carpet; furniture once belonging to Marie-Antoinette; and a collection of Vincennes, Sèvres, and Dresden porcelain. The villa's most splendid aspect, however, is its themed gardens—seven of them. The French garden is the most seductive one, complete with a Temple of Love replicating the Trianon at Versailles. The main ticket admits you to the ground floor and gardens. For a few more euros, you get a guided tour of the first floor, including the tapestry room and the *singeries* room, decorated with monkeys. *villa-ephrussi.com* 🅰 163 C2 ✉ 1 av. Ephrussi-de-Rothschild, St.-Jean-Cap-Ferrat ☎ 04 93 01 33 09 🆂 $$

Ste.-Agnès

Clinging to a pinnacle 2,559 feet (780 m) above sea level, this is Europe's highest seaside village; the views from the southern parking lot are breathtaking. Once a Saracen stronghold, the town is a medieval haven of cobbled lanes, vaulted archways, and underground caverns. Peek into the **Éspace Culture et Traditions** (Center of Culture and Tradition) at the Office de Tourisme for displays of local artifacts. **Fort Maginot de Ste.-Agnès** *(tel 04 93 51 62 31, open daily July–Sept., Sat.–Sun. rest of year, $)* was built in 1932 as part of the French military's futile defense effort against Italy. 🅰 163 E2 **Visitor Information** ✉ Office de Tourisme, 51 rue des Sarrasins ☎ 04 93 28 35 31

Just Desserts

A province so rich in natural flavors bodes well for sweets and desserts. Lavender and thyme appear in crème brûlée, as well as in jams and honey, while nougat made from black honey is considered essential for the Noël meal. But the fun comes in tasting different regional specialties. *Navettes* from Marseille are cookies flavored with anise and orange blossom, and *gâteaux secs aux amands* from Nîmes are almond biscuits. The Aix specialty is *calisson*, a melon-and-almond sweet glazed in sugar. Apt is known for its *fruits confits* (crystallized glazed fruit), while the Vaucluse features Cavaillon melon accompanied by muscat from Beaumes-de-Venise. St.-Tropez offers *tarte Tropézienne*, a cream-filled sandwich cake. Nearby Massif des Maures focuses on chestnuts: *Glace aux marrons glacé* is chestnut ice cream and *crème des marrons* is chestnut cream. Nice offers *socca*, a chickpea crêpe; *berlingots* are mint-and-lemon hard caramels from Carpentras. And that's just a start.

Provence's Alpine realm, with snowy, knife-edged peaks, a wild gorge and wilder still national park, and fields and fields of lavender

Alpes Provençales

Wheat-speckled lavender blooms

Alpes Provençales

The southern Alps end abruptly just inland from the Mediterranean Sea, providing an unexpected foray into remote mountainscapes—the domain of chamois, ibex, and bearded falcons. Towns are few and far between, in this region where hiking, skiing, white-water rafting, and canyoning reign. But here, too, you'll find fields of lavender, faïence, and other celebrated icons of Provence.

Perhaps the greatest surprise is Parc National du Mercantour, a wilderness escape where jaggy peaks rise abruptly to the sky. Roads are tortuous and steep, with many *lacets* (hairpin turns)—providing magnificent, white-knuckle views. This is a world of rare and endangered flowers, endless hiking trails, and high-altitude camps. Isola 2000 is the

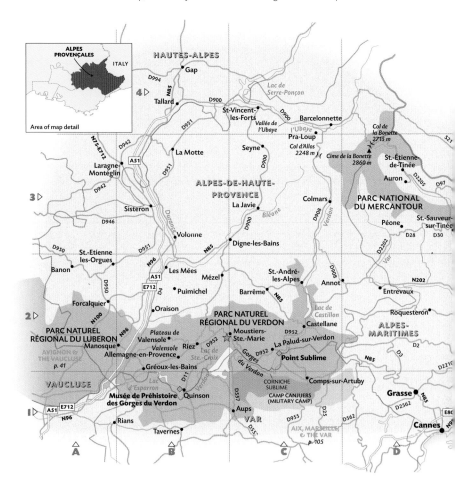

Sheep graze on the Col d'Allos, deep in the southern Alps.

famous ski resort where the Niçois head in winter, while the Vallée des Merveilles harbors some of the world's oldest etchings, dating from the Bronze Age.

The mountains taper farther west, setting the scene for the Gorges du Verdon, Europe's largest canyon. This is an outdoor enthusiast's dream, with white-water

rafting, bungee jumping, and rock climbing.

A popular base at the canyon's eastern edge, the village of Castellane is Provençal in feel, with its central *pétanque* court, terrace cafés, and warm-hued buildings. Moustiers-Ste.-Marie, on the canyon's western side, has been world famous for its faïence for centuries. Shop after shop features the exquisite porcelainware, some better quality than others.

Westward, the plateau de Valensole is a bucolic world of medieval villages and forested hills ... and rows and rows of lavender. During their peak bloom in late June and July, the air fills with a purple-blue aura and, as the harvest begins, their distinct pungent aroma. ■

NOT TO BE MISSED:

Parc National du Mercantour

High up in the rocky peaks behind Menton and Nice, only 25 miles (40 km) from the sea, Mercantour National Park is one of Provence's best kept secrets. In this spectacular Alpine realm, spreading across seven valleys and covering more than 171,250 acres (69,300 ha), you'll find an amazing diversity of scenery, from wild canyons to olive groves to lily-scattered prairies; more than 2,000 species of flora; profuse wildlife; and amazing archaeological treasures.

Nicknamed the Switzerland of Nice, St. Martin-Vésubie has been a mountaineering center since the 19th century.

Created in 1979, the park is one of France's seven national parks. It borders on Italy's Parco Naturale Alpi Marittime, so that the two parks create a vast protected area in the heart of the Maritime Alps.

Wildlife is abundant here (see sidebar opposite). The diversity of flora is just as incredible. This is the only place in France you can travel from the Mediterranean biosphere all the way up to the Alpine, experiencing all the flora in between: from lavender and olive trees below 2,300 feet (700 m); to fir trees, Norway spruce, and Norway pine between 2,300 and 5,000 feet (700–1,500 m); giving way to larch trees above that; and, above 8,000 feet (2,500 m), scrabbly patches of rhododendron, Alpine grass, and lichens.

Of 4,200 known plant species in France, 2,000 are found here, 200 of which are rare, and 30 endemic (found nowhere else in the world). For example, the *Saxifraga florulenta moretti,* which flowers once every ten years, grows only here, specifically at elevations between 8,000 and 10,000 feet (2,500–3,000 m). The Bérard thistle is one of the blooms that have survived from the Tertiary period, adapting to the cold climate. In the meantime, species such as the Asian lily have been brought from far away by wind or birds.

There is an abundance of outdoor activities: hiking, mountain biking, spelunking, canyoning, white-water rafting, kayaking, paragliding, and, in winter, skiing—and that's just a start. You can join guided tours of archaeological sites, birds-of-prey evenings, and much more. Seek out the different Maisons du Parc (visitor centers) throughout the park for information.

From the south, you will most likely enter the park via Menton (through Sospel) or via Nice (through the Vallée de la Vésubie or the Vallée de la Tinée).

Vallée de la Roya

One of Mercantour's most striking valleys, the Roya Valley, on the park's eastern edge, became French in 1947. Until then, King Victor Emmanuel II of Italy used

it for his hunting grounds. A string of medieval towns dot the River Roya from south to north, with St.-Dalmas-de-Tende being the gateway to the fabled Vallée des Merveilles.

In the valley's south, linked to the coast via Sospel (see p. 198), is charming **Breil-sur-Roya,** feeling very much like a 17th- or 18th-century mountain town with its ancient buildings. Seek out 18th-century **Sancta-Maria-in-Albis,** a dazzlingly baroque church with frescoed ceilings and gilded decorations; the magnificent altarpiece dates from the 12th century. With the turbid River Roya running through town, it's no surprise that Breil is a hub of kayaking and white-water rafting.

From Breil the N204 heads north along the Roya through the **Gorges de Saorge,** leading to the spectacular village of **Saorge,** its boxy little houses holding dearly to

Parc National du Mercantour

🗺 186 C3, D3–D4, E2–E3

Visitor Information

✉ Administrative headquarters, 23 rue d'Italie, Nice

☎ 04 93 16 78 88

parc-mercantour.com

Mercantour's Wild Side

Located at the crossroads of Mediterranean and Alpine biomes, Mercantour harbors a profusion of varied wildlife species. Ermines, marmots, boars, and foxes are some of the most common critters. Six *ongulés* (hoofed animals) also live here—the most celebrated being the nimble, sure-footed chamois, a small antelope that can leap as high as 6.5 feet (2 m) and as far as 20 feet (6 m); wild mountain sheep *(mouflon),* introduced in 1950 from Corsica for hunting purposes and, despite its name, poorly adapted to mountain life; and ibex, a wild mountain goat with large recurved horns.

But perhaps the most exciting creature is the wolf. The wolf has migrated back from Italy after 50 years of absence, having been hunted nearly to extinction. There's a wolves welcome center near St.-Martin-Vésubie, called Parc Alpha *(Le Boréon, RD 89, tel 04 93 02 33 69, alpha-loup.com, closed mid-Nov.–mid-Dec., $$$),* dedicated to restoring the region's wolf population. The nature reserve features hiking trails and observation huts, and you can also devote a morning to helping care for a wolf as well as observing wolves under the full moon.

In the skies above, look for golden eagles, falcons, and vultures—including the *Gypaète barbu* (bearded vulture), with a wingspan of up to 10 feet (3 m).

the sheer cliff. The only way to get here is from behind, via the village of Fontan. Don't miss the **Couvent des Franciscains** (tel 04 93 04 55 55, closed Tues. & Oct.–April, $), south of the village, with its baroque church and cloister adorned in 18th-century frescoes showing the life of St. Francis.

Northward, the spectacularly Alpine **Gorges de Bergue** brings you to **St.-Dalmas-de-Tende,** the main gateway to the Vallée des Merveilles (see below). Farther on you pass through picturesque La Brigue to **Tende,** with its medieval bourg; the ruins above the village are those of a castle once belonging to the counts of Tende. Don't miss the **Musée des Merveilles** (av. du 16 Septembre 1947, Tende, tel 04 93 04 32 50, closed Tues., 2 weeks March, & 2 weeks Nov., $),

with its thorough account of the geological and archaeological history of the Vallée des Merveilles through displays, dioramas, and a film. Copies of the valley's ancient etchings help identify the petroglyphs.

Vallée des Merveilles

Sometime between 2800 and 1300 B.C, during the Bronze Age, shepherds migrated seasonally to the remote Vallée des Merveilles, where they scratched tens of thousands of rock carvings into stone walls at the foot of Mont Bégo. Among the drawings are pointed shapes identified as knives, arrows, and other weapons, and witchlike figures called *orants.* The site's original purpose is unknown, though possibly it was used for worship.

You can walk in yourself, but the rugged region is extremely high in altitude—it's not for amateurs. From St.-Dalmas-de-Tende, take the D91 to Lac des Meshes, then proceed on foot or by 4WD vehicle approved by the

---

EXPERIENCE:
Skiing the Southern Alps

Blessed with snow-glistening, sky-high mountain peaks and a Provençal blue sky, the Alpes de Haute-Provence boast 447 miles (720 km) of ski trails in nine Alpine resorts just beyond Mercantour's borders. Conditions are typically snowy and sunny, making this an ideal place to strap on some skis and join *les Français* in a swoosh down the slopes. Favorite *stations de ski* include **Allos** (valdallos.com), south of Barcelonnette; **St.-Dalmas-le-Selvage** (saintdalmasleselvage.com) and **Auron** (winter.auron.com), near St.-Étienne-de-Tinée; **Valberg** (valberg.com), near Péone; and, perhaps the most famous, snuggled up against the Italian border, **Isola 2000** (winter.isola2000.com). Visit the Alps-Provence website for additional information: *tourism-alps-provence.com.*

national park. You can also access it from Madone de Fenestre, in the Vallée de la Vésubie to the west. Mountain shelters are available for overnight stays. The less adventurous can take a guided walk, arranged through Merveilles Gravures et Découvertes *(10 montée des Fleurs, Tende, tel 06 86 03 90 13, vallee-merveilles.com);* half-day and full-day tours leave regularly June to September. There are also 4WD tours.

Vallée de la Vésubie

The Vésubie Valley, accessed via the D2565 north of Nice, weaves in and out of park boundaries. Less wild than its counterparts, the green valley still has its share of heart-stopping views. Its main outdoor base is the medieval village of **St.-Martin-Vésubie,** where you can hike in summer and ski in winter. Don't miss the view out onto the valley from place de la Frairie, behind the church.

Vallée de la Tinée

In winter, Niçois head to the slopes of Isola 2000 via the narrow D2205, through the heart of the Tinée Valley. Isola village, 11 miles (18 km) from the slopes, is charmingly medieval, with cobbled streets and the chapel of Ste.-Anne. Northwest of Isola village, St.-Étienne-de-Tinée offers ample summertime walking adventures around the 9,383-foot (2,860 m) **Cime de la Bonette.**

Vallée de l'Ubaye

Seven mountain passes link the Ubaye Valley to the outside world,

The Couvent des Franciscans' church choir, Saorge

including Col de la Bonette, one of Europe's highest passes, at 8,900 feet (2,715 m). Barcelonnette is this remote valley's only town, founded by the count of Barcelona in 1231. Some 5,000 Barcelonnette residents followed the lead of the Arnaud brothers, who emigrated in 1821 to Mexico and established a textile empire. In time, some returned home, building Mexican-style villas and farmhouses. This curious history is retold at the **Musée de la Vallée** *(10 av. de la Libération, tel 04 92 81 27 15, closed Sun.–Mon. & a.m. Sept.–June, & mid-Nov.–mid-Dec., $).* ∎

Tende
⛰ 187 F3
✉ 1 place du Général de Gaulle
☎ 04 93 04 73 71

tendemerveilles.com

St.-Martin-Vésubie
⛰ 187 E3
✉ Place du Général de Gaulle
☎ 04 93 03 21 28

saintmartin vesubie.fr

Gorges du Verdon

At first glance, the River Verdon's unearthly light jade color takes your breath away. Its name—meaning "gift of green"—couldn't be more apt. Vertiginous limestone cliffs loom high above, some more than 2,300 feet tall (700 m)—the ensemble creating Europe's wild Grand Canyon. This natural paradise, located within an hour of the Côte d'Azur, is among France's unsung secrets, perhaps because the only way in—and out—is along one of France's scariest roads. Sporting types will love the outdoor opportunities.

Europe's largest canyon does not disappoint, with plunging limestone walls, vertiginous views (especially along the Route des Crêtes, seen here), and a plethora of outdoor adventures.

Parc Naturel Régional du Verdon

🗺 186 B1–B2, C1–C2

✉ BP 14, Domaine de Valx, Moustiers-Ste.-Marie

✉ 04 92 74 68 00

parcduverdon.fr

A Bit of Background

The canyon provided a refuge as far back as the Paleolithic period, when people were living in caves near Quinson. In the second century B.C., Ligurians hid out here from Romans. In the fifth century, monks lived in the canyon's caves as hermits. More recently, the only humans who knew the deepest gorges were 19th-century woodcutters, who rappelled down cliffs looking for boxwood stumps for *boules*. French explorer Edouard Martel (1859–1938) was the first to penetrate the canyon's length, during a three-day expedition in 1905. His group braved torrents, navigated chaotic rocks—and not one member could

Adventure Checklist

Aquatic Hiking (*randonée aquatique*) This adventure trek can include sliding down waterfalls and paddling through rapids.

Bungee Jumping (*saut en élastique*) The most popular spot is the Pont de l'Artuby, 600 feet (182 m) above the water, considered one of Europe's best drops.

Canyoning Guides take you hiking, climbing, and rappelling down ravines.

Climbing (*escalade*) More than 900 climbing routes have been classified on the Verdon cliffs. The most famous, Falaise de l'Escales (Stopover Cliff), is 1,000 vertical feet high (300 m).

Hiking (*randonée*) You can walk most of the canyon's length on the difficult GR4. There are two must-do hikes for serious hikers: the 9-mile (14 km) Martel Trail,

which roughly follows Martel's 1905 route into the gorge; and the 3.4-mile (5.5 km) Imbut Trail, which ends at the Imbut, where the River Verdon disappears into rocks.

White-Water Rafting The trip through the 18.6-mile-long (30 km) canyon drops several hundred yards down between rock walls—passing through impressively named rapids, such as Niagara and Cyclops. This trip—passing through Class III and IV rapids—is for experienced boaters only, or those on a guided trip.

Other Activities Horseback riding, trout fishing, hang gliding, kayaking, canoeing, parasailing, hot-air ballooning.

Information Ask at regional outfitters, or visit ProvenceWeb (*provenceweb.fr*).

INSIDER TIP:

The Artuby Bridge is the tallest bridge in Europe. The greatest thrill? A bungee jump from it!

—CHRISTEL CHERQAOUI
National Geographic Books

swim! A plaque commemorates their accomplishment at **Point Sublime,** on the Rive Droite. Only with the construction of the Corniche Sublime in 1948 could the gorge be reached by car. The entity was made a *parc naturel régional* in 1977.

Visiting

The canyon's most impressive section zigzags 13 miles (21 km) between **Moustiers-Ste.-Marie**

(see p. 196) and **Castellane.** Both towns are good bases, with Castellane being a camper's haven, and pretty Moustiers, famous for its faïence, catering more to the inn crowd. Both towns offer a choice of outfitters—you will definitely want to get out to hike or take advantage of the gorge's other outdoor activities. See pages 194–195 for a driving tour around the gorge.

One place that history lovers will not want to miss is the fabulous **Musée de Préhistoire des Gorges du Verdon.** State-of-the-art information terminals and computer-generated images shed light on how early humans lived, while a prehistoric village has been re-created. The museum offers guided tours of the nearby **Grotte de la Baume Bonne,** a major prehistoric site. ∎

Castellane

🅰 186 C2

Visitor Information

✉ Office de Tourisme, rue Nationale

☎ 04 92 83 61 14

castellane.org

Musée de Préhistoire des Gorges du Verdon

🅰 186 B1

✉ Rte. de Montmeyan, Quinson

☎ 04 92 74 09 59

🕐 Closed mid-Dec.–Jan.

💲 $$

museeprehistoire .com

Driving the Gorges du Verdon

This circuit around the canyon begins in Moustiers-Ste.-Marie and proceeds along the Rive Droite, highlighting the spectacular Route des Crêtes. You can detour to (or overnight in) Castellane before returning along the Rive Gauche, fittingly called the Corniche Sublime. Lookout points *(belvédères)* along the way provide the perfect opportunities to stop and admire the endless views.

Rive Droite (North)

From the pretty town of **Moustiers-Ste.-Marie ❶** (see p. 196), follow the D952 toward the Rive Droite. On this tiny, twisty road high above the gorge, generally lacking guard rails, you climb past views of far-off Lac de Ste.-Croix, then descend on the edge of a cliff, with the raft-filled **River Verdon** far below.

The road makes a hairpin turn at **Belvédère de Mayreste ❷**, where, if you scramble 500 feet (150 m) up the rocks, you get your first overall view of the canyon. Farther along, the road climbs past the **Relais des Gorges,** a snack bar. Beyond, the landscape flattens into a plateau, wide enough for fields of lavender, and then you descend to **La Palud-sur-Verdon ❸**, one of the canyon's major activities hubs.

Just out of town is where you pick up the D23—the **Route des Crêtes ❹**. The dizzyingly high, 14-mile (23 km) road follows the plateau's edge, where sometimes only empty space exists between you and the valley floor, 2,300 feet (700 m) below. Keep an eye out for raptors soaring on thermals beneath you. Wild goats may also be spotted. A little more than midway along the Route des Crêtes, the **Refuge des Malines** offers snacks and drinks overlooking one of the canyon's most sublime views (no bathroom, though). The trailhead for the popular **Sentier Martel** is found here. Back in the car, you are treated to a couple more gorge views before turning back toward town.

Back at La Palud, turn right on the D952 (ignoring the Route des Crêtes sign this time) and proceed through woods, past valley views and wildflower fields, snaking down to **Point Sublime ❺**. Park at the designated lot and

---

NOT TO BE MISSED:

Route des Crêtes • Point Sublime • Tunnel de Fayet

---

walk up the hill, following the blue blazes, to the grand view of **Couloir Samson**—the entrance to the Grand Canyon.

Beyond the tunnel, the road slips into the narrow **Clue de Carejuan** and from there you have a choice—continue on the D952 to Castellane or cross over the Pont de Soleils to begin the drive along the Rive Gauche.

Rive Gauche (South)

The D955 takes you through tiny Soleils, beyond which you see Trigance's crenelated castle topping a hill. Turn right on the D90, which winds to medieval **Trigance ❻**—pleasant enough with a couple of restaurants. The castle is home to a gourmet restaurant *(tel 04 94 76 91 18)*.

Beyond, the road climbs through fields and woods, with far-off mountain views. At the D71, turn right toward Aiguines. The road descends, and you come to the **Balcons de la Mescla ❼**. A short path leads to an overview of where the Artuby and Verdon Rivers meet. Just down the road, more views await, as well as a snack bar-restaurant.

The road then winds down to **Pont de l'Artuby** (Artuby Bridge), 600 feet (180 m) above the river. The bridge is Europe's highest, a popular spot for bungee jumpers. Beyond, you are on the gorge's edge, with pullouts from which to safely admire the views. Climbing a bit,

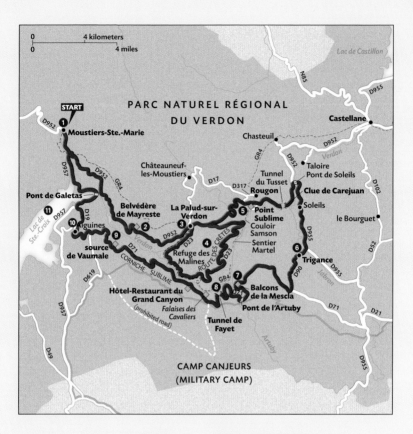

0   4 kilometers
0   4 miles

PARC NATUREL RÉGIONAL
DU VERDON

Lac de Castillon

START ❶
Moustiers-Ste.-Marie

Castellane

Chasteuil

Châteauneuf-
les-Moustiers

Tunnel
du Tusset

Taloire
Pont de Soleils

Rougon

Clue de Carejuan

Pont de Galetas

Belvédère
de Mayreste

La Palud-sur-
Verdon

❺ Point
Sublime

Soleils

le Bourguet

❶❶

Aiguines ❷ ❸

Couloir
Samson

❿

❾

❹

Sentier
Martel

❻ Trigance

source
de Vaumale

Refuge des
Malines

❼

Hôtel-Restaurant du
Grand Canyon

❽

Balcons
de la Mescla

Falaises des
Cavaliers

Pont de l'Artuby

(prohibited road)

Tunnel de
Fayet

CAMP CANJEURS
(MILITARY CAMP)

you come to the **Tunnel de Fayet** ❽; pull over at its exit for a magnificent view of the Verdon 1,000 feet (300 m) below.

Moving away from the gorge, the road follows **Falaises des Cavaliers**, bringing you to the **Hôtel-Restaurant du Grand Canyon** (tel 04 94 76 91 31), a concrete concoction with vistas from its terrace. Behind the hotel, the Rive Gauche footpath begins its journey to the bottom of the gorge.

The road closely traces the canyon, with pullouts offering chances to stop. Fill your water bottles with cool, sweet water at the **source de Vaumale** ❾ (Vaumale spring), then proceed to the road's highest point—more than 2,625 feet (800 m) above the Verdon. Far away lie the turquoise waters of Lac de Ste.-Croix, one of the artificial lakes created by dams.

▲ See area map p. 186
▶ Moustiers-Ste.-Marie
🕐 A full day
↔ 50 miles (80 km)
▶ Moustiers-Ste.-Marie

From here, the road twists down to **Aiguines** ❿, a pleasant town with a centuries-old legacy of "turning boxwood" to make *boules* (lawn-bowling balls).

Beyond town you enter the watery wonderland of **Lac de Ste.-Croix** ⓫, where all kinds of water-sports equipment can be rented. Take a dip before taking the quick jaunt back to Moustiers via the D957—with one last stop: the **Pont de Galetas,** where you can stand on the bridge and watch the lake spilling into the river.

Moustiers-Ste.-Marie

Moustiers is known far and wide for finely painted, tin-glazed ceramics, or faïence. Every historical museum in Provence boasts some sample from Moustiers's heyday, between 1689 and the late 19th century. In the age-old tradition, more than 20 *poteries* flourish here once again, selling their wares in tiny boutiques on oft-crowded lanes. Nonetheless, Moustiers remains one of Provence's most picturesque villages, with its red-roofed buildings clutching a steep hillside beneath two towering cliffs, a gold star strung between.

Market Day
Fri.

Moustiers-Ste.-Marie
🅰 186 C2

Visitor Information
✉ Office de Tourisme, place de l'Église
☎ 04 92 74 67 84

moustiers.eu

No one knows for sure who hung the star, which dangles directly above the Romanesque **Chapelle Notre-Dame-de-Beauvoir,** the little church tucked hard among the rocks above the village. Legend describes it this way: During the Crusades, the knight Blacas d'Aups was taken prisoner in the Holy Land. He vowed that if he returned safely to his hometown, he would suspend a chain bearing a star between the two cliffs

overhanging his village. Ever since, the star has been replaced when it falls. In the Middle Ages, pilgrims flocked to the church following an increase of miracles taking place here. A steep, winding path leads from rue Bourgade to the church, with 14 Stations of the Cross along the way.

Back in the center of town, Moustiers is a fine place to stroll, its tiny, pedestrian-only lanes lined with old taupe buildings and tiny, flowery squares. Water runs in abundance through numerous fountains and basins, and a rushing mountain stream drops right through the heart of it all. With 30-odd shops selling faïence, you will quickly become an expert—some are obviously better quality than others. Most of the shops make their own pottery, in workshops outside town.

A stop at the small **Musée de la Faïence** *(rte. du Seigneur de la Clue, tel 04 92 74 61 64, closed Tues., Jan., & a.m. Sat.–Sun., $)* provides a good overview. A video (in French) explains the process of faïence making, and display cases show some of the city's finest historical pieces.

Moustiers also serves as an outfitting base for the Gorges du Verdon (see pp. 192–195). ∎

Moustiers' Famous Faïence

In 1668 a monk from Faenza shared the secret of porcelain glazing with Pierre Clérissy of Moustiers. As the economy suffered during the Spanish Wars of Secession, Louis XIV encouraged nobility to melt down their gold and silver to help finance the war and to use Moustiers faïence—entire suites of pitchers, plates, saucers, cups—instead. The town's earthenware industry was never the same again. At first, blue and pale cream were used in designs depicting hunting and biblical scenes. The 18th century saw more detailed scenes, followed by a period of grotesque figures, clowns, and birds. Along the way, new colors were introduced: red, orange, purple, green, yellow. With the hardships of the revolution and exhaustion of local clay quarries, alas, the last oven went cold in 1874. Thankfully, Marcel Provence reestablished a kiln in 1927, heralding the arrival of Moustiers' modern porcelain era.

Plateau de Valensole

The plateau de Valensole is legendary for its fields and fields of summertime-blooming lavender. A cluster of unspoiled historic villages make visiting this region a delight.

Lavender potpourri, grown on the plateau de Valensole

Valensole is the plateau's main city, built on a site previously occupied by Romans. Stroll the medieval streets around the **Église St.-Blaise.**

In **Riez,** an old lavender-distilling center to the south, you'll find a typical Provençal town through medieval gates, with vaulted passages and tiny streets. Among its fine buildings, **Hôtel de Mazan** (*12 rue Grande*) dates from the Renaissance. In a field on the town's southern outskirts, four granite columns are believed to have been part of a first-century A.D. temple of Apollo. Opposite, you'll spot one of the oldest baptisteries in France, from the sixth century; a small museum of archaeological finds is inside.

Nearby **Allemagne-en-Provence** has a Renaissance château (*tel 04 92 77 46 78, closed Nov.–March, $$*), begun in the late 12th century; tours and *chambres d'hôtes* are offered. The town's name dates back to the Wars of Religion, when

the baron of Germany besieged the place.

The genteel spa town of **Digne-les-Bains** offers pleasant cafés along shady boulevard Gassendi. Don't miss the **Cathédrale Notre-Dame-du-Bourg** (*rue du Prévôt*), dating from the 12th and 13th centuries; faint fresco fragments from the 14th and 15th centuries still adorn its walls. World traveler Alexandra David-Néel began her explorations in 1883 at the age of 15 and rarely let up. Having spent much of her life in East Asia, she settled in Digne, at her "Samten Dzong," or "Castle of Meditation," just south of town. It's now the **Musée Alexandra David-Néel** (*27 av. Maréchal Juin, tel 04 92 31 32 38, alexandra-david-neel.com*), filled with exhibits on Tibetan art and culture.

To learn more about exploring the region's lavender fields, see pages 60–61 and sidebar page 198. ∎

Valensole

🗺 186 B2

Visitor Information

✉ Office de Tourisme, place Héros de la Résistance

☎ 04 92 74 90 02

valensole.fr

Riez

🗺 186 B2

Visitor Information

✉ Office de Tourisme, place de la Mairie

☎ 04 92 77 99 09

ville-riez.fr

Allemagne-en-Provence

🗺 186 B2

Visitor Information

✉ Office de Tourisme, place de Verdun

☎ 04 92 77 43 10

Digne-les-Bains

🗺 186 C3

Visitor Information

✉ Office de Tourisme, place du Tampinet

☎ 04 92 36 62 62

ot-dignelesbains.fr

More Places to Visit in the Alpes Provençales

Entrevaux

Full of charm with its drawbridge entrance, tall and narrow houses, and tiny squares, Entrevaux has a few shops and restaurants without being touristy. At the behest of King Louis XIV, Vauban (see sidebar p. 152) fortified the town in the 17th century as part of the defensive line blocking the Alpine pass to defend France from the Savoy (Italy). A serpentine climb up ramps and through fortified doorways brings you high above town to his pinnacle-top **citadel** (*$*); its ghostly ruins are in a slow state of restoration. 🅰 186 D2 **Visitor Information** *entrevaux.info* ✉ Office de Tourisme, Porte Royale ☎ 04 93 05 46 73

Gréoux-les-Bains

Celebrated since Roman days for the curative power of its waters, this affluent spa town is best known for the rather clinical **Thermes de Gréoux-les-Bains** (*rue Eaux Chaudes, tel 08 26 46 81 85, closed Sun. & Jan.–Feb., chainethermale.fr/greoux-les-bains.html*). More than a million gallons (4 million L) of

Lavender Festivals

Games, competitions, music, floats, and food, all having to do with lavender, celebrate the height of the lavender bloom. These are some of the season's best festivals throughout Provence:

- **Digne-les-Bains:** beginning of Aug., *ot-dignelesbains.fr*
- **Esparron-sur-Verdon:** mid-Aug., *esparrondeverdon.com*
- **Ferrassières:** end of June, *saultenprovence.com*
- **Riez:** second half of July, *tourism-alps-provence.com*
- **Sault:** mid-Aug., *saultenprovence.com*
- **Valensole:** end of July, *valensole.fr*
- **Valréas:** beginning of Aug., *ot-valreas.fr*

bubbling sulfurous water a day fill its white marble baths, enjoyed by the rheumatic, arthritic, and other sufferers. Shop-lined **rue Grande** crosses the old town, along which you'll find the **Maison de Pauline** (*47 rue Grande, closed weekends, $*), an 1827 house furnished in 19th-century Provençal style. Overlooking the town is a 12th-century **Templar castle,** which you can visit by guided tour (*ask at the tourism office*). 🅰 186 B2 **Visitor Information** *greoux-les-bains.com* ✉ Office de Tourisme, 5 av. des Maronniers ☎ 04 92 78 01 08

Manosque

Housing developments and industrial parks are your first impressions of this bustling city. Its town center, however, remains picturesque. **Rue Grande** is the main shopping street, along which, at No. 14, a plaque marks the house where Provençal writer Jean Giono (1895–1970) was born. At No. 21 is a branch of **L'Occitane,** the Manosque-based purveyor of Provence-inspired cosmetics. 🅰 186 B2 **Visitor Information** *ville-manosque.fr* ✉ Office de Tourisme, place du Dr. Joubert ☎ 04 92 72 16 00

Sospel

The mountain gateway to the Roya Valley, this sleepy Alpine town straddles the River Bévéra. You can't miss the 11th-century **Pont Vieux** (Old Bridge). Its tiny tower was a tollhouse on the medieval salt road between the coast and Italy; today it holds temporary art exhibitions. On place St.-Michel rises **Église St.-Michel,** the epitome of baroque frothiness. Inside, the pride of place is the magnificent 16th-century retable by François Bréa, "Immaculate Virgin." 🅰 187 E2 **Visitor Information** *sospel-tourisme.com* ✉ Office de Tourisme, 19 av. Jean Médecin ☎ 04 93 04 15 80

Travelwise

Traditional transport

TRAVELWISE

PLANNING YOUR TRIP

When to Go

See sidebar p. 10 and Major Events, pp. 202–203.

What to Take

You should be able to buy anything you need in France. Pharmacies offer a wide range of drugs, medical supplies, and toiletries, along with expert advice, but you should bring any prescription drugs you might need. If you wear them, a second pair of glasses or contact lenses is a good idea (and a legal requirement if you plan to drive). Sunscreen and anti-mosquito products are advisable in summer. A warm sweater is useful early and late summer evenings. In the mountains bring a light, waterproof garment. If you're headed to the Camargue, bring binoculars and lots of mosquito repellent. Lastly, don't forget the essentials: passport, driver's license, ATM card (and/or traveler's checks), and insurance documentation.

Insurance

Make sure you have adequate coverage for medical treatment and expenses including repatriation, and baggage and money loss.

Passports

U.S. and Canadian citizens need only a passport to enter France for up to 90 days' stay. No visa is required. Nationals of the European Union have no entry requirement; a national ID is sufficient.

HOW TO GET TO PROVENCE

By Plane

All the major airlines have direct flights to Paris, including American, Delta, United, and Air France. Delta, Aer Lingus, and Air France fly direct to Nice from New York, though it's often cheaper to fly to Paris and then catch a cheap internal flight or take the TGV train south.

Major Airports

Aéroport Marseille–Provence
Tel 08 20 81 14 14
marseille-aeroport.com
Located 15.5 miles (25 km) northwest of Marseille, the airport offers 30 daily flights to Paris, with a travel time of 65 minutes. Direct flights to 60 destinations.
Airport shuttle bus service:
Tel 04 42 14 31 27
navettemarseilleaeroport.com
• To and from Marseille's Gare St.-Charles: shuttle every 20 minutes; travel time 25 minutes. Depart from Platform 2. €8.20.
• To and from Aix-en-Provence: shuttle every 30 minutes; travel time 30 minutes. Depart from Platform 1. €8.20.

Aéroport Nice–Côte d'Azur
Tel 08 20 12 33 33
nice.aeroport.fr
Located 3.7 miles (6 km) west of Nice.

Airlines in France

Air France *airfrance.com*
American Airlines *aa.com*
Delta *delta.com*
EasyJet *easyjet.com*
Ryanair *ryanair.com*
United *united.com*

By Train

The French national railroad, the SNCF (Société Nationale des Chemins de Fer), links Paris and all major cities. There are numerous daily train connections between Paris and Provence via the TGV, with a travel time of 3 hours between the Gare de Lyon and Marseille (see below). You can buy train tickets in advance from your travel agent or SNCF office, at a station or travel agency (*agence de voyage*) in France, or online (*sncf.com*).

Ticket Information

If you buy your train ticket in France, you must punch it at the time-stamping machine (*composteur*) at the platform entrance, before you begin the journey. Once stamped, a ticket is valid for 24 hours. An unstamped ticket is not valid (and can result in an on-the-spot fine).

North Americans have a wide choice of passes, including Eurailpass, Flexipass, and Saver Pass, which can only be purchased in the U.S. (information and reservations: 888-382-7245, *raileurope .com*). Discounts are available for students and senior citizens with a student card or passport.

SNCF Information

Tel 36 35 (in France only), *sncf.fr*

TGV (Train à Grande Vitesse): The Paris–Méditerranée train will whisk you to Marseille in three hours, with stops (depending on the train) at Avignon and Aix-en-Provence. There are separate schedules from Paris–Charles de Gaulle airport and Paris–Gare de Lyon. Information: tel 36 35. You can reserve your seats and buy tickets directly from the SNCF website (*sncf.fr*), or purchase them at train stations in larger towns. Reservations are required.

Provence's TGV Stations

Avignon TGV Located at the town's southern edge, between ring-road and Durance River, 2 miles (3 km) from town center. A train shuttle to Avignon Central Station, running 35 times a day, takes six minutes and can be included in your train ticket upon purchase.

Aix-en-Provence TGV The train station is about 6 miles (10 km) west of town, with *navettes* providing direct links to Aix and Marseille. There are also other buses, taxis, and easy access to the A8 autoroute.

Marseille TGV The train station is at the Gare St.-Charles, in the center of town. Buses and taxis can transport you elsewhere, and a navette will take you to the Marseille–Provence airport.

GETTING AROUND PROVENCE

By Train

The major cities of Provence and the Côte d'Azur are linked by excellent rail services (see inside back cover map). Nice is the major rail hub along the Côte d'Azur, and Cannes and Monaco are linked by frequent service.

By Bus

To get off the tourist path without a car, your best bet is the frequent bus service that links smaller towns and villages. Buses run most frequently Monday to Saturday; there are very few buses on Sunday. Visit *pacamobilite.fr* for local bus information.

By Car

Provence has a good network of roads, from small and often picturesque D roads to autoroutes, often called *péages*, because a toll (*péage*) must be paid. Occasionally you pay a fixed fee upon entering a section of autoroute; more often you are given a ticket as you enter, and you pay as you leave according to the distance traveled. Credit cards are accepted in the pay booths. The autoroutes may only be two lanes in each direction, but are the quickest routes.

There are gas stations with 24-hour service approximately every 12 miles (20 km), but there are also, more frequently, well-designed parking and picnic places (called *Aires*). The main *routes nationales* between towns and cities (N on maps) are generally in excellent condition. Many are two-lane for at least part of their length.

Renting a Car

Renting a car in France is expensive. Arrange a car rental with your local travel agent or online before leaving home; it can be much cheaper. Otherwise there are desks in airports and major railroad stations in France. There are fly-drive options with most flights, and the SNCF offers a train-car rental package.

To rent a car in France you must have a current driver's license (held for at least three years) and be at least 21 years old. Some companies will not rent to people under 26 or over 60. Make sure you have information about what to do in case of an accident or breakdown; telephone numbers in case of emergencies; and the procedure to follow. You must carry the relevant car documents with you, and some identification. It is recommended that you purchase the collision-damage waiver, which costs extra per day, but, in the case of accidental damage to the car, your responsibility will be a few hundred euros at most. Your credit card company may also cover you. Automatic transmission and air-conditioning are luxuries in Europe and come at a price.

Central Offices

The largest rental agencies are located at the Marseille–Provence airport.

ADA *ada.fr*
Avis *avis.com*
Europcar *europcar.com*
Hertz (at Marseille *gare*) *hertz.com*
Rent-a-Car *rentacar.com*

Driving Information

Accidents See p. 206.

Age limits and licenses The minimum age limit for driving in France is 18 years (21 if you are renting a car). Visitors from North America and the U.K. do not need an international driver's license but must carry their home driver's license.

Breakdown assistance Autoroutes and routes nationales have emergency telephones every mile (2 km). Police stations (*gendarmeries*) can give information about breakdown services or garages— call them at 17.

Busy periods French roads will be busy from the beginning of July, when school vacations begin, and at their worst around August 15, a major national holiday. Special routes attempt to relieve summer traffic congestion; watch for the small green BIS (Bison Futé) signs that indicate these alternative routes. A brochure in English on the Bison Futé routes is available from French government tourist offices.

Children Children under ten must travel in the rear seat.

Distances All distances on signposts in France are shown in kilometers (1 km = 0.6 mile).

Drunk driving The French drunk-driving limit is 50 mg alcohol per 100 mL of blood. This can mean that as little as one glass of beer can take you up to the limit.

Gas Gas is expensive. Sold by the liter (there are 3.75 L to an American gallon), you'll need either leaded *(avec plomb)* or unleaded *(sans plomb)*. Most gas stations accept credit cards.

Headlights All vehicles must carry a spare set of lightbulbs.

On-the-spot fines On-the-spot fines may be levied by police for several offenses, including speeding, not wearing seat belts, and not having the car's documentation with you.

Parking Some French towns and cities have blue zones where parking is free for up to an hour. You need to display a parking disk *(disque de stationnement)*, which you obtain from garages, *tabacs*, and tourist offices. Otherwise most towns have on-street parking machines *(horodateurs)* from which you buy a ticket to display in your car. Coins required vary from 20 cents to €2. Multistory parking garages are common; check closing times: Some close overnight and may shut by 8 p.m.

Priorité à droite Traditionally, priority on French roads was given to vehicles approaching from the right, except where otherwise indicated. Nowadays, on main roads, the major road will normally have priority, with traffic being halted on minor approach roads with one of the following signs:

- *Cedez le passage:* yield
- *Vous n'avez pas la priorité:* you do not have right of way
- *Passage protégé:* no right of way

A yellow diamond sign indicates that you have priority; the diamond sign with a diagonal black line indicates that you do not have priority.

Take care in small towns and rural areas without road markings where you may be expected to yield to traffic coming from the right—especially farm vehicles. If oncoming drivers flash their headlights, it is to indicate that they have priority, not the other way around. Priority is always given to emergency and public utility vehicles.

Road conditions For information about current road conditions, telephone the Inter Service Route line or tune into the local radio frequency (often indicated on signs beside roads). Autoroutes information, tel 08 92 68 10 77, *autoroutes.fr.*

Road signs

- *Access interdit:* no entry
- *Allumez vos feux:* switch on lights
- *Interdiction de stationner:* no parking
- *Passage pour piétons:* pedestrian crossing
- *Rappel* (remember): reminder of a previous restriction
- *Ralentissez:* slow down
- *Sens unique:* one-way traffic
- *Virages sur ... km:* curves for ... km
- *Zone bleue:* parking disk required

Seat belts The wearing of seat belts is mandatory in both the front and rear seats.

Speed limits There are different speed limits for normal weather and times of poor visibility (heavy rain or fog).

- Autoroutes have limits of 75–85 miles (110–130 km) an hour; slower limit applies in poor visibility. Two-lane roads: 60–75 miles (90–110 km) an hour
- Other open roads: 50–55 miles (80–90 km) an hour
- Towns (from entry name sign to exit name sign): 30 miles (50 km) an hour

Traffic circles Vehicles already on a traffic circle have priority, except very occasionally in small towns where priorité à droite still applies.

Traffic lights These are sometimes suspended high over the road and can easily be missed.

MAJOR EVENTS

Festivities in the south of France are far too numerous to list in their entirety. What follows is a selection of the largest and most well-known events throughout the region. Ask at the local tourist office or check websites to confirm dates and find information on some of the more obscure events that are set to take place.

January

Festival International du Cirque de Monte-Carlo (Éspace Fontvieille, Monaco; *Office de Tourisme: tel 377 92 05 23 45, www.montecarlofestival.mc*) International circus artists compete.

February

Le Chandeleur (2, Basilique St.-Victor, Marseille; *tel 04 96 11 22 60, saintvictor.net*) Candlelit procession behind black virgin of Basilique St.-Victor.

Le Corso Fleuri (3rd Sun., Bormes-les-Mimosas; *Office de Tourisme: tel 04 94 01 38 38, bormeslesmimosas .com*) Flower-adorned floats parade through town.

Menton Lemon Festival (3 weeks in Feb.; *tel 04 92 41 76 76, menton .fr*) Lemon-decorated floats, lemon-decorated gardens, and more, all related to lemons.

Carnaval de Nice (month before Lent, Nice; *tel 892 707 407, nicecarnaval.com*) Floats, fireworks, and performers in the region's most celebrated festival.

April

Féria Pascale (Easter Sat.–Mon., Les Arènes, Arles; *tel 91 70 03 70, arenes-arles.com*) Course Camarguaise and Spanish bullfights.

May

Fête des Gardians (1, Arles; *Office de Tourisme: tel 04 90 18 41 20, arlestourisme.com*) Camargue cowboys parade in the streets of the city and show in the arena.

Féria de Pentecôte (Pentecost weekend, Les Arènes, Nîmes; *tel 04 66 21 82 56, arenesdenimes.com*) Bullfighting, music, and art.

Fête de la Transhumance (Pentecost Mon., St.-Rémy-de-Provence) Traditional festival in which shepherds herd sheep to greener pastures.

Grand Prix de Monaco (Ascension weekend; *tel 377 97 70 74 75, acm.mc;* see sidebar p. 178) Formula One racing cars speed around Monte-Carlo's narrow streets.

Cannes Film Festival (2nd week; *www.festival-cannes.fr*) Annual international film festival.

La Bravade (mid-May, St.-Tropez; *Office de Tourisme: tel 08 92 68 48 28, sainttropeztourisme.com*) Celebration of the arrival of headless Christian martyr Torpes (Tropez) in A.D. 68.

Pélerinage de Mai (24–25; Les Stes.-Maries-de-la-Mer; *tel 04 90 97 82 55, saintesmaries .com*) Gypsies from all over come to honor Sara, their patron saint.

June

Fête de la Musique (21; *fetedela musique.culture.fr*) Celebration of music throughout France on the summer solstice.

Les Baroquiales (end June–early July; *tel 04 93 04 45 80*) Baroque music in Alpine valley churches.

July

Festival d'Avignon (3 weeks in July, Avignon; *tel 04 90 27 66 50, festival-avignon.com*) Famous theater festival.

Festival Piano (mid-July–mid-Aug., La Roque d'Anthéron; *tel 04 42 50 51 15, festival-piano.com*) Classical piano under the stars.

Jazz à Juan (2 weeks in July; *tel 04 22 10 60 10, antibesjuanlespins .com*) Legendary jazz festival.

Nice Jazz Festival (2 weeks in July, Place Masséna, Nice; *nicejazzfestival.fr*) One of world's most prestigious jazz festivals, held annually since 1948, now centering on place Masséna.

Bastille Day (14, throughout France) French national holiday, with balls and fireworks.

Festival de la Sorgue (L'Isle-sur-la-Sorgue; *Office de Tourisme: tel 04 90 38 04 78, oti-delasorgue .fr*) Folklore, street theater, and a floating market.

Les Chorégies d'Orange (July–Aug., Théâtre Antique & other venues; *tel 04 90 34 24 24, choregies.fr*) Lyric opera in ancient amphitheater.

Festival International d'Art Lyrique (Aix-en-Provence; *tel 04 34 08 02 17, festival-aix.com*) Basic opera with a modern twist.

August

La Féria Provençale (mid-Aug., St.-Rémy-de-Provence; *Office de Tourisme: tel 04 90 92 05 22, saint-remy-de-provence.com*) Three days of bull races.

Festival de Musique (Aug., parvis St.-Michel, Menton; *tel 04 92 41 76 76, menton.fr*) Concerts in ancient church square.

October

Fiesta des Suds (last 3 weeks, Marseille; *dock-des-suds.org*) Marseille's world and contemporary music festival.

December

La Pastorale (Dec.–Jan., throughout Provence) Theatrical announcement to shepherds of Christ's birth.

Fêtes de la Lumière à St.-Raphaël (2 weeks in Dec., St.-Raphaël; *Office de Tourisme: tel 04 94 19 52 52, saint-raphael-lumieres.com*)

PRACTICAL ADVICE

COMMUNICATIONS

Post Offices

La Poste is open from 9 a.m. to 6 p.m. on weekdays and from 9 a.m. to noon on Saturdays (in smaller towns offices will close for lunch and in villages may only be open for two or three hours on weekday mornings). Mail can be delivered to you at a post office if it is marked "Poste Restante" and with the postal code of the Bureau de Poste at which you collect it. The postal code is essential. You will have to pay a fee for each item of mail.

Mailboxes Yellow *boîtes postales* (mailboxes) are located outside every post office and on walls in larger towns. They may have separate compartments for local mail, *départemental* (mail within the département), and *autres départements/déstinations* (elsewhere in France and foreign).

Telephones

Telephone numbers have ten digits usually written into pairs, for example 04 23 45 67 89.

Numbers in Provence begin with 04.

To call a French number (for example, 04 23 45 67 89) from abroad, dial the international code (011 from U.S. and Canada, 00 from U. K.), then the code for France (33), followed by the number, omitting the first 0:

011 33 4 23 45 67 89.

To call Monaco, the international prefix 00 377 (011 377 from U.S. and Canada) must be dialed, followed by the 8-digit number.

Phone booths *Cabines téléphoniques* stand outside larger post offices, in railroad stations and airports, and near roads and parking garages in towns and villages (though there are fewer and fewer of them). They take either phone cards or credit cards and occasionally money. Phone cards (*télécartes*) can be bought at any tobacconist (*bureau de tabac*).

Making a call Follow the instructions that will appear on the telephone's screen: *décrochez* (pick up the receiver); *inserrez votre carte* (insert your card or coin); *patientez* (wait); *numérotez* (dial the number); *raccrochez* (hang up).

International calls To make an international call from France, dial 00 followed by the country's international code. These can be found in the front of the Pages Jaunes section of the *annuaire* or posted in a telephone booth. Some useful ones are: Australia 61; Canada 1; Ireland 353; U.K. 44; U.S. 1.

For operator services dial 12. For international directory assistance, dial 32 12, followed by the country code.

To dial toll-free numbers (*numéros verts),* insert a card or money to make the connection (coins will be returned, units will not be registered against cards). Reduced rate calls in France and Europe: 7 p.m.–8 a.m. weekdays, noon Sat.–8 a.m. Mon. For calls to the U.S. and Canada: 7 p.m.– 1 p.m., Mon.–Fri., and all day Sat. & Sun. Reduced rates also apply on public holidays.

Cell Phones

Many cell phones can be used in France so long as there is network coverage. Don't rely on it in rural or mountainous regions. Making or receiving international calls can be very expensive. Consult your provider before you travel. If you need to make a lot of local calls, consider buying a SIM card from local operators. Or you can use Skype (skype.com) or other web-based service. Viber (viber.com) is also an inexpensive way to converse with folks back home, on any device and network.

Conversions

1 kilogram = 2.2 pounds
1 liter = 0.2642 U.S. gallon
1.6 kilometer = 1 mile

Women's clothing

| American | 8 | 10 | 12 | 14 | 16 | 18 |
| French | 38 | 40 | 42 | 44 | 46 | 48 |

Men's clothing

| American | 36 | 38 | 40 | 42 | 44 | 46 |
| French | 46 | 48 | 50 | 52 | 54 | 56 |

Women's shoes

| American | 6-6.5 | 7-7.5 | 8-8.5 | 9-9.5 |
| French | 38 | 39 | 40-41 | 42 |

Men's shoes

| American | 8 | 8.5 | 9.5 | 10.5 | 11.5 | 12 |
| French | 41 | 42 | 43 | 44 | 45 | 46 |

Electricity

In France, electricity is 220 volts, 50 Hz, and most plugs have two round prongs. If you bring electrical equipment, you will need an adapter, and, for U.S. appliances, a transformer.

Email & Internet

If you bring your own computer, you will need a universal AC adapter, plus an adapter between your telephone plug and the standard T-shape French receptacle.

Wi-Fi is widely available in hotels.

Internet cafés exist in major cities and smaller towns; often, they are simply a computer or two hooked up in a café (or even at McDonald's). Ask at the local tourist office for the nearest location.

Etiquette & Local Customs

Etiquette is very important in France: Always be ready to shake hands when you are introduced, and when you meet friends and acquaintances. Kissing on both cheeks is also very common. When entering any establishment it is polite to offer a general *Bonjour, messieurs/dames.* Remember to use the titles Monsieur and Madame. Young women are addressed as Mademoiselle, a woman in her 20s or older is addressed as Madame. Address a waiter as Monsieur, and call a waitress either Madame or Mademoiselle. Garçon (boy) is not acceptable.

When visiting churches and cathedrals, dress appropriately and respect the sensitivities of those who are there for devotional purposes. Visitors are requested not to walk around religious buildings during services. Even though in most cases no fee is charged to visit a church or cathedral, it is polite to contribute to one of the boxes requesting donations.

Media

English-Language Newspapers
Newspapers and magazines are sold in tabacs and *maisons de la presse,* many of which stock American or British newspapers (often the previous day's edition). International newspapers are available in airports, major railroad stations, and most large hotels.

The main national dailies are *Le Monde,* conservative *Le Figaro,* and left-wing *Libération* and *L'Humanité.* American and British dailies—*International Herald Tribune, The Times,* and *Daily Telegraph*—are widely available in Nice, Marseille, and most coastal resorts.

Regional newspapers contain national and international as well as local news, and are often read more than the national press. *Nice-Matin* is the leading regional daily newspaper; there is also the Toulon-based Var edition called *Var-Matin;* and the *Vaucluse Matin* in the Vaucluse. *La Provence* has local editions for Bouches-du-Rhône, Vaucluse, and Alpes-de-Haute-Provence. *Riviera Reporter* is a good English-language Côte d'Azur magazine.

Radio

National channels are broadcast from Marseille (France Bleu Provence, RFM Provence). Local French-language radio stations include Radio Provence (103.6 MHz and 102.9 MHz FM) and Cannes Radio (91.5 MHz FM). Popular music channels include Nostalgie FM (98.3 MHz FM) and Chérie FM (100.1 MHZ FM). Riviera Radio (106.3 and 106.5 kHz) broadcasts 24 hours a day in English. In some areas, BBC Radio 4 can be received on long wave (198 kHz). Radio Traffic (107.7 MHz FM) broadcasts traffic reports in English, French, and Italian.

TV Channels

French television offers five TV channels: TF1, France 2, France 3, 5 or La Cinquième (in the evening this one becomes Arte, a combined Franco-German transmission), and M6. TF1 occasionally shows undubbed American films with French subtitles, Arte more frequently shows subtitled international films and art programs. Most American films shown on French television are dubbed into French, as are all the American soaps and serials that make up the bulk of French TV. France 3 Région has good shows about Provence. A subscription channel, Canal+, has a monthly program of films, shown at least once in the original language (marked VO—*version original*), as well as sports. The main television news programs are at 1 p.m. and 8 p.m.

Money Matters

The euro is available in 500, 200, 100, 50, 20, 10, and 5 euro notes; 2 and 1 euro coins; and 50, 20, 10, 5, and 1 centime coins.

Most major banks have ATMs outside for bank (ATM) cards and international credit cards with instructions in a choice of languages. You will need a four-digit PIN number: Arrange this with your bank before you leave home. Currency can be exchanged in banks, and Bureaux de Change in train stations and airports. If you're going to use traveler's checks, buy them in euros before you leave home. To cash traveler's checks at the bank have some form of ID (passport) ready. To use a check you will not need a check card, but you may be asked for photo ID.

Visa is the most common credit card accepted. MasterCard (Access/Eurocard) is also widely accepted, while American Express is less popular. Carte Bancaire (CB) is a French card encompassing both Visa and MasterCard.

These days, most European cards are chip cards, embedded with a security chip. The down side of this for Americans is that some ATMs and other automated payment machines reject U.S. cards. This can be a problem on tollways, in parking garages, in subway and train stations, and at self-serve gas pumps. You'll typically find a cashier nearby, and the machines should take cash as well.

National Holidays

All banks, post offices, and many museums, galleries, and stores close on these national holidays:
January 1 (Jour de l'An)
Easter Sunday and Monday
   (Pâcques)
May 1 (Fête du Travail)
May 8 (Victoire 1945)
Ascension Thursday (Jeudi de
   l'Ascension)
May or June (Lundi de Pentecôte)
July 14 (Fête Nationale)
August 15 (Assomption)
November 1 (Toussaint)
November 11 (Armistice 1918)
December 25 (Noël)

Opening Times

Nearly all stores and offices close for lunch from noon to 2 p.m., even until 3 p.m. or 4 p.m. Many stores close for the morning or all day Mon. or Wed.
Banks 9 a.m.–5 p.m. Mon.–Sat., closing for lunch
Bureaux de tabac and maisons de la presse 8 a.m.–7 p.m. Mon.–Sat., 8 a.m.–noon Sun.
Gas stations usually close at 9 p.m. except on autoroutes.
Grocery stores 9 a.m.–7 p.m. Mon.–Sat., some closing for lunch except Sat. and sometimes Fri.
Museums Closed for lunch noon–2 p.m., except perhaps during the months of July and/or Aug. Municipal museums usually close on Mon., national museums on Tues.
Post offices 9 a.m.–6 p.m. weekdays, closing for lunch, 9 a.m.–noon Sat.
Stores 9 a.m.–7 p.m. Mon.– Sat., closing for lunch; some food stores also open Sun. a.m.

Restrooms

Public restrooms vary considerably—some are still old-fashioned squat toilets. Towns generally have public restrooms near the *mairie* (town hall) of major towns. Self-cleaning toilet cabins are sometimes available on the street (not wheelchair accessible) for 20 cents. Large department stores have public restrooms. You can always use the toilet in a bar or café, signposted *les toilettes* or *les WC* (the acceptable thing to do is purchase a drink in exchange). There may be an attendant; tip with small change.

Time Differences

Provence, as the rest of France, runs to CET (Central European

Time), 1 hour ahead of Greenwich Mean Time, 6 hours ahead of Eastern Standard Time. New York is 6 hours behind. Remember that France uses the 24-hour clock.

Tipping
See p. 10.

Tourist Offices
See p. 9.

Travelers With Disabilities
A national website (tourisme-handicaps.org) presents France's program for travelers with disabilities. An information sheet published by the French Government Tourist Office, "Où Ferons-Nous Étape?" (in French), lists accommodations suitable for travelers with disabilities, including wheelchair users. It is available by mail from the Association des Paralysés.
APF (Association des Paralysés de France) 17 blvd. Auguste Blanqui, Paris 75013, tel 01 40 78 69 00, apf.asso.fr
APF des Bouches-du-Rhône (Marseille) Tel 04 91 79 99 99
APF des Alpes-de-Hautes-Provence (Manosque) Tel 04 92 71 74 50

EMERGENCIES

Embassies in France
British Embassy 35 rue du Faubourg St.-Honoré, Paris 75008, tel 01 44 51 31 00, embassy-paris.com
Canadian Embassy 35 av. Montaigne, Paris 75008, tel 01 44 43 29 00, canadainternational.gc.ca/france
Canadian Consulate 37 av. Montaigne, Paris 75008, tel 01 44 43 29 16, canadainternational.gc.ca/france
U.S. Embassy 2 av. Gabriel, Paris 75008, tel 01 43 12 22 22, france.usembassy.gov

U.S. Consulate 12 blvd. Paul-Peytral, Marseille 13006, tel 04 91 54 92 00

Emergency Phone Numbers
Ambulance (Service d'Aide Médicale d'Urgente, or SAMU): 15
Police secours (police rescue): 17
Pompiers (fire rescue): 18
SOS Help (in English): 01 46 21 46 46
Standard European Emergency: 112

What to Do in a Car Accident
There is no need to involve the police if you have an accident in which no one has been hurt. The official procedure is for each driver to fill out a constat à l'amiable, each signing the other's copy. Phone the rental company and explain what has happened.

If you are involved in a serious road accident, phone the police (17) or fire rescue (18). These numbers are free but in a phone booth you need to insert a calling card to make a connection (no credit is taken).

A number and address in the telephone booth will say where you are, and you may be asked the name of the nearest town so that the operator can identify which département you are in. Alternatively, you may find the local police secours number posted in the phone booth.

Lost Property
If you lose your passport, report first to the police, then to the nearest embassy or consulate (see above). If you are detained by the police for any reason, you are entitled to call the nearest consulate for a member of the staff to come to your assistance.

Lost Credit Cards
American Express: tel 01 47 77 72 00, americanexpress.com
MasterCard: tel 08 00 90 13 87, mastercard.com
Visa: tel 08 00 90 11 79, visaeurope.com

Health
Check that your health insurance covers visits to France.

Pharmacies—recognizable by a green cross sign—are staffed by qualified pharmacists who can recommend treatment, and will tell you if you need to see a doctor and where to find one.

For serious physical injury, go to a hospital emergency room (urgences). A pharmacy will be able to direct you. To renew a prescription, take your medicine in its package to a pharmacy. If they do not have that product, they will try to find its equivalent. If they can only sell it to you with a prescription, they will direct you to the nearest doctor.

International Association for Medical Assistance to Travelers (IAMAT) is a nonprofit organization that anyone can join free of charge. Members receive a directory of English-speaking IAMAT doctors on call 24 hours a day, and are entitled to services at set rates.

IAMAT offices
U.S.: 1623 Military Rd. #279, Niagara Falls, NY 14304, tel 716-754-4883
Canada: 1287 St. Claire Ave., W. Toronto, Ontario M6E 1B8, tel 416-652-0137

Medical Emergencies
For an ambulance, dial 15, Service d'Aide Médicale d'Urgente.

French medical treatment is of a high standard, and facilities are generally excellent.

Hotels & Restaurants

Finding a place to stay in Provence will be a challenge—not because choice is limited, but rather because there is such an enormous selection of appealing hotels. From reconverted medieval châteaus to stately country inns, and Riviera palaces to clifftop villas, there's no shortage of accommodation available for all budgets and tastes. The same goes for restaurants: The legendary *cuisine du soleil* has innumerable disciples in the fertile south, and dining here never fails to be an unforgettable experience.

HOTELS

The following is a selection of good quality hotels throughout Provence and the Côte d'Azur (listed in each region by price, then in alphabetical order). Wherever possible we have chosen hotels that are both individual and typical, perhaps with notable local or historic associations.

No matter when you visit, reservations will be essential. This is particularly the case during July and August, when contacting hotels and restaurants well in advance is imperative. It's also a good idea to check whether or not a town festival is taking place during your trip. Quintessentially French, these are not to be missed, but be forewarned they can make finding accommodation difficult, and in addition might radically change the face of an otherwise sleepy, rural town. November is the traditional time for the tourist industry to go on vacation themselves—meaning hotels and restaurants close up shop.

Grading System

French hotels are officially graded according to a star system, from one to five stars, as well as the special designation of Palace. The system is based on room size and lobby size, with other amenities counted on a weighted scale. The requirements of the lesser grades are assumed in the higher ones. Some B&Bs and unique hotels in this section fall outside of the rating system and therefore do not indicate any stars.

What to Expect of Starred Hotels:

Palace Five star hotels with exceptional amenities that go above and beyond.

✪✪✪✪✪ Staff speaks at least two European languages including English. All rooms have air-conditioning.

✪✪✪✪ Certain amenities like hair dryers and luggage porters must be provided. Restaurant on the premises.

✪✪✪ All rooms have en suite bathrooms.

✪✪ Bathroom may be en suite or shared. Staff speaks at least one other European language (besides French).

✪ Must have a small reception area. Bathrooms may be en suite or shared.

Credit & Debit Cards

Many hotels accept all major cards, though some smaller ones accept only cash. Abbreviations used are:
AE (American Express), MC (MasterCard), V (Visa).

Hotel Chains & Groups

Airbnb.com
Au.chateau.com
chateauxhotels.com
Concorde-hotels.com
Gites-de-france.com
Hilton.com
Hotels.com
lhw.com
Logishotels.com
Relaischateaux.com
Venere.com

You can also book through local branches of the French tourist office. Most hotels listed have websites; it is preferable to book with them directly if possible.

RESTAURANTS

Our selection (listed in each region by price, then in alphabetical order) suggests good regional restaurants offering typical local dishes, as well as including some of the great stars of French cuisine. It is always worth seeking out typical local restaurants and sampling the specialties of the area.
L = lunch   D = dinner

Dining Hours

Lunch usually starts around midday and continues until 2 p.m. Dinner is eaten around 8 p.m. but may start about 7 p.m.; in smaller places or in the countryside you may be too late after 9 p.m.

At the height of the season, or if you have a particular place in mind, make a reservation.

Restaurants often have outdoor tables for good weather, and even in towns and cities you may find yourself sitting on the sidewalk or in a courtyard. Facilities for outside dining are mentioned here only where the view, or perhaps the garden, is of particular note.

Most restaurants offer one or more prix-fixe menus, set meals at a fixed price, sometimes including wine. Otherwise (and usually more expensively), you order individual items à la carte—from the menu.

The French usually eat a salad after the main course and sometimes with the cheese course, which always comes before dessert. Bread and water are supplied free. (Tap water is safe to drink.)

Local wines dominate wine lists, and all restaurants offer a *vin de pays* by the carafe or by the glass. Smoking is forbidden by law in all public places in France except outdoor terraces.

Cafés

Cafés remain a French institution, good for morning coffee, leisurely drinks, or modest meals. In small towns and villages they are very much the center of local life. Note that drinking at the bar is cheaper than sitting at a table.

Useful Websites

www.idealgourmet.fr
www.lefooding.com
www.resto.fr
www.restoenfrance.com

Tipping

See p. 10.

AVIGNON & THE VAUCLUSE

APT

 CHEZ SYLLA
$
406 AV. DE LANÇON
TEL 04 90 04 60 37
A wine cellar that takes tastings a step further with farm-fresh lunches based on local cheeses and seasonal salads.
🕒 Closed D & Sun. Sept.–June 🅖 All major cards

AVIGNON

🏨 **DE LA MIRANDE**
🍴 **$$$$$ ✪✪✪✪**
4 PLACE DE LA MIRANDE
TEL 04 90 14 20 20
FAX 04 90 86 26 85

la-mirande.fr
An 18th-century hotel close to the Palais des Papes, with luxurious rooms and tasteful furnishings. Dine in its fine restaurant or in the basement kitchen on Tuesday and Wednesday evenings where the chef prepares an intimate meal for a table that seats 15.
🛏 27 🅿 🅢 🅖 All major cards

SOMETHING SPECIAL

🏨 **L'EUROPE**
🍴 **$$$/$$$$$ ✪✪✪✪**
12 PLACE CRILLON
TEL 04 90 14 76 76
FAX 04 90 14 76 71
heurope.com
Avignon's top hotel—even Napoléon stayed here. The grand entrance to this 16th-century mansion leads onto the peaceful terrace, and tapestries hang in the elegant salon. The Michelin one-star restaurant, **La Vieille Fontaine,** lives up to the splendor.
🛏 39 + 5 suites 🅿 🕒 Restaurant closed Mon., Sun. D, & 2 weeks in Aug. 🅢 🅖 All major cards

---

🏨 **CLOÎTRE ST.-LOUIS**
$$$ ✪✪✪✪
20 RUE DU PORTAIL BOQUIER
TEL 04 90 27 55 55
FAX 04 90 82 24 01
cloitre-saint-louis.com
A perfect blend of classical and modern French aesthetic sensibilities. Situated in a 16th-century Jesuit cloister, its contemporary touches include a rooftop pool and sundeck.
🛏 80 🅿 Limited 🄴 🅢 ⬚ 🅖 All major cards

🏨 **DE L'HORLOGE**
$ ✪✪✪✪
1 RUE FÉLICIEN DAVID
TEL 04 90 16 42 00
FAX 04 90 82 17 32
hotel-avignon-horloge.com
Just off place de l'Horloge

PRICES

HOTELS

An indication of the cost of a double room in the high season is given by **$** signs.

$$$$$	Over $400
$$$$	$300–$400
$$$	$200–$300
$$	$100–$200
$	Under $100

RESTAURANTS

An indication of the cost of a three-course meal without drinks is given by **$** signs.

$$$$$	Over $200
$$$$	$100–$200
$$$	$75–$100
$$	$50–$75
$	Under $50

---

in the heart of Avignon, this charming, stylish hotel occupies a rambling, 19th-century building. Room 505 overlooks the Palais des Papes.
🛏 66 🅿 Fee 🄴 🅢 🅖 All major cards

🍴 **L'AGAPE**
$$
21 PLACE DES CORPS SAINTS
TEL 04 90 85 04 06
Elaborate market-fresh dishes are served in a relaxed bistro-style, neo-industrial ambience. In season, dine *en plein air* beneath plane trees by a trickling fountain. Fish is the chef's specialty.
🕒 Closed Mon.–Tues. Nov.–March 🅖 All major cards

🍴 **L'ÉPICERIE**
$$
10 PLACE ST.-PIERRE
TEL 04 90 82 74 22
Opposite the 16th-century Église St.-Pierre, this tiny café

🏨 Hotel   🍴 Restaurant   🛏 No. of Guest Rooms   🅿 Parking   🕒 Closed   🅢 Nonsmoking   🄴 Elevator

offers local dishes such as lamb in apricot sauce and a tempting selection of cheeses. Closed Sun. & Nov.–March All major cards

L'ESSENTIEL
$–$$
2 RUE DE LA PETITE FUSTERIE
TEL 04 90 85 87 12
This sweet homey restaurant offers rustic Provençal dishes such as duck confit served with black olive jam and lemon zest, with pear cake and baked apple for dessert. Ask for a courtyard table. Closed Sun.–Mon. All major cards

46
$
46 RUE DE LA BALANCE
TEL 04 90 85 24 83
A wine bar–bistro with an impressive list of over 160 wines and innovative cuisine based on seasonal ingredients. Dine on the quaint street side or inside for a sleek and modern ambience. Closed Sun. & Mon.–Fri. L All major cards

Across the river in Villeneuve-lez-Avignon:

LE PRIEURÉ
$$$ 0000
7 PLACE DU CHAPITRE
TEL 04 90 15 90 15
FAX 04 90 25 45 39
leprieure.fr
This upscale hotel in a 14th-century priory offers chic rooms, some overlooking the garden. The one-Michelin-star restaurant is a superb choice for an elegant dinner. 36 All major cards

L'ATELIER
$$ 00
5 RUE DE LA FOIRE
TEL 04 90 25 01 84
hoteldelatelier.com
A charming, restful,

16th-century house. 23 Closed Jan.–Feb. All major cards

BONNIEUX

LA BASTIDE DE CAPELONGUE
$$$ 0000
LE VILLAGE
TEL 04 90 75 89 78
FAX 01 90 75 93 03
capelongue.com
One of the only hilltop hotels in the Petit Luberon, its light, airy rooms, with typical Provençal furniture, look out on the old village. The upscale, two-Michelin-star restaurant's menu features refined dishes fresh from the farm and garden: guinea fowl in truffle sauce and generously seasoned baked John Dory. 17 Closed Nov.–Feb. All major cards

LE FOURNIL
$$$
5 PLACE CARNOT
TEL 04 90 75 83 62
The fountain-graced terrace is an exquisite place to enjoy a southern, three-hour lunch. Closed Mon.–Tues., and Sat. L Nov.–Feb. V

BUOUX

AUBERGE DE LA LOUBE
$$
D113 TOWARD LOURMARIN
TEL 04 90 74 19 58
Below the hamlet of Buoux, this out-of-the-way restaurant has a 35-year legacy of simple but delicious cooking culled from seasonal local products. Most famous for its Provençal hors d'oeuvres. Meals are served on the terrace in summer, by the fireplace in winter. Reservations recommended. Closed Wed.–Thurs. & Jan. No credit cards

CAVAILLON

PRÉVÔT
$$$
353 AV. DE VERDUN
TEL 04 90 71 32 43
Well known for its themed seasonal menus, summer is M. Prévôt's brightest moment, showcasing his seven-course menu centered around cantaloupe–Cavaillon's specialty. One Michelin star. Closed Sun.–Mon. All major cards

CHÂTEAUNEUF-DU-PAPE

LE CHÂTEAU DES FINES ROCHES
$$$ 0000
RTE. DE SORGUES
TEL 04 90 83 70 23
FAX 04 90 83 78 42
chateaufinesroches.com
Several kilometers out of town amid cypress trees and vineyards, the castlelike manor house features spacious, rustic-style rooms. 11 All major cards

LE VERGER DES PAPES
$$$
04 RUE DU CHÂTEAU
TEL 04 90 83 50 40
Classic Provençal food served on the terrace in season, a few steps down from the castle ruins. The vista takes in a sea of vineyards as far as Avignon. Closed Sun. D, Mon., & Tues. L All major cards

LE PISTOU
$
15 RUE JOSEPH-DUCOS
TEL 04 90 83 71 75
An unassuming lunch stop could quite easily turn into a memorable meal—the suggestion du jour here rarely disappoints. Closed Sun. D & Mon., and Tues.–Fri. D Nov.–March All major cards

---

Air-Conditioning Indoor Pool Outdoor Pool Health Club Credit Cards

GARGAS

🏨 LA COQUILLADE
🍴 $$$$ ✪✪✪✪✪
HAMEAU LE PERROTET
TEL 04 90 74 71 71
coquillade.fr
Occupying a beautifully restored, centuries-old hamlet tucked among vineyards, this luxurious resort offers the epitome of tranquillity and luxury. Two outdoor swimming pools, three restaurants, winery, and bird-seranaded walking paths.
🛏 63 🅿 🔲 🏊 🏊 🎾
🚭 MC, V

GIGONDAS

🏨 LES FLORETS
🍴 $$/$$$
RTE. DES DENTELLES
TEL 04 90 65 85 01
hotel-lesflorets.com
An attractive, quiet restaurant with Provençal decor and a flowery terrace. The menu features natural, typical products and old-time recipes: monkfish braised with orange butter, lamb on a bed of eggplant. Clean, comfortable rooms available.
🕐 Closed Sun. D & Mon., & Tues.–Fri. D Nov.–March 🚭 All major cards

GORDES

🏨 LA BASTIDE DE
🍴 GORDES & SPA
$$$$$ ✪✪✪✪
RTE. DE COMBE
TEL 04 90 72 12 12
FAX 01 90 72 05 20
bastide-de-gordes.com
A restored brick *bastide* in the village, with spacious rooms decorated with antiques. Its three-story spa includes a sauna, hammam, and meditation room. Provençal and Mediterranean cuisine in the well-appointed restaurant.
🛏 39 🅿 🕐 Closed Jan.–Feb.
🔲 🏊 🚭 All major cards

SOMETHING SPECIAL

🏨 LA BASTIDE
DE VOULONNE
$$
CABRIÈRES-D'AVIGNON
TEL 04 90 76 77 55
FAX 04 90 76 77 56
bastide-voulonne.com
An 18th-century farmhouse centering on a fountain-graced courtyard, with huge rooms decorated in fresh natural colors. Join the owner-chef and his wife for a spectacular dinner available only to guests.
🛏 10 + 3 suites 🅿 🕐 Closed mid-Nov.–Dec., open Jan.–Feb. by arrangement only
🔲 🏊 🚭 All major cards

🏨 DOMAINE DE L'ENCLOS
$$ ✪✪✪✪
RTE. DE SÉNANQUE
TEL 06 83 67 89 13
FAX 04 90 72 03 03
domainedelenclos.com
Private gardens, a *boules* court, and a heated pool make this an excellent family choice. Rooms are spacious, each with an individual touch. Five-minute walk to town.
🛏 17 🅿 🔲 🏊 🚭 All major cards

🍴 LE MAS TOURTERON
$$
LES IMBERTS
CHEMIN ST.-BLAISE
TEL 04 90 72 00 16
This old Provençal *mas* with a walled garden serves light, imaginative seasonal cuisine.
🕐 Closed Mon.–Tues. Sept.–June, Nov.–March, & Sun. L
🚭 All major cards

L'ISLE-SUR-LA-SORGUE

🏨 MAS DE CURE BOURSE
🍴 $$ ✪✪✪
RTE. DE CAUMONT
TEL 04 90 38 16 58
FAX 04 90 38 52 31
masdecurebourse.com
Comfort and tranquillity abound at this 18th-century post office surrounded by orchards. The restaurant serves traditional Provençal fare.
🛏 13 🕐 Restaurant closed Sun. D, Mon. & Tues. L, & Nov.
🚭 🚭 MC, V

🍴 LE CARRÉ D'HERBES
$
13 AV. DES QUATRE OTAGES
TEL 04 90 38 23 97
This chic bistro alongside the antique dealers won't disappoint a hungry appetite.
🕐 Closed Wed.–Thurs. & Jan.
🚭 MC, V

LAGARDE D'APT

🍴 BISTROT DE LAGARDE
D'APT
$$
RTE. DEPARTEMENTALE 34
TEL 04 90 74 57 23
A serpentine road brings you to this delightful, remote, one-Michelin-star restaurant near Apt. Talented young chef Lloyd Tropeano serves up a fresh, imaginative menu that changes every three months.
🕐 Closed Mon.–Tues. & Dec.–Feb. 🚭 MC, V

LOURMARIN

🏨 AUBERGE LA FENIÈRE
🍴 $$$/$$$$$ ✪✪✪✪
RTE. DE CADENET
TEL 04 90 68 11 79
FAX 04 69 96 20 96
reinesammut.com
A stylish *mas* restored with care, taste, and elegance. Reine Sammut's garden-fresh kitchen is what really put this luxury spot on the map. Her daughter, Nadia, has joined her in the kitchen exclusively to create gluten-free fare.
🛏 16 🕐 Closed Nov.–Jan.; restaurant closed Mon.–Tues. L
🚭 All major cards

🏨 Hotel 🍴 Restaurant 🛏 No. of Guest Rooms 🅿 Parking 🕐 Closed 🚭 Nonsmoking 🛗 Elevator

MAS DE GUILLES

$$ ✪✪✪

RTE. DE VAUGINES
TEL 04 90 68 30 55
FAX 04 90 68 37 41
guilles.com

A 50-acre (20 ha) estate for those intent on enjoying the countryside's blooming flowers and whirring cicadas. Charming rooms in Provençal style; restaurant.

ℹ 29 🅿 ⊕ Closed Nov.–March 🏊 🆂 All major cards

ORANGE

HÔTEL ARÈNE

$$ ✪✪✪

PLACE DE LANGES
TEL 04 90 11 40 40
FAX 04 90 11 40 45
hotel-arene.fr

The quiet, simple, Provençal-style rooms at this newly renovated Best Western are among Orange's most pleasant accommodations.

ℹ 30 🅿 ⊕ 🆂 All major cards

LE PARVIS

$$$

3 COURS POURTOULES
TEL 04 90 34 82 00

Braised sea bass is just one of the choices on a haute cuisine menu renowned for its use of top-notch ingredients.

⊕ Closed Sun. D & Mon. 🆂 MC, V

L'ORANGERIE

$

4 PLACE DE L'ORMEAU PIOLENC
TEL 04 90 29 59 88

This 18th-century auberge with a stone-walled courtyard provides a traditional atmosphere for inventive cuisine: Langoustine with truffle sauce and osso buco of langoustine are favorites.

⊕ Closed Mon. L 🆂 MC, V

ROUSSILLON

LA CLÉ DES CHAMPS

$$ ✪✪✪

RTE. DE ST.-SATURNIN
TEL 04 90 05 63 22
FAX 04 90 05 70 01
hotelcledeschamps.com

Small, cozy hotel with bold-colored rooms each dedicated to a Provençal herb. Each room has a private terrace overlooking the Luberon.

ℹ 9 🅿 ⊕ 🏊 🆂 All major cards

SAIGNON

CHAMBRE AVEC VUE

$$

RUE DES BOURGADES
TEL 04 90 04 85 01
chambreavecvue.com

A breathing work of art, this B&B is also a renowned retreat for writers and artists. Rooms, living areas, and gardens inspire creation and relaxation with bold colors, artful design, unique sculptures, and a chic aire du sud.

ℹ 5 🆂 All major cards

SÉGURET

DOMAINE DE

CABASSE

$$$ ✪✪✪

ST.-JOSEPH
TEL 04 90 46 91 12
FAX 04 90 46 94 01
cabasse.fr

An established Dentelles vineyard that also takes in boarders. Perfect for wine lovers and those who appreciate Provençal home cooking.

ℹ 12 🅿 ⊕ Closed Nov.–March 🏊 🆂 MC, V

AMOUR PROVENCE

$$

CHEMIN DE ST.-JOSEPH
TEL 04 90 46 89 39
amourprovence.com

A restored Provençal farmhouse nestled among olive trees and vineyards with large rooms, amiable hosts, and views of the Dentelles de Montmirail.

ℹ 4 ⊕ Closed mid-Nov.–mid-March 🆂 All major cards

VAISON-LA-ROMAINE

LE BEFFROI

$$ ✪✪✪

RUE DE L'ÉVÊCHÉ, HAUTE VILLE
TEL 04 90 36 04 71
FAX 04 90 36 24 78
le-beffroi.com

A 16th-century mansion perched high up in the medieval town: Country-style antiques, wooden rafters, and ceramic tiles set the mood. The restaurant makes ample use of local products (such as lavender honey).

ℹ 22 🅿 🏊 🆂 All major cards

BISTRO DU Ô

$

LA HAUTE VILLE
RUE DU CHÂTEAU
TEL 04 90 41 72 90

This tiny restaurant set in the stables of the old château gets big raves for its modern, seasonal cuisine sourced from local producers. Try the raviole de foie gras (ravioli with foie gras) or the tartare de saumon, croustillant de gambas (salmon tartare with crispy prawns).

⊕ Closed Wed. & Sun. 🆂 All major cards

VÉNASQUE

LE CHÂTEAU DE

MAZAN

$$ ✪✪✪✪

PLACE NAPOLEON IN MAZAN,
NEAR VENASQUE
TEL 04 90 69 62 61
FAX 04 90 69 76 62
chateaudemazan.com

Located at the base of Mont Ventoux, this château built in 1720 was once the residence of the Marquis de Sade. It's now

---

a hotel with old-world effects and a fine dining restaurant.
ⓘ 30 ◈ MC, V

■ SOUTH ALONG THE RHÔNE

AIGUES-MORTES

🏨 LES TEMPLIERS
$$$ ✪✪✪
23 RUE DE LA RÉPUBLIQUE
TEL 04 66 53 66 56
FAX 04 66 53 69 61
A thoughtfully restored old hotel within the ramparts, with stone walls, painted beams, and fireplaces in many of the rooms. The courtyard is a haven of tranquillity.
ⓘ 11 🅿 🚭 ⊜ ◈ All major cards

🏨 LES ARCADES
$$ ✪✪✪
23 BLVD. GAMBETTA
TEL 04 66 53 81 13
FAX 04 66 53 75 46
les-arcades.fr
Above the arcades housing Aigues-Mortes's best seafood restaurant are nine individually decorated rooms. The building dates from the 16th century, with modern furnishings.
ⓘ 9 🅿 🕛 Closed Mon.–Tues., & Thurs. L 🚭 ⊜ ◈ All major cards

ARLES

🏨 LE MAS DE PEINT
🍴 $$$$ ✪✪✪✪✪
LE SAMBUC
TEL 04 90 97 20 62
FAX 04 90 97 22 20
masdepeint.com
Former stables attached to an old Camargue farmhouse hold exquisite rooms with wood ceilings, white linen furnishings, and antiques. The restaurant offers innovative regional cuisine with garden views.
ⓘ 8 + 2 suites 🅿 🕛 Closed

early Jan.–March 🚭 ◈ All major cards

🏨 GRAND HÔTEL NORD-PINUS
$$$/$$$$$ ✪✪✪✪
14 PLACE DU FORUM
TEL 04 90 93 44 44
FAX 04 90 93 34 00
nord-pinus.com
Although brought up-to-date, this luxury hotel remains traditionally Provençal at heart. Very popular with bullfighters at festival time. The rooms in front can be noisy in summer.
ⓘ 25 🅿 🚭 Some rooms ◈ All major cards

🏨 D'ARLATAN
$$ ✪✪✪
26 RUE SAUVAGE
TEL 04 90 96 90 03
FAX 04 90 49 68 45
hotel-arlatan.fr
This 15th-century town house in the heart of Arles overflows with history and furnishings fit for Provençal nobility. Fine touches include a walled garden and Roman excavations.
ⓘ 47 🅿 🕛 Closed Nov.–Feb. 🚭 ◈ All major cards

🍴 LA GUEULE DU LOUP
$$$
39 RUE DES ARÈNES
TEL 04 90 96 96 69
First-floor wood-beamed restaurant above the kitchen serves Midi classics with an original twist like *charlotte d'agneau* with eggplant and red pepper coulis; and tarte tatin of turnips with foie gras. Reservations recommended.
🕛 Closed Jan., Sun., & Mon. L ◈ MC, V

🍴 LA CHASSAGNETTE
$$–$$$
RTE. DU SAMBUC
TEL 04 90 97 26 96
Michelin-starred chef Armand Arnal produces fanciful cuisine direct from the expansive kitchen garden and orchards of

this Provençal farmhouse.
🕛 Closed Tues.–Wed. & Jan.–Feb. ◈ All major cards

🍴 LE GALOUBET
$$
18 RUE DU DOCTEUR FANTON
TEL 04 90 93 18 11
Industrial lamps and vintage armchairs create the scene at this hip bistro serving modern Provençal cuisine with a great local wine list. The tomato-and-herb octopus salad gets consistently rave reviews.
🕛 Closed Sun.–Mon. ◈ All major cards

🍴 BODEGUITA
$
49 RUE DES ARÈNES
TEL 04 90 96 68 59
A lively and popular Spanish bistro, near the place du Forum, specializing in top-notch tapas at reasonable prices with local and Spanish wines.
🕛 Closed Sun. & winter ◈ All major cards

PRICES

HOTELS
An indication of the cost of a double room in the high season is given by $ signs.

$$$$$	Over $400
$$$$	$300–$400
$$$	$200–$300
$$	$100–$200
$	Under $100

RESTAURANTS
An indication of the cost of a three-course meal without drinks is given by $ signs.

$$$$$	Over $200
$$$$	$100–$200
$$$	$75–$100
$$	$50–$75
$	Under $50

LES-BAUX-DE-PROVENCE

🏨 DOMAINE DE
🍴 MANVILLE
$$$$

LES-BAUX-DE-PROVENCE
TEL 04 90 54 40 20
domainedemanville.fr
An ultraluxe, sunny, five-star resort on a 100-acre (40 ha), olive-tree-dotted estate. *Très chic* rooms, a glass-walled breakfast room, and an 18-hole golf course. Restaurants include a gastropub bar, locally sourced dining room, and buzzing bistro.
🛏 39 🅿 ❄ 🏊 ⬥ All major cards

SOMETHING SPECIAL

🏨 OUSTAU DE
🍴 BAUMANIÈRE
$$$$

MAUSSANE-LES-ALPILLES
TEL 04 90 54 33 07
FAX 04 90 54 4046
oustaudebaumaniere.com
This legendary hotel beneath towering cliffs charms with three stone houses set on pretty grounds. The two-Michelin-star restaurant is famous for its *gigot d'agneau en croûte* (lamb in pastry) and truffle ravioli.
🛏 30 ❄ Restaurant closed Jan.–Feb. ❄ ➖ 🏊 ⬥ All major cards

🏨 LA BENVENGUDO
$$$ ☆☆☆☆

1 MILE (2 KM) S OF LES BAUX
TEL 04 90 54 32 54
FAX 04 90 54 42 58
benvengudo.com
Tucked beneath the Alpilles, a manor-hotel with an elegant garden. The lounge and dining room are in Provençal style; some rooms have private terraces. Tennis courts.
🛏 20 + 3 suites 🅿 ❄ Closed Nov.–Dec. ❄ 🏊 ⬥ All major cards

🏨 LE MAS D'AIGRET
$$ ☆☆☆

D27A
TEL 04 90 54 20 00
FAX 04 90 54 44 00
masdaigret.com
Part of the hotel is built into the cliffside, in keeping with the rocky-themed village above. Breakfast is served in the troglodyte dining room.
🛏 17 🅿 ❄ Closed Nov.–March ❄ 🏊 ⬥ All major cards

NÎMES

🏨 JARDINS SECRETS
$$$ ☆☆☆☆

3 RUE GASTON MARUEJOLS
TEL 04 66 84 82 64
FAX 04 66 84 27 47
jardinssecrets.net
A peaceful retreat in the heart of town expertly adorned with lavish antiques and furnishings. Known for its service, copious breakfasts, spa, and songbirds in the garden.
🛏 14 ⬥ All major cards

🏨 MARQUIS
🍴 DE LA BAUME
$$$ ☆☆☆

21 RUE NATIONALE
TEL 04 66 76 28 42
FAX 04 66 76 28 45
In old Nîmes, the New Hotels group has added a sensual, urban chic to this former *hôtel particulier*. A good location for visiting the city's monuments.
🛏 34 🅿 ❄ 🏊 ⬥ All major cards

🍴 L'ENCLOS DE LA
FONTAINE
$$

HÔTEL IMPERATOR
QUAI DE LA FONTAINE
TEL 04 66 21 90 30
Restaurant of the Hôtel Imperator favored by bullfighters at *féria* time. Try local specialties such as *brandade de morue* (creamy salt cod),

escabèche (marinated fish), or sea bass with fennel compote.
⬥ All major cards

🍴 LE 9
$$

9 RUE DE L'ÉTOILE
TEL 04 66 21 80 77
Hidden away in the old town, this chic, theatrical restaurant serves Mediterranean-style cuisine till late.
❄ Closed Nov.–April ❄ ⬥ V

ST.-RÉMY-DE-PROVENCE

🏨 CHÂTEAU DES ALPILLES
$$$$ ☆☆☆☆☆

D31
TEL 04 90 92 03 33
FAX 04 90 92 45 17
chateaudesalpilles.com
The castle, chapel, and farmhouse all hold spacious, elegant rooms caringly restored and decorated with period furnishings by a mother-daughter duo.
🛏 22 🅿 ❄ Closed mid-Nov.–mid-Feb. ❄ 🏊 ⬥ All major cards

🏨 LES ATELIERS DE
L'IMAGE
$$$ ☆☆☆☆

36 BLVD. VICTOR HUGO
TEL 04 90 92 51 50
FAX 04 90 92 43 52
hotel-image.fr
This contemporary hotel uses photography as a central theme, and includes a private collection and gallery on the premises. The modern rooms are a wonder of sophisticated architectural style.
🛏 11 🅿 ❄ Closed Jan. ❄ 🏊 ⬥ All major cards

🏨 SOUS LES FIGUIERS
$$ ☆☆☆

3 AV. TAILLANDIER
TEL 04 32 60 15 40
FAX 04 32 60 15 39
Fig trees shade rustic and cool rooms perfect for siestas and

lazy days in this quaint hotel in the heart of town. Most rooms have terrace or private garden. Art classes offered.
🛏 12 🅿 🕐 Closed Jan.–mid-March 🚭 ⛵ 🚹 MC, V

🍴 LA MAISON JAUNE
$–$$$
15 RUE CARNOT
TEL 04 90 92 56 14
A St.-Rémy classic in an 18th-century town house, featuring such delectables as roasted monkfish garnished with sun-dried tomatoes and cumin.
🕐 Closed Sun., Mon. & Tues. L 🚹 MC, V

🍴 LA GOUSSE D'AIL
$
6 BLVD. MARCEAU
TEL 04 90 92 16 87
The Garlic Clove gets rave reviews from just about everybody for its inexpensive gastronomical treats, family-run atmosphere, and occasional live music.
🕐 Closed Thurs. 🚹 All major cards

STES.-MARIES-DE-LA-MER

🏨 LE MAS DE LA FOUQUE
$$$$ ✪✪✪✪
RTE. DU PETIT RHÔNE
TEL 04 90 97 81 02
FAX 04 90 97 96 84
masdelafouque.com
A traditional Camargue hotel, with large rooms, tiled floors, and wooden beams. Private terraces overlook the lagoon and park.
🛏 14 🅿 🕐 Closed Nov.–March, open during Christmas ⛵ 🚹 All major cards

🏨 L'AUBERGE CAVALIÈRE
🍴 DU PONT DES BANNES
$$$ ✪✪✪✪
D570
TEL 04 90 97 88 88
FAX 04 90 97 89 28
aubergecavaliere.com

Individual lodges constructed in the *gardian* tradition, with adobe walls and thatched roofs—but modern interiors. Situated on the edge of the wetlands. Two restaurants.
🛏 69 🅿 ⛵ 🚹 All major cards

🍴 LE BRÛLEUR DE LOUPS
$$$
9 AV. LÉON GAMBETTA
TEL 04 90 97 83 31
One of the best spots in town to sample local seafood. Grilled sea bream with fennel butter and scorpion fish topped with a tomato-basil sauce are specialties.
🕐 Closed Tues. D & Wed. 🚹 All major cards

◼ AIX, MARSEILLE, & THE VAR

AIX-EN-PROVENCE

🏨 LE PIGONNET
🍴 $$$$ ✪✪✪✪✪
5 AV. DU PIGONNET
TEL 04 42 59 02 90
FAX 04 42 59 47 77
hotelpigonnet.com
A quintessential Provençal country château surrounded by exquisite gardens, just half a mile (0.8 m) from the old town. Local fabrics and furniture decorate the well-appointed rooms. **La Table du Pigonnet** restaurant serves exquisite Mediterranean and local cuisine, with dining on the garden terrace in summer.
🛏 44 🅿 🚭 ⛵ 🚹 All major cards

🏨 BASTIDE DU COURS
🍴 $$$ ✪✪✪✪
43–47 COURS MIRABEAU
TEL 04 42 91 57 56
FAX 04 42 91 57 51
bastideducours.com
Gorgeous B&B in a historic mansion along cours Mira-beau, with king-size beds fit-ted in fine linen. Its renowned

eponymous restaurant serves deceivingly simple creations such as roast duck with pump-kin chutney.
🛏 5 🅿 🚭 🚹 All major cards

🏨 GRAND HÔTEL NÈGRE COSTE
$$ ✪✪✪
33 COURS MIRABEAU
TEL 04 42 27 74 22
FAX 04 42 26 80 93
hotelnegrecoste.com
One of Aix's better values, this 18th-century town house has friendly service and quiet rooms decorated in lovely Provençal style.
🛏 38 🅿 🚹 All major cards

🍴 LE CLOS & LE COMPTOIR DU CLOS
$$$
RENAISSANCE HOTEL
320 AV. W. A. MOZART
TEL 04 86 91 55 00
Celebrated chef Jean-Marc Banzo moved his signature Provençal style to Aix's new Renaissance Hotel in 2014. He now presides over the gastronomic Le Clos restaurant, as well as the hip Le Comptoir du Clos bistro.
🕐 Closed Sun., Mon. D 🚹 All major cards

🍴 LE PASSAGE
$$
10 RUE VILLARS
TEL 04 42 37 09 00
le-passage.fr
Reine Sammut's hip restaurant cum culinary center (with cooking classes, wine cellar, and tearoom) offers a rare combina-tion: It's stylish, delicious, and affordable.
🚹 All major cards

🍴 LES DEUX GARÇONS
$
53 COURS MIRABEAU
TEL 04 42 26 00 51
Artists and intellectuals have frequented this classic terrace

---

🏨 Hotel   🍴 Restaurant   🛏 No. of Guest Rooms   🅿 Parking   🕐 Closed   🚭 Nonsmoking   🛗 Elevator

café on the cours Mirabeau since the 18th century.
🃏 All major cards

🍽 LE FORMAL
$
32 RUE ESPARIAT
TEL 04 42 27 08 31
Tucked away on a quiet street, this reconverted cellar promises romantic dining. Foie gras of duck accompanied with stewed apples and walnuts is the appetizer par excellence.
🕐 Closed Sat. L & Sun.–Mon.
🃏 MC, V

Along the rte. de Cézanne in Le Tholonet:

🏨 LES LODGES SAINTE
🍽 VICTOIRE
$$$$ ✪✪✪✪
2250 RTE. DE CÉZANNE
TEL 04 42 24 80 40
FAX 04 42 24 80 41
leslodgessaintevictoire.com
This 18th-century structure opened as a modern hotel and spa with a serious take on Provençal tranquillity in 2013. On the road to Montagne Ste.-Victoire, its Michelin-starred restaurant **Le Saint-Estève** merits a detour its due.
🛏 12 🅿 🕐 Restaurant closed Mon. 🆒 🏊 🃏 All major cards

LES ARCS

🍽 LE RELAIS DES MOINES
$$
RTE. DE STE.-ROSELINE
TEL 04 94 47 40 93
Housed in a 16th-century stone sheepfold in the midst of truffle country, the Michelin-starred Sèbastien Sanjou gives the earthy mushroom its due respect while also calling on the briny flavors of the nearby sea. A shaded terrace offers views of the medieval village and Massif des Maures.
🕐 Closed Sun., Sat. L, & Sun.–Mon. Sept.–June 🃏 All major cards

CASSIS

🏨 LES ROCHES
🍽 BLANCHES
$$$ ✪✪✪✪
RTE. DES CALANQUES
TEL 04 42 01 09 30
FAX 04 42 01 94 23
roches-blanches-cassis.com
White cliffs, an ivy-covered facade, gardens down to the sea's edge, and quiet ocean views make this a much sought-after locale. The sea-food restaurant has to-die-for sea views. It's located several kilometers west of Cassis toward Les Calanques.
🛏 24 🅿 🆒 🏊 🃏 All major cards

🍽 NINO
$$
1 QUAI BARTHÉLEMY
TEL 04 42 01 74 32
One of Cassis' several alluring portside restaurants, offering seafood platters, grilled fish, and pasta, accompanied by local crisp white wine.
🕐 Closed Mon. & Sun. D
🃏 All major cards

HYÈRES & ÎLES DES PORQUEROLLES

🏨 LE MANOIR DU
🍽 PORT-CROS
$$$ ✪✪✪
ÎLE DE PORT-CROS
TEL 04 94 05 90 52
FAX 04 94 05 90 89
The island's only hotel, where D. H. Lawrence supposedly met the Englishwomen whose confessional conversations inspired *Lady Chatterley's Lover*. The restaurant offers a romantic terrace ideal for sunset-watching.
🛏 25 🕐 Closed Oct.–April
🃏 MC, V

🏨 LE MAS DU
🍽 LANGOUSTIER
$$$ ✪✪✪✪
CHEMIN DU LANGOUSTIER
ÎLE DES PORQUEROLLES
TEL 04 94 58 30 09
FAX 04 94 58 36 02
langoustier.com
This luxury island hotel, with its own vineyard, sits on a rocky spur overlooking the sea. Its one-Michelin-star restaurant offers the light Provençal cuisine of chef Julien Le Goff; meals served in the garden. Half-board only. Tennis courts.
🛏 44 + 5 suites 🕐 Closed Oct.–May 🃏 All major cards

🏨 HÔTEL DU SOLEIL
$$ ✪✪
RUE DU REMPART, HYÈRES
TEL 04 94 65 16 26
FAX 04 94 35 46 00
hoteldusoleil.com
Simple rooms in an ivy-covered *bastide* set on 12th-century ramparts overlooking Hyères's *vieille ville*.
🛏 22 🅿 🃏 All major cards

🍽 LES JARDINS DE
BACCHUS
$
32 AV. GAMBETTA, HYÈRES
TEL 04 94 65 77 63
A good place to indulge, as the name implies. Swordfish, scampi, and other coastal specialties are prepared with finesse. In the modern town.
🕐 Closed Sun.–Mon. 🃏 All major cards

LA GARDE-FREINET

🏨 LA SARRAZINE
$$ ✪✪✪
D588
TEL 04 94 49 04 29
FAX 04 94 55 58 18
hotellasarrazine.fr
A luxury hotel situated above the medieval village in the heart of the undeveloped Massif des Maures—a walker's paradise.
🛏 9 🅿 🕐 Closed Nov.–March
🆒 🃏 MC, V

🆒 Air-Conditioning 🏊 Indoor Pool 🌊 Outdoor Pool 🏋 Health Club 🃏 Credit Cards

LORGUES

SOMETHING SPECIAL

🍴 CHEZ BRUNO
$$$–$$$$
RTE. DES ARCS
TEL 04 94 85 93 93
The restaurant where truffle king Bruno Clément created his black-diamond-based cuisine. Try the foie gras raviolis in truffle juice or roasted shoulder of lamb with truffles.
🕐 Open daily June–Sept., closed Sun. D & Mon. Sept.–June 🅂 All major cards

MARSEILLE

🏨 LE PETIT NICE
🍴 $$$$$ ⬤⬤⬤⬤⬤
ANSE DE MALDORMÉ
CORNICHE J. F. KENNEDY
TEL 04 91 59 25 92
FAX 04 91 59 28 08
passedat.fr
Two luxurious Greek-style villas along the corniche are perfectly situated for contemplating the Mediterranean expanse—every room has sea views. Gerald Passedat's eponymous restaurant offers contemporary cuisine with a regional twist: sea anemone beignets, for starters.
🛈 16 🅿 🅂 🛆 🅂 All major cards

🏨 INTERCONTINENTAL
🍴 HÔTEL-DIEU
$$$ ⬤⬤⬤⬤⬤
1 PLACE DAVIEL
TEL 04 13 42 42 42
marseille.intercontinental.com
Overlooking the Vieux Port, this majestic hotel occupies the 18th-century Hôtel-Dieu. Every corner has been refurbished with a sophisticated touch—showcasing its monumental staircase, vaulted passageways, and curved archways. Michelin-starred **Alycone** serves Mediterranean gastronomy.

🛈 172 + 22 suites
🅿 🅂 🛆 🛇 🅂 All major cards

🏨 ALIZÉ
$$ ⬤⬤⬤
35 QUAI DES BELGES
TEL 04 91 33 66 97
FAX 04 91 54 80 06
alize-hotel.com
Simple, comfortable rooms conveniently located off the harbor's main quay.
🛈 39 🅿 🅂 🅂 🅂 All major cards

🏨 BOMPARD
$$ ⬤⬤⬤⬤
2 RUE DES FLOTS BLEUS
TEL 04 91 99 22 22
FAX 04 91 31 02 14
new-hotel.com
A stately bourgeois house on hilly wooded grounds overlooking the sea, this lovely hotel is an oasis of calm. Rooms are decorated with Provençal flair.
🛈 46 🅿 🅂 🛆 🅂 All major cards

🏨 RÉSIDENCE DU VIEUX PORT
$$ ⬤⬤⬤⬤
hotel-residence-marseille.com
18 QUAI DU PORT
TEL 04 91 91 91 22
FAX 04 91 56 60 88
Traditional hotel with large bay windows and great views over the harbor. Rooms are spacious and equipped with modern amenities.
🛈 41 🅿 🅂 🅂 🅂 All major cards

SOMETHING SPECIAL

🍴 LE MIRAMAR
$$$$
12 QUAI DU PORT
TEL 04 91 91 10 40
Simmering pots of authentic bouillabaisse have been the specialty of the house for more than 40 years. A classy, not-to-be-missed way of expe-

---

PRICES

HOTELS
An indication of the cost of a double room in the high season is given by $ signs.

$$$$$	Over $400
$$$$	$300–$400
$$$	$200–$300
$$	$100–$200
$	Under $100

RESTAURANTS
An indication of the cost of a three-course meal without drinks is given by $ signs.

$$$$$	Over $200
$$$$	$100–$200
$$$	$75–$100
$$	$50–$75
$	Under $50

---

riencing Marseille at its best.
🕐 Closed Mon. 🅂 All major cards

🍴 UNE TABLE AU SUD
$$$
2 QUAI DU PORT
TEL 04 91 90 63 53
Chef Lionel Levy handed over the reins of this fine establishment to the young duo Ludovic and Karine Turac in 2013 (Ludovic made his fame on the show *Top Chef*). The inventive menu centers on local seafood. The dining room, with floor-to-ceiling windows, offers privileged views of the port and Mediterranean.
🕐 Closed Mon., Sun. D 🅂 All major cards

🍴 LES ARCENAULX
$
25 COURS ESTIENNES D'ORVES
TEL 04 91 59 80 30
A restaurant, wine cellar, and rare books shop with a classy

---

lunch *menu du terroir* in an elegant setting.
🕐 Closed D & Mon. 🅐 All major cards

🍽 LA PART DES ANGES
$
33 RUE SAINTE
TEL 04 91 33 55 70
A popular wine bar and eatery run by three friends with a healthy respect for the bottle and food pairing. Glasses range from €2 to infinity with choices from charcuterie and cheese plates to fish and chips.
🕐 Closed Sun.–Mon. 🅐 All major cards

ST.-TROPEZ

🏨 LE BYBLOS
🍽 $$$$$ 😊😊😊😊😊
AV. PAUL-SIGNAC
TEL 04 94 56 68 00
FAX 04 94 56 68 01
byblos.com
The famous hotel where Mick Jagger married Bianca; designed like a village with sumptuous Moroccan decor, a chic nightclub, and two restaurants offering dinner only.
🛏 86 + 11 suites 🅿 🕐 Closed mid-Oct.–April 🅐 🅐 🅐 All major cards

🏨 LA PONCHE
$$$$$ 😊😊😊😊
PLACE RÉVELIN
TEL 04 94 97 02 53
FAX 04 94 97 78 61
laponche.com
Charming ensemble of former fishermen's cottages behind the port, with stylish, surprisingly large guest rooms.
🛏 13 + 5 suites 🅿 🕐 Closed Nov.–mid-Feb. 🅐 🅐 All major cards

🏨 LE YACA
$$$$$ 😊😊😊😊
1 BLVD. D'AUMALE
TEL 04 94 55 81 00
FAX 04 94 97 58 50

hotel-le-yaca.fr
Old Provençal house in the town center, built around a swimming pool and garden.
🛏 27 🅿 🕐 Closed mid-Oct.–Easter 🅐 🅐 All major cards

🍽 LE CAFÉ
$$
PLACE DES LICES
TEL 04 94 97 44 69
The former star-studded Café des Arts, whose adjoining restaurant in the back is reputedly still frequented by the occasional celebrity. The most regular patrons, however, are the *boules* players from the square out front.
🅐 All major cards

🍽 CAFÉ SÉNÉQUIER
$$
QUAI JEAN-JAURÈS
TEL 04 94 97 00 90
A favorite port café that's pricey but good for evening apéritifs and watching celebrities on yachts drinking theirs.
🅐 No credit cards

🍽 LA TABLE DU MARCHÉ
$$
11 RUE DE COMMERCANTS
TEL 04 94 97 91 91
Chef Christophe Leroy has added a gourmet note to many French standards: lobster and macaroni au gratin, shepherd's pie with duck and foie gras.
🅐 All major cards

In Gassin:

🍽 BELLO VISTO
$
PLACE DEI BARRYS
TEL 04 94 56 17 30
Perched in the hills overlooking the St.-Tropez peninsula, the Bello Visto has a view that defies believable. If you can peel your eyes away, enjoy a meal of grilled John Dory or rabbit sautéed with thyme.
🕐 Closed Tues. 🅐 MC, V

In Ramatuelle:

🏨 VILLA MARIE
$$$$/$$$$$ 😊😊😊😊😊
CHEMIN VAL RIAN
TEL 04 94 97 40 22
villamarie.fr
Luxurious hotel in soft terra-cotta shades overlooking Pampelonne Bay. The pool has a waterfall. Spa.
🛏 45 🕐 Closed Oct.–March 🅐 🅐 🅐 All major cards

TOURTOUR

🏨 LA BASTIDE DE
🍽 TOURTOUR
$$$ 😊😊😊😊
MONTÉE ST.-DENIS
TEL 04 98 10 54 20
FAX 04 94 54 02 09
verdon.net
Sublime vistas from an exquisitely refurbished château outside one of the Var's loftiest villages. Surrounded by several acres of pine trees, olive groves, and lavender. Tennis courts. The restaurant serves traditional Provençal cuisine, and there's a cooking school.
🛏 25 🅿 🅐 🅐 🅐 🅐 🅐 All major cards

▮ CÔTE D'AZUR: CANNES & AROUND

ANTIBES

🏨 HOTEL ROYAL
🍽 ANTIBES
$$$ 😊😊😊😊
16 BLVD. MARÉCHAL LECLERC
TEL 04 83 61 91 91
hotelroyal-antibes.com
This beachfront hotel has all the contemporary standards: beach chairs, waterfront dining, spa, and airy, minimalist design rooms.
🛏 39 🅐 All major cards

LE CESAR

$$$

CHEMIN DE LA GAROUPE

TEL 04 93 61 33 74

Specialties include fish cooked in salt crust, pasta flambé, and artichoke ravioli. Just up a small staircase above Keller Beach.

🕓 Closed Oct.–March

🚫 MC, V

OSCAR'S

$$

8 RUE DU DOCTEUR ROSTAN

TEL 04 93 34 90 14

Stone walls, copper cookware, and Roman-style sculptures set the tone for this cheery Italian seafood eatery in the old town. Among seasonal delicacies: *scampi tortellini*, scallop raviolis, and sea perch and lemongrass lasagna.

🕓 Closed Sun.–Mon.

🚫 MC, V

CHEZ MARGUERITE

$

31 RUE SADE

TEL 04 93 34 33 58

Mediterranean restaurant with paella and bouillabaisse in spring and summer, and various pasta dishes in the fall and winter.

🕓 Closed Mon. 🚫 All major cards

In Cap d'Antibes:

DU CAP-EDEN-ROC

$$$$$ ⬤⬤⬤⬤⬤

BLVD. KENNEDY

TEL 04 93 61 39 01

FAX 04 93 67 13 83

hotel-du-cap-eden-roc.com

Favored by Cannes film stars, this is the last word in luxury, especially the 1930s terrace and the pool hewn out of the rocks where Zelda Fitzgerald used to swim. Tennis courts.

🛏 121 + 9 suites 🅿

🕓 Closed Nov.–April

🚭 🏊 🛗

BIOT

LES TERRAILLERS

$$$$

11 RTE. DU CHEMIN-NEUF

TEL 04 93 65 01 59

Imaginative cuisine at this large farmhouse restaurant south of Biot has gained it one Michelin star. Try baby rabbit with *fines herbes*, foie gras ravioli with *fumet de morilles*, or monkfish with thyme butter.

🕓 Closed Wed.–Thurs. & Nov.

🚭 🚫 All major cards

CAGNES: HAUT-DE-CAGNES

LE CAGNARD

$$$ ⬤⬤⬤⬤

RUE SOUS BARI

TEL 04 93 20 73 22

FAX 04 93 22 06 39

Attached to the Grimaldi castle, the former haunt of artists and writers such as Modigliani and Renoir. Rooms have a medieval touch.

🛏 26 🅿 🕓 Closed Nov.–mid-Dec. 🚭 🚫 All major cards

JOSY-JO

$$

2 PLACE PLANASTEL

TEL 04 93 20 68 76

Bistro in the old town with rustic decor and a huge fireplace. Superb ingredients simply cooked such as peppers marinated in olive oil, and *petits farcis* (stuffed vegetables).

🕓 Closed Sun.–Mon., & L July–Aug. 🚭 🚫 All major cards

CANNES

INTERCONTINENTAL CARLTON

$$$$$ ⬤⬤⬤⬤

58 BLVD. DE LA CROISETTE

TEL 04 93 06 40 06

FAX 04 93 06 40 25

intercontinental-carlton-cannes.com

The last word in luxury, the legendary Carlton is where film moguls do deals during the festival. The bathrooms are all marble, and many rooms have views overlooking the bay. Private beach.

🛏 295 + 18 suites 🅿 🚫
🚭 🚭 🚫 All major cards

MAJESTIC

$$$$$ ⬤⬤⬤⬤⬤

10 BLVD. DE LA CROISETTE

TEL 04 92 98 77 00

FAX 04 92 98 77 60

lucienbarriere.com

One of the mythic beachside resorts that packs in the film industry during festival time, with all the luxurious trappings one would expect.

🛏 305 🅿 🚭 🚭 🚫 🛗
🚫 All major cards

3.14

$$$ ⬤⬤⬤⬤

6 RUE FRANÇOIS EINESY

TEL 04 92 99 72 00

314cannes.com

A pebble's toss from the beach, each color-saturated floor of this unique, globally themed hotel depicts a different continent. The hotel restaurant reflects the mixing of cultures.

🛏 94 🅿 🚭 🏊 🚭 🛗 🚫 All major cards

HÔTEL DE PROVENCE

$$$ ⬤⬤⬤

9 RUE MOLIÈRE

TEL 04 93 38 44 35

FAX 04 93 39 63 14

hotel-de-provence.com

A secret oasis in the middle of Cannes, this charming hotel has clean, refreshing rooms in Provençal style. It has access to a private beach.

🛏 30 🅿 🕓 Closed mid-Nov.–mid-Dec. 🚭 🚫 All major cards

SPLENDID

$$$ ⬤⬤⬤⬤

4 RUE FELIX FAURE

TEL 04 97 06 22 22

FAX 04 93 99 55 02

🏨 Hotel 🍴 Restaurant 🛏 No. of Guest Rooms 🅿 Parking 🕓 Closed 🚭 Nonsmoking 🚭 Elevator

splendid-hotel-cannes.fr
Cannes's oldest hotel is pleasantly unpretentious and an excellent alternative to some of La Croisette's larger resorts. Rooms are stylishly decorated. Ask for an ocean view.

ⓘ 34 🅿 🔄 🔊 All major cards

🍴 LA PALME D'OR
$$$$
HÔTEL MARTINEZ
73 BLVD. DE LA CROISETTE
TEL 04 92 98 74 14
Contemporary art deco decor and Riviera allure combine with an exceptional menu (rabbit with rosemary and chickpeas) to make this a top dining spot in Cannes.

🕐 Closed Sun.–Mon.
🔊 All major cards

🍴 L'ECHIQUIER
$$$
14 RUE ST.-ANTOINE
TEL 04 93 39 77 79
An intimate, candlelit restaurant in Suquet that caters to stars and locals alike. Standards include foie gras, bouillabaisse, sea bass, and *magret de canard*.

🕐 Open D only, closed Sun.
🔄 All major cards

🍴 JW GRILL
$$
JW MARRIOTT
50 BLVD. DE LA CROISETTE
TEL 04 92 99 70 92
An elegant steakhouse in the fashionable JW Marriott, with a terrace overlooking the Mediterranean.
🔊 All major cards

🍴 LA MÈRE BESSON
$$
13 RUE DES FRÈRES PRADIGNAC
TEL 04 93 39 59 24
A Cannes institution, this popular little bistro serves a different fish dish every day.
🕐 Closed Sun. 🔄 🔊 All major cards

🍴 LA BROUETTE DE GRAND-MÈRE
$
9 BIS RUE D'ORAN
TEL 04 93 39 12 10
Traditional French cooking, as good as *grand-mère* used to make. A convivial atmosphere, helped along by plenty of wine and roast quail.
🕐 Open D only, closed Sun.
🔊 MC, V

GRASSE

SOMETHING SPECIAL

🏨 LA BASTIDE SAINT
🍴 ANTOINE
$$$$ ⬤⬤⬤⬤⬤
48 AV. HENRI DUNANT
TEL 04 93 70 94 94
FAX 04 93 70 94 95
jacques-chibois.com
Jacques Chibois's two-Michelin-star restaurant is what first gave this 18th-century country house a name, but the regional-styled rooms are just as luscious as the food. Try the artfully prepared lobster in black olive fondue or lemon sea bream with truffle purée and hibiscus juice.

ⓘ 11 🅿 🏊 🔊 All major cards

🏨 MOULIN STE.-ANNE
$$ ⬤⬤⬤⬤
9 CHEMIN DES PRÉS
TEL 04 92 42 01 70
moulin-sainte-anne.com
A beautifully restored 18th-century stone olive oil mill with modern rooms in a tranquil and rustic setting.
ⓘ 5 🔊 All major cards

JUAN-LES-PINS

🏨 HÔTEL JUANA
🍴 $$$$$ ⬤⬤⬤⬤⬤
LA PINÈDE, AV. GALLICE
TEL 04 93 61 08 70
FAX 04 93 61 76 60
hotel-juana.com
Enchanting art deco monument

dating back to 1931, with contemporary furnishings to match the state-protected facade. **Bistro Terrasse** boasts the Cap's best dining experience—try the baked turbot with truffles or clam and *supion* cannelloni in squid ink.
ⓘ 40 🅿 🕐 Hotel closed mid-Dec.–mid-Jan.; restaurant closed L & Nov. 🔄 🏊 🎽 🔊 All major cards

🏨 DES MIMOSAS
$$ ⬤⬤⬤
RUE PAULINE
TEL 04 93 61 04 16
FAX 04 92 93 06 46
A quiet, 19th-century house with large modern rooms, many with balconies, and a shady garden.
ⓘ 34 🕐 Closed Oct.–late April 🏊 🔊 All major cards

MOUGINS

🏨 LE MAS CANDILLE
🍴 $$$$ ⬤⬤⬤⬤
BLVD. CLÉMENT REBUFFEL
TEL 04 92 28 43 43
FAX 04 92 28 43 40
lemascandille.com
An 18th-century farmhouse transformed into a therapeutic getaway complete with spa—a gorgeous accommodation in a tranquil country setting. Two restaurants on the premises.
ⓘ 39 🅿 🕐 Closed Jan.
🔄 🏊 🔊 All major cards

🍴 LE MOULIN DE MOUGINS
$$$–$$$$
1028 AV. DE LA VALMASQUE
TEL 04 93 75 78 24
Founded by *cuisine du soleil* master Roger Vergé in a 16th-century mill, Le Moulin de Mougins is one of the region's best known restaurants. It's now run by chef Erwan Louaisil, a Vergé disciple.
🕐 Closed Mon.–Tues. Oct.–April 🔊 All major cards

🔄 Air-Conditioning 🏊 Indoor Pool 🏊 Outdoor Pool 🎽 Health Club 🔊 Credit Cards

🍴 **L'AMANDIER DE MOUGINS**

$$–$$$

48 AV. JEAN-CHARLES MALLET
TEL 04 93 90 00 91
An elegant Provençal home serving fresh cuisine with a Roger Vergé cooking school, lounge, and tribute menu to the great chef who created *cuisine du soleil*.
🕐 Closed Wed. Sept.–June
⧆ All major cards

ST.-PAUL-DE-VENCE

🏨 **LE ST.-PAUL**

$$$ ○○○○○

86 RUE GRANDE
TEL 04 93 32 65 25
FAX 04 93 32 52 94
lesaintpaul.com
A secluded, exquisitely furnished 16th-century town house, within the village walls.
🛏 15 + 3 suites 🚭 ⧆ All major cards

🏨 **LE HAMEAU**

$$ ○○○

528 RTE. DE LA COLLE
TEL 04 93 32 80 24
FAX 04 93 32 55 75
le-hameau.com
Excellent family hotel with large swimming pool and secluded location; some rooms have a private terrace.
🛏 19 P 🕐 Closed Nov.–Dec.
🚭 ⛴ ⧆ All major cards

SOMETHING SPECIAL

🍴 **COLOMBE D'OR**
🏨 $$$–$$$$$ ○○○

PLACE DES ORMEAUX–
PLACE DE GAULLE
TEL 04 93 32 80 02
FAX 04 93 32 77 78
la-colombe-dor.com
Dine on the terrace at this celebrity-haunted hotel-restaurant amid a priceless collection of art donated as payment for meals and rooms by Picasso, Calder, Braque, and more. Try the serving of 15

hors d'oeuvres and the souf-flés. Reserve rooms in advance.
🛏 16 + 10 suites 🕐 Closed Nov.–late Dec. ⧆ All major cards

VENCE

🏨 **CHÂTEAU DU**
🍴 **DOMAINE ST.-MARTIN**

$$$$$ ○○○○○

AV. DES TEMPLIERS
TEL 04 93 58 02 02
FAX 04 93 24 08 91
chateau-st-martin.com
Built on the site of a Knights of Templar fort, the large suites of this contemporary château have Louis XV–style furnish-ings, with balconies overlook-ing the Mediterranean. The one-Michelin-star restaurant serves up excellent roast prawns in balsamic vinaigrette and grilled turbot with cocoa bean and apricot purée.
🛏 38 P 🕐 Closed mid-Oct.–mid-Feb. 🚭 ⛴ ⧆ All major cards

🍴 **LES BACCHANALES**

$$

247 AV. DE PROVENCE
TEL 04 93 24 19 19
Market cooking shines at this Michelin-starred restaurant housed in a villa with modern and playful decor.
🕐 Closed Wed., & Mon.–Fri. L July–Aug. ⧆ All major cards

■ CÔTE D'AZUR: NICE TO MENTON

BEAULIEU-SUR-MER

🏨 **LA RÉSERVE**
🍴 **DE BEAULIEU**

$$$$$ ○○○○○

5 BLVD. DU MARÉCHAL LECLERC
TEL 04 93 01 00 01
FAX 04 93 01 28 99
reservebeaulieu.com
Fabulous Riviera hotel on the seafront, founded by James

Gordon Bennett, the famous proprietor of the *New York Herald Tribune*. It's called La Réserve for the seawater tank (*réserve*), where the chef used to keep live fish. The restau-rant, which has one Michelin star, still specializes in fish.
🛏 33 P 🕐 Closed mid-Nov.–mid-Dec. 🚭 Some rooms ⛴ ⧆ All major cards

🏨 **FRISIA**

$$ ○○○

5 CHEMIN CAMIN DE LA BEGUDA
TEL 04 93 79 08 11
FAX 04 93 79 37 79
This little coastal hotel on the port is classic, clean, and framed by a mountainous horizon.
🛏 34 ⧆ All major cards

🍴 **L'ESCENTIEL**

$$

26 BLVD. MARÉCHAL LECLERC
TEL 04 93 01 17 33
After 30 years of working in upscale restaurants on the

PRICES

HOTELS

An indication of the cost of a double room in the high season is given by $ signs.

$$$$$	Over $400
$$$$	$300–$400
$$$	$200–$300
$$	$100–$200
$	Under $100

RESTAURANTS

An indication of the cost of a three-course meal without drinks is given by $ signs.

$$$$$	Over $200
$$$$	$100–$200
$$$	$75–$100
$$	$50–$75
$	Under $50

Côte d'Azur, chef Charles Séméria returned home to open this tiny restaurant focusing on simple and fresh cuisine. ⊕ Closed Thurs., Tues. & Wed. D, & Sun. L 🕸 All major cards

ÈZE

🏨 CHÂTEAU DE LA
🍴 CHÈVRE D'OR
$$$$$ ✪✪✪✪✪
RUE DU BARRI
TEL 04 92 10 66 66
FAX 04 93 41 06 72
chevredor.com
High atop the eagle's nest village of Èze, this collection of restored, stone village houses clusters around the original manor house. Rooms are luxurious, including pink-marble bathrooms. The gourmet restaurant's menu changes with the seasons; plate glass windows look out on stunning sea views all around.
ⓘ 33 🅿 ⊕ Closed Nov.–March 🔲 ⬛ 🔳 🕸 All major cards

MENTON

🏨 AIGLON
$$$ ✪✪✪
7 AV. DE LA MADONE
TEL 04 93 57 55 55
FAX 04 93 35 92 39
hotelaiglon.net
A converted belle époque villa showcases a rococo-gilt lobby and luxurious gardens. Rooms are well appointed; ask for a garden view in summer. Dine by candlelight beside the pool.
ⓘ 29 🅿 ⊕ Closed mid-Nov.–mid-Dec. 🔲 ⬛ 🕸 All major cards

🏨 NAPOLÉON
$$$ ✪✪✪✪
29 PORTE DE FRANCE
TEL 04 93 35 89 50
napoleon-menton.com
A modern Riviera hotel with private terrace views of sea and mountains. Rooms are

bright and hung with the art of Menton lovers Jean Cocteau and Graham Sutherland.
ⓘ 44 🕸 All major cards

🍴 LE BISTROT
DES JARDINS
$$
14 AV. BOYER
TEL 04 93 28 28 09
Fresh Mediterranean cuisine that follows the market seasons. The terrace is a garden in the city.
⊕ Closed Sun. D & Mon.
🕸 All major cards

🍴 L'ULIVO
$
21 PLACE DU CAP
TEL 04 93 35 45 65
Convivial Italian trattoria serving a variety of pasta dishes. Steamed mussels are a specialty.
⊕ Closed Sun. D & Mon.
🕸 MC, V

MONACO: MONTE-CARLO

🏨 HERMITAGE
$$$$$ ✪✪✪✪✪
PLACE BEAUMARCHAIS
TEL 377 98 06 59 70
FAX 377 98 06 59 70
hotelhermitagemontecarlo.com
A luxurious belle époque palace with a huge, glass-domed winter garden, opulent restaurant, and terrace of cool marble.
ⓘ 209 + 18 suites 🅿 🔲 🕸 All major cards

🏨 METROPOLE
$$$$$ ✪✪✪✪
4 AV. DE LA MADONE
TEL 377 93 15 15 15
FAX 377 93 25 24 44
metropole.com
Historic palace renovated in 2004 to include a spa and even more sumptuous rooms. Gardens are an oasis of calm in the heart of Monte-Carlo.
ⓘ 146 🅿 🔲 🔳 ⬛ 🔳 🕸 All major cards

🏨 COLUMBUS
$$ ✪✪✪
23 AV. DES PAPALINS
TEL 377 92 05 90 00
FAX 377 92 05 91 67
columbushotels.com
The bourgeois answer to Monaco's old-fashioned, aristocratic tradition. Modern, chic, and seductively comfortable.
ⓘ 192 🅿 🔲 🔳 ⬛ 🔳 🕸 All major cards

🍴 LOUIS XV
$$$$$
HÔTEL DE PARIS
PLACE DU CASINO
TEL 377 98 06 88 64
Monaco's most famous restaurant, a three-Michelin-star establishment presided over by the celebrated Alain Ducasse. If you need to look at the prices, don't go. Typical dishes might be Provençal vegetables with black truffles, or pigeon with *foie gras de canard*.
⊕ Closed Tues.–Wed. Oct.–mid-Dec. 🕸 All major cards

🍴 LE BLUE BAY
$$$$
MONTE CARLO BAY HOTEL
4 AV. PRINCESSE GRACE
TEL 377 98 06 03 60
A colorful and stylish terrace on the water with inventive, well-prepared cuisine. Sunday brunch is popular.
⊕ Closed Mon., Sun. D, & Tues.–Sat. L 🕸 All major cards

🍴 CAFÉ DE PARIS
$$$
PLACE DU CASINO
TEL 377 98 06 76 23
Monte-Carlo's front-and-center brasserie with an enormous terrace and extravagant fin-de-siècle interior.
🕸 All major cards

NICE

🏨 LA PÉROUSE
$$$$$ ⭐⭐⭐⭐
11 QUAI RAUBA-CAPÉU
TEL 04 93 62 34 63
FAX 04 93 62 59 41
For a sea view that won't
break the bank. Flowery terrace and garden restaurant.
🛏 64 ⛔🏊⛔ All major cards

SOMETHING SPECIAL

🏨 NÉGRESCO
$$$$ ⭐⭐⭐⭐⭐
37 PROMENADE DES ANGLAIS
TEL 04 93 16 64 00
FAX 04 93 88 35 68
hotel-negresco-nice.com
The most famous and
expensive hotel in Nice. This
magnificent belle époque
building on the promenade des
Anglais has sumptuous furnishings and impeccable service. As
grand as it gets—look for the
vast Baccarat chandelier.
🛏 134 + 18 suites ⛔⛔
⛔ All major cards

🏨 BEAU RIVAGE
$$$ ⭐⭐⭐⭐
24 RUE ST.-FRANÇOIS-DE-PAULE
TEL 04 92 47 82 82
FAX 04 92 47 82 83
hotelnicebeaurivage.com
Ideally located on the edge
of the old town, with views
over the sea, this large hotel
has its own private beach
club. It was here that Matisse
stayed on his first few visits
to Nice.
🛏 118 ⛔⛔⛔ All major
cards

🏨 HI
$$$ ⭐⭐⭐⭐
3 AV. DES FLEURS
TEL 04 97 07 26 26
hi-hotel.net
This boutique hotel with
postmodern design and
informal service offers themed
bedrooms for music lovers,

computer freaks, or movie
fans. No restaurant but DIY
bar on each floor.
🛏 38 ⛔ All major cards

🏨 WINDSOR
$$ ⭐⭐⭐⭐
11 RUE DALPOSSO
TEL 04 93 88 59 35
FAX 04 93 88 94 57
hotelwindsornice.com
Individually designed rooms
by famous and not-so-
famous artists alike in a sleek
postmodern hotel three
blocks from the beach. With
hammam, massages, and
beautiful tropical garden.
🛏 57 🅿⛔⛔🏊⛔ All
major cards

🍽 LA MÉRENDA
$$
3 RUE RAOUL BOSIO
A tiny bistro famous for its
traditional Niçois dishes:
stockfish, beignets, stuffed
sardines, beef daube. No
phone and no reservations.
Get there early.
🕐 Closed Sat.–Sun. Aug.,
& late Nov.–mid-Dec. ⛔
⛔ No credit cards

🍽 LE SAFARI
$$
1 COURS SALEYA
TEL 04 93 80 18 44
Big café with Mediterranean
blue shutters, close to the
market on cours Saleya. Great
for alfresco dining. Try the
deep rich calamari daube, or
bagna cauda, a hot anchovy
dip with raw vegetables.
⛔ All major cards

🍽 BISTROT D'ANTOINE
$
27 RUE DE LA PRÉFECTURE
TEL 04 93 85 29 57
Good friends meet here for
a convivial atmosphere and
a good dose of southern
French cooking.
🕐 Closed Sun.–Mon. ⛔ All
major cards

🍽 TERRES DE TRUFFES
$
11 RUE ST.-FRANÇOIS-DE-PAULE
TEL 04 93 62 07 68
Chef Bruno Clément's
boutique selling truffle-related
products. The truffle-tasting
bar inside has appetizers in
addition to full-course meals—
look for tortellini soup with
truffles and the ever popular
truffle ice cream.
🕐 Closed Sun. ⛔ All major
cards

PEILLON

🏨🍽 AUBERGE DE LA MADONE
$$ ⭐⭐⭐
2 PLACE AUGUSTE ARNULF
TEL 04 93 79 91 17
FAX 04 93 79 99 36
Top pick of the tiny hotels
dotting Nice's backcountry.
With views looking out onto
the village, and a restaurant
serving local specialties.
🛏 20 🕐 Closed mid-Oct.–
Dec.; restaurant closed Wed.
⛔ MC, V

ST.-JEAN-CAP-FERRAT

🏨🍽 GRAND HÔTEL DU CAP FERRAT
$$$$$ ⭐⭐⭐⭐
BLVD. DU GÉNÉRAL DE GAULLE
TEL 04 93 76 50 50
FAX 04 93 76 04 52
grand-hotel-cap-ferrat.com
One of the Riviera's legendary grand hotels, secluded
in its own tropical gardens
overlooking the sea, with a
private funicular down to a
terrace and the seawater pool.
Magnificent interior furnishings and a one-Michelin-star
restaurant. Tennis courts.
🛏 44 + 9 suites 🅿 🕐 Closed
Oct.–April ⛔ ⛔ All major
cards

HÔTEL LE PANORAMIC
$$ ✪✪✪
3 AV. ALBERT 1ER
TEL 04 93 76 00 37
FAX 04 93 76 15 78
hotel-lepanoramic.com
All rooms in this friendly, quiet hotel have balconies facing the Mediterranean sunrise.
🛏 20 🕐 Closed Nov.–Dec.
🃏 All major cards

▌ ALPES PROVENÇALES

BARCELONNETTE

AZTECA
$$ ✪✪✪
3 RUE FRANÇOIS ARNAUD
TEL 04 92 81 46 36
azteca-hotel.fr
Centrally located 19th-century villa with Mexican-style rooms. Free shuttle to the ski slopes in season.
🛏 27 🅿 🕐 Closed Nov.
🃏 MC, V

BREIL-SUR-ROYA

CASTEL DU ROY
$$ ✪✪
RTE. DE L'AIGARA
TEL 04 93 04 43 66
castelduroy.com
The most comfortable choice for those visiting the Vallée des Merveilles. Simple rooms, but the peaceful setting in the forested slopes just outside of town make for a lovely stay.
🛏 19 🅿 🕐 Closed Nov.–April
🃏 MC, V

DIGNE-LES-BAINS

LE GRAND PARIS
🍴 **$$ ✪✪✪✪**
19 BLVD. THIERS
TEL 04 92 31 11 15
FAX 04 92 32 32 82
hotel-grand-paris.com
A 17th-century monastery

has been transformed into a luxurious retreat with a superb restaurant. Tennis courts and golf.
🛏 20 🕐 Closed Dec.–March
🅿 🔄 🏊 📺 🃏 All major cards

VILLA GAIA
$$
RTE. DE NICE
TEL 04 92 31 21 60
FAX 04 92 32 32 82
hotel-villagaia-digne.com
An 18th-century home with a garden, library, and quiet rooms without televisions. Gourmet dinners for guests only.
🛏 10 🃏 All major cards

MOUSTIERS-STE.-MARIE

SOMETHING SPECIAL

LA BASTIDE DE
🍴 **MOUSTIERS**
$$$/$$$$ ✪✪✪✪
CHEMIN DE QUINSON
TEL 04 92 70 47 47
FAX 04 93 70 47 48
bastide-moustiers.com
Alain Ducasse transformed this 17th-century farmhouse into one of Provence's most beautiful country inns. The one-Michelin-star restaurant is worth a trip in itself.
🛏 12 🅿 🕐 Closed Dec.–Feb.
📶 🔄 🏊 🃏 All major cards

🍴 LES SANTONS
$–$$
PLACE POMEY
TEL 04 92 74 66 48
A tiny restaurant with gorgeous views of the village church and stream. Its most famous dish is wild hare stuffed with foie gras and truffles. Reservations required.
🕐 Closed Mon. D & Tues. mid-Nov.–mid-Feb. 🃏 All major cards

LA PALUD-SUR-VERDON

HÔTEL DES GORGES DU VERDON
$$$ ✪✪✪
LA PALUD
TEL 04 92 77 38 26
FAX 04 92 77 35 00
hotel-des-gorges-du-verdon.fr
Ideally situated near the edge of the Gorges du Verdon, this excellent mid-range choice has modern, colorful rooms with sweeping views.
🛏 27 🅿 🕐 Closed Nov.–March 🏊 🃏 MC, V

ST.-DALMAS-DE-TENDE

LE PRIEURÉ
🍴 **$ ✪✪**
RUE JEAN MÉDECIN
TEL 04 93 04 75 70
FAX 04 93 04 71 58
leprieure.org
Serving fresh trout and *magret de canard*, this is one of the better restaurants near the Vallée des Merveilles. Pleasant rooms available.
🛏 24 🅿 🕐 Closed Nov.–March 🃏 All major cards

VALENSOLE

HOSTELLERIE DE
🍴 **LA FUSTE**
$$ ✪✪✪✪
LIEU-DIT DE LA FUSTE
TEL 04 92 72 05 95
FAX 04 92 72 92 93
lafuste.com
This 17th-century farmhouse was converted into an oasis of luxury amid fields of lavender, almond trees, and sun-drenched hills. Excellent service. Enjoy gastronomic cuisine *en plein air*.
🛏 12 🅿 🕐 Closed mid-Nov.–mid-Dec. 📶 Some rooms 🏊 🃏 All major cards

Shopping

Provence has been marketed to the outside world for centuries, so it's not surprising that many of its traditional products are already well known even to first-time visitors. Lavender, *herbes de Provence,* and olive oil all bespeak the intense sunlight and distinctive aromas of the area. Handicrafts are prolific as well: terra-cotta *santons,* woven baskets, and Provençal linens to name a few examples. In addition to these regional products are numerous department stores and chic boutiques, catering to the well-heeled international clientele that has made Provence and the Côte d'Azur a home away from home for the past several decades. Nice, Cannes, St.-Tropez, and Aix-en-Provence are the top cities in which to window-shop and see the latest in French fashion trends.

Markets

Markets are still the best way to shop in Provence. Most towns and villages have at least a weekly market, and in bigger cities they may even be daily (town and village markets are noted in the margin information throughout the book). See sidebar p. 181.

Weekly Flea Markets

Provence has several flea markets (*marchés aux puces* or *brocantes*) selling secondhand goods, antiques, and local curios. Arrive early to find the bargains.

Aix-en-Provence
Place du Verdun, Tues., Thurs., & Sat.

Cannes
Rue Forville, Mon.

L'Isle-sur-la-Sorgue
Sun. (see sidebar p. 62)

Marseille
Av. du Cap Pinède, Sun.

Nice
Cours Saleya, Mon.

Nîmes
Blvd. Jean-Jaurès, Mon.

Dégustations

Dégustation means "tasting." All over France you will see signs inviting you to sample the local produce, particularly the wine. You are not obliged to buy, but it would be thought uncivil not to purchase at least one bottle.

Opening Hours

Food stores, especially bakers (*boulangeries*), open early, around

7 a.m. Small stores and department stores (*grands magasins*) usually open at 9 a.m. Most stores close for lunch between noon and 2 or 3 p.m., staying open until 7 or 7:30 in the evening. Hypermarkets will usually stay open all day until quite late.

Many stores close on Mondays; food shops—especially bakers—open on Sunday mornings, when it is fun to watch everyone buying their tarts and cakes for Sunday lunch.

Payment

Supermarkets accept credit cards, but smaller stores often do not. Check the signs on the door before you go in. Some traders are reluctant to accept payment by American Express cards.

Exports

Most purchases include TVA (VAT or value-added tax) at a base rate running currently at 20 percent. Visitors from outside the European Union may claim back TVA if they spend more than 300 euros in one place: Ask the store for a completed *bordereau* (export sales invoice), which must be shown, together with the goods, to customs officers when you leave the country. You then mail the form back to the retailer, who will refund the TVA—though this may take some time. Or you can get an immediate refund (minus a percentage) from merchants who use refund services like Global Blue or Premier Tax Free.

WHAT TO BUY

Antiques & Flea Markets

The best place for serious antique hunting is L'Isle-sur-la-Sorgue, where more than 300 dealers have set up shop (open Sat.–Mon.), in addition to the huge weekly antique flea market on Sundays along the quays of the River Sorgue. The items on sale range from furniture and paintings to curios and clothes.

Le Village des Antiquaires
2 bis av. de l'Égalité
L'Isle-sur-la-Sorgue
Tel 04 90 38 04 57
levillagedesantiquairesdelagare.com
Close to 100 antique dealers are stuffed into this market space, specializing in everything from china to bathroom furnishings.

Ceramics

Pottery has been a regional export since Roman times. The art began to die out around the turn of the 20th century, but underwent a major renaissance following the end of World War II. Picasso was largely responsible for its popular rebirth in Vallauris along the Côte d'Azur; Moustiers-Ste.-Marie specializes in the altogether different tradition of faïence, meticulously painted tableware. There are many pottery shops here along route de Riez. Other *poteries* include:

Galerie Sassi-Milici
65 av. Georges Clemenceau
Vallauris 06220
Tel 04 93 64 65 71
sassi-milici.com

Ceramics individually decorated by international artists.

Syndicat des Potiers
Rue Jean Gerbino
Vallauris 06220
Tel 04 93 64 88 30

English-Language Books
Antibes Books
24 rue Aubernon
Antibes 06600
Tel 04 93 34 74 11
Book in Bar
1 bis rue Cabassol
Aix-en-Provence 13100
Tel 04 42 26 60 07
www.bookinbar.com
Camili Books & Tea
155 rue Carreterie
Avignon 84000
Tel 04 90 27 38 50
camili-booksandtea.com
Cannes English Bookshop
11 rue Bivouac Napoléon
Cannes 06400
Tel 04 93 99 40 08
cannesenglishbookshop.com

Fabric
Today, you can find fabric shops in most major towns. See sidebar p. 69.
Les Indiennes de Nîmes
2 blvd. des Arènes
Nîmes 30000
Tel 04 66 21 69 57
indiennesdenimes.fr
Sells home accessories and clothing; fabric by the meter also available.
La Maison des Lices
2 & 18 blvd. Louis Blanc
St.-Tropez 83990
Tel 04 94 97 64 64
blancdivoire.com
Fine linens and other household products.
Les Olivades
12 rue Granet
Aix-en Provence 13100
Tel 04 42 23 29 02
lesolivades.fr
The largest traditional fabrics

manufacturer with stores in all the major towns of Provence. See website for other locations.
Souleïado
18 blvd. de Lices
Arles 13200
Tel 04 90 18 25 91
Traditional linens with outlets all over Provence.
Tissus Grégoire
309 av. du 19 mars 1962
St.-Saturin-les-Avignon 24450
Tel 04 90 85 56 45
Offers a wide range of Provençal fabrics.

Glass
Cristallerie d'Èze
8 rue Principale
Èze 06360
Tel 04 93 41 20 34
Crystal and glassware.
La Verrerie de Biot
Chemin des Combes
Biot 06410
Tel 04 93 65 03 00
verreriebiot.com
Glassblowing factory with products for sale in the showroom; guided tours also available.

Paper
Vallis Clausa, Moulin à Papier
Chemin de la Fontaine
Fontaine-de-Vaucluse 84800
Tel 04 90 20 34 14
An old-fashioned paper mill here is used to produce handmade paper and related products.

Perfume
The three main perfume houses of Grasse all sell individual perfumes and gift sets created by their *parfumeurs-in-residence*. See sidebar p. 145.
Florame
34 blvd. Mirabeau
St.-Rémy 13210
Tel 04 32 60 05 18
florame.com
Essential oils, aromatherapy, and soaps in the Musée des Arômes.

Fragonard
20 blvd. Fragonard
Grasse 06130
Tel 04 93 36 44 65
fragonard.com
Galimard
73 rte. de Cannes
Grasse 06130
Tel 04 93 09 20 00
galimard.com
Molinard
60 blvd. Victor Hugo
Grasse 06130
Tel 04 93 36 01 62
molinard.com

Sandals
Les Sandales Tropéziennes
18 bis rue Georges Clemenceau
St.-Tropez 83990
Tel 04 94 97 19 55
chaussure-tropeziennes.fr
Handmade leather sandals since 1927.

Santons
Family-run workshops still make each santon by hand (see sidebar p. 109). Christmas santon fairs also are the perfect place to pick up a figurine or two; Marseille's is the oldest, dating back to 1803 (*marseille-tourisme.com*).
Arterra
3 rue du Petit Puits
Marseille 13002
Tel 04 91 91 03 31
santons-arterra.com
La Cité de l'Art Santonnier
Thérèse Neveu
Aubagne 13400
Tel 04 42 03 43 10
A museum dedicated to the tradition of santons, with a directory of modern santon makers in Aubagne.
Santons Fouque
65 cours Gambetta
Aix-en-Provence 13100
Tel 04 42 26 33 38
santons-fouque.com
One of the most acclaimed santon workshops of Provence.

Santons Girault
35 rue Bédarrides
Aix-en-Provence 13100
Tel 04 42 27 17 35
santons-girault.com
Carries a full line of santons in various sizes.

Santons Richard
955 chemin Bouenhoure-Haut
Aix-en-Provence 13090
Tel 04 42 20 10 15
santons-richard.com
A maker of santons since 1968. The workshop is open for visits during the week.

Soap

The highly successful L'Occitane chain found its niche exporting the aroma of Provence with soaps, creams, and other beauty products. When the French think of Provençal soap, however, the first image that springs to mind is the olive green block of *savon de Marseille;* see sidebar p. 117.

Compagnie de Provence
18 rue Davso
Marseille 13001
Tel 04 91 33 04 17
compagniedeprovence.com
Carrying the time-honored cubes of Marseille soap.

L'Occitane
21 rue Grande
Manosque 04100
Tel 04 92 72 41 02
loccitane.com
The home store of the renowned producer of Provence-related beauty supplies.

Savonnerie Marius Fabre Jeune
148 av. Paul Bourret
Salon-de-Provence 13300
Tel 04 90 53 24 77
marius-fabre.com
Like Marseille, Salon-de-Provence was also a major producer of soap in the 19th century.

FOOD & WINE
Chocolate, Jams, & Pastries

Delectable chocolates, homemade jams, candied fruits, honey, and a mind-boggling variety of pastries are just some of the many sweets that southern France has perfected over the years.

La Bonbonnière
57 rue Sous Préfecture
Apt 84400
Tel 04 90 74 12 92
labonbonniere84.com
Candied fruits, jams, and chocolate.

Calissons du Roy René
330 rue Guillaume du Vair
Aix-en-Provence 13545
Tel 04 42 39 29 89
calisson.com
Aix's own almond-flavored *calissons* and other pastries.

Chocolatier Schies
125 rue d'Antibes
Cannes 06400
Tel 04 93 39 01 03

Chocolatiére de Marseille
35 rue Vacon
Marseille 13001
Tel 04 91 11 96 24

Clavel Confiseur
Place Aristide Briand
Carpentras 84200
clavel-confiserie.com
Maker of famous citrus and mint flavored candies called *berlingots.*

Confiserie Bono
280 allée Jean-Jaurès
Carpentras 84200
Tel 04 90 63 04 99
confiseriebono.com
Candied fruits and jams.

Confiserie Florian
14 quai Papacino
Nice 06300
Tel 04 93 55 43 50
confiserieflorian.com
The most well-known producer of candied fruits on the Riviera.

Four des Navettes
136 rue Sainte
Marseille 13007
Tel 04 91 33 32 12
fourdesnavettes.com
One of Marseille's oldest bakeries, specializing in boat-shaped *navettes.*

Joel Durand
3 blvd. Victor Hugo
St.-Rémy de Provence 13210
Tel 04 90 92 38 25
joeldurand-chocolatier.fr
Maker of fine chocolates with letters of the alphabet that correspond with the flavor inside. L is for lavender, etc. Tip: Choose flavors that spell a message in your box of chocolates.

Puyricard
Av. Georges de Fabry
Aix-en-Provence 13100
Tel 04 42 28 18 18
Chocolate and other sweets.

Venturini Fougassettes
1 rue Marcel Journet
Grasse 06130
Tel 04 93 36 20 47
Sweet flatbreads flavored with orange blossom.

Herbs & Other Specialties

Most herbs can be found at local markets, though in the lavender country around Sault and Valensole, you can also buy lavender-related products (including honey) direct from the farmers themselves at roadside stalls. Little sachets of *herbes de Provence* are ubiquitous in tourist shops.

Alziari
14 rue St.-François-de-Paule
Nice 06100
Tel 04 93 85 76 92
alziari.com
Actually an olive oil producer, Alziari also sells about everything one could ever want from inland Provence: herbs, soaps, honey, and tapenade.

Boutique de l'Abbaye de Lérins
Île St.-Honorat 06400
Tel 04 92 99 54 00
abbayedelerins.com

The place to buy the famous 45-herb liqueur made by the monks, wine, and other regional products.

Cannolive
16 rue Vénizélos
Cannes 06400
Tel 04 93 39 08 19
cannolive.fr
Inland Provençal specialties.

Les Délices du Luberon
1 av. du Partage des Eaux
L'Isle-sur-la-Sorgue 84800
Tel 04 90 20 77 37
delices-du-luberon.fr
Tapenades, sun-dried tomatoes, and pesto.

L'Herbier en Provence
Montée La Castre
St. Paul 06570
Tel 04 93 32 91 51
lherbierenprovence.com

Musée de la Lavande
276 rte. de Gordes
Coustellet 84220
Tel 04 90 76 91 23
museedelalavande.com
Extensive boutique full of lavender-related items.

Au Père Blaize
4 rue Méolan
Marseille 13001
Tel 04 91 54 04 01
pereblaize.fr
Pharmacy and traditional herbalist.

Olive Oil

The best place to buy olive oil is from *moulins à huile,* oil presses, which are often signposted off backroads throughout Provence. The two major areas of olive cultivation center around St.-Rémy and Nyons (in the Vaucluse), though mills exist even along stretches of the Riviera. See sidebar p. 102.

Castelas
Les Baux de Provence 13520
tel 04 90 54 50 86
castelas.com

Château d'Estoublon
Rte. de Maussane

Fontvieille 13990
Tel 04 90 54 64 00
estoublon.com

Huilerie Sainte-Anne
138 rte. de Draguignan
Grasse 06130
Tel 04 93 70 21 42
huilerie-sainte-anne-boutique.com

Moulin à Huile Lottier
102 av. des Acacias
Menton 06500
Tel 04 93 35 79 15

Moulin Jean-Marie Cornille
Maussane-les-Alpilles 13520
Tel 04 90 54 32 37
moulin-cornille.com

Moulin d'Opio
2 rte. de Châteauneuf
Opio 06650
Tel 04 93 77 23 03
moulin-dopio.com

Pastis

The two major brand names in the industry are Ricard and Pernod. Bottles are available in all supermarkets. See sidebar p. 93.

Wine

Some of the finest French wines originate in Provence, and the opportunity to stop in and visit individual *domaines* and walk off with a crate of a wine you'd never find anywhere else is one of the great delights of the area. The *maisons des vins* listed below are good starting points to sample the regional appellations. See sidebar p. 75.

La Carré du Palais
(Côtes du Rhône)
Place de l'Horloge
Avignon 84000
carredupalaisavignon.com

Caveau du Gigondas
Place du Portail
Gigondas 84190
Tel 04 90 65 82 29
caveaudugigondas.com
Comprehensive selection of Gigondas wines at cellar-door prices.

Château Vignelaure
(Côteaux d'Aix)
Rte. Jouques
Rians 83560
Tel 04 94 37 21 10
vignelaure.com

Domaine de la Ferme Blanche
(Vignoble de Cassis)
D559
Cassis 13260
Tel 04 42 01 00 74

Domaine de la Genestière
Chemin de Cravailleux
Tavel 30126
Tel 04 66 50 07 03
domaine-genestiere.com

Domaine des Terres Blanches
(Côteaux des Baux)
Off D99
St.-Rémy 13210
Tel 04 90 95 91 66
terresblanches.com

Domaine de Trévallon
(Côteaux d'Aix)
Chemin Romain Arles
St.-Etienne-du-Gres 13210
Tel 04 90 49 06 00
domainedetrevallon.com

Maison des Vins
(Côtes de Provence)
N7
Les Arcs 83460
Tel 04 94 99 50 20
maison-des-vins.fr

Vignerons de Beaumes de Venise
Quartier Ravel
Beaumes-de-Venise 84190
Tel 04 90 12 41 00
beaumes-de-venise.com

Vinadéa
8 rue Marechal Foch
Châteauneuf-du-Pape 84230
Tel 04 90 83 70 69
www.vinadea.com
A hundred Châteauneuf-du-Pape estates sold at cellar-door prices.

La Vinothèque
18 rue Jean Reboul
Nîmes 30900
Tel 04 66 67 20 44
la-vinotheque-nimes.fr

Entertainment

Entertainment possibilities vary from sophisticated opera billings to traditional bullfights, with several towns transforming ancient Roman monuments into impressive outdoor venues. Nonstop festival lineups ensure something for everyone, with jazz concerts, Gypsy pilgrimages, photography exhibits, and theater performances year-round. Casinos and movie theaters round off the list of after-dark entertainment choices, and, for the real night owls, there are always the clubs of Marseille, St.-Tropez, Cannes, and Nice.

Bullfights

Known as *tauromachie* in French, the bullfights staged in the Roman arenas of Arles and Nîmes are an excellent way of experiencing a real slice of traditional Provençal life. Decidedly less gruesome than the bullfights of Spain, it's for the most part the *raseteurs,* not the animals, who get hurt. The best times to see a bullfight are the Féria de Pentecôte in Nîmes; and Féria de Pâques and Féria du Riz in Arles. Tickets are available at the ticket offices of the arenas; otherwise you can also ask the tourist office for more information.

Casinos

Casinos are all part of the allure of the French Riviera, the most famous and over-the-top of them all being Le Casino, in Monte-Carlo.

Le Casino
Place du Casino
Monte-Carlo, Monaco
Tel (377) 98 06 21 21
casinomontecarlo.com

Casino de Bandol
2 place Lucien Artaud
Bandol 83150
Tel 04 94 29 31 31
casinobandol.com

Casino de Cavalaire
Promenade Port
Cavalaire-sur-Mer 83240
Tel 04 94 01 92 40
casinodecavalaire.com

Casino de Grasse
Blvd. Jeu de Ballon
Grasse 06130
Tel 04 93 36 91 00

Casino Ruhl
1 promenade des Anglais
Nice 06000
Tel 04 97 03 12 22
lucienbarriere.com

Children's Entertainment

Kids, of course, don't need much more than a sandy strip of sand to frolic all day long, but here are some family-friendly places should the little ones tire of the surf.

Aqualand Fréjus
Quartier le Capou - RN98
Fréjus
Tel 04 94 51 82 51
aqualand.fr
Slides, fun pool, food and drink, and more.

Aqualand Sainte-Maxime
Route Plan de la Tour
Ste.-Maxime
Tel 04 94 55 54 54
aqualand.fr
Another member of the Aqualand family (see above).

Canyon Forest
Villeneuve-Loubet
Tel 04 92 02 88 88
canyonforest.com
Adventure park extraordinaire, with rock climbing, cycling, and zip-lining.

Marineland
306 av. Mozart
Antibes 06600
Tel 0892 42 62 26
marineland.fr
Sharks, penguins, dolphins, plus water park and zoo.

Parc Aventure de la Coudou
Rond point du lycée de la Coudoulière, Bois de la Coudoulière
Six-Fours-les-Plages

Tel 06 63 77 02 06
coudouparc.com
Seaside adventure park comprising treetop courses connected with ladders, rope slides, and bridges.

Parc Spirou
800 allée de Beaulieu, Monteux
parc-spirou.com
A compact amusement park based on the comic-book adventures of the popular, Franco–Belgian Spirou and Fantasio characters.

Splashworld Provence
800 allée de Beaulieu, Monteux
parcs-aquatiques.com/splashworld-provence
A seasonal, ecological waterpark including a surfing simulator.

Cinema

The interest that the French display in cinema is on par with the attention that other cultures devote to professional sports, and Provence is no exception. The following theaters screen movies in V.O., meaning they're shown in their original language with French subtitles. Not only will you find Hollywood's latest blockbusters, but also independent and classic films that rarely make it to the big screen elsewhere. Cannes's world-famous International Film Festival takes place each May, but without some sort of relevant credentials, getting a seat borders on impossible.

Cinéma Mazarin
6 rue Laroque
Aix-en-Provence 13100
Tel 08 92 68 72 70
lescinemasaixois.com

Cinéma Mercury
16 place Garibaldi
Nice 06300
Tel 08 36 68 81 06
Cinéma Olympia
5 rue d'Antibes
Cannes 06400
Tel 04 93 39 13 93
cinemaolympia-cannes.fr
Cinéma Renoir
24 cours Mirabeau
Aix-en-Provence 13100
Tel 08 92 68 72 70
lescinemasaixois.com
Cinéma Rialto
4 rue de Rivoli
Nice 06000
Tel 08 92 68 00 41
Cinéma Utopia
4 rue Escaliers Ste.-Anne
Avignon 84000
Tel 04 90 82 65 36
cinemas-utopia.org
Cinéma Les Variétés
37 rue Vincent Scotto
Marseille 13001
Tel 08 92 68 05 97
Entrevue
23 quai Marx Dormoy
Arles 13200
Tel 04 90 93 37 28
lentrevue-restaurant.com
Bookstore, hammam, and
movie theater.

Opera, Ballet, & Classical Music

In addition to the main opera houses and classical music venues, be on the lookout for signs posted outside churches and cathedrals, which make for intimate and enchanting concert spaces. During the summer a number of music festivals take place throughout the south, many staged in spectacular outdoor locations such as the Roman theater in Orange.
Ballet National de Marseille
20 blvd. Gabès
Marseille 13008
Tel 04 91 32 73 27
ballet-de-marseille.com

Opéra de Marseille
2 rue Molière
Marseille 13001
Tel 04 91 55 11 10
opera.marseille.fr
In a 20th-century art deco building downtown.
Opéra de Monte-Carlo
Place du Casino
Monaco 98000
Tel 377 98 06 28 00
opera.mc
Opéra de Nice
4 rue St.-François-de-Paule
Nice 06300
Tel 04 92 17 40 40
opera-nice.org
Opera and music concerts in Vieux Nice.
Opéra-Théâtre
1 rue de Racine
Avignon 84007
Tel 04 90 14 26 40
operagrandavignon.fr
Built in 1847, boasting a year-round bill of opera, music, and theater performances.
Palais de l'Europe
8 av. Boyer
Menton 06500
04 92 41 76 50
Menton's cultural center, hosting operas, ballets, and music concerts.
Théâtre Antique
Rue Madeleine Roch
Orange 84100
Tel 04 90 51 17 60
theatre-antique.com
Ticket office for events staged in Orange's majestic Roman theater, including the Chorégies music festival in July and Aug.
Théâtre du Jeu de Paume
21 rue de l'Opéra
Aix-en-Provence 13100
Tel 04 42 99 12 00
lestheatres.net
Beautiful 18th-century theater with a varied program.

Stadium Events

Follow the crowds to big-name stadium events.

Stade Vélodrome
3 blvd. Michelet
Marseille 13008
Tel 04 13 64 64 71
lenouveaustadevelodrome.com
Home to the Olympique de Marseille football club, a 67,000-seat multipurpose stadium.
Zénith-Oméga
Blvd. Commandant Nicolas
Toulon 83000
Tel 04 94 22 66 77
zenith-omega-toulon.com
Popular concert hall with 8,875 seats.

FURTHER READING

Countless books have been written about Provence. Here are just a few:
Collected Short Stories (1990), by Somerset Maugham. Includes "The Fact of Life" and "Three Fat Women from Antibes," which take place in Provence by the St.-Jean-Cap-Ferrat resident.
The Count of Monte Cristo (1845) and *The Man in the Iron Mask,* by Alexandre Dumas. Two classics set partly in 19th-century Marseille.
A Little Tour in France (1885), by Henry James. A lively personal account of James's solo trip through France, including nine chapters about Provence.
Perfume (2001) by Patrick Suskind. The fascinating, horrifying tale of a gifted boy in 18th-century Grasse who sets out to create his own perfume.
Provence (1935) by Ford Madox Ford. A florid, rambling account of Provence between the wars.
Tender is the Night (1934), by F. Scott Fitzgerald. The decadent '20s Jazz Age on Cap d'Antibes.
Two Towns in Provence (1983), by M. F. K. Fisher. Fisher's classic and unforgettable portraits of Aix-en-Provence and Marseille.
Wine & War (2002), by Don and Petie Kladstrup. How French winemakers saved the nation's vineyards from WWII invaders.

Activities

A wide variety of activities can be pursued in Provence and along the Mediterranean, ranging from the inert (lying on the beach) to the extreme (bungee jumping). Virtually everywhere in the region you can walk, ride, and play golf, and the coasts offer a huge variety of marine and bathing activities. Most towns have excellent public swimming pools and sports facilities.

A good place to pick up general information is the local tourist office. However, for a more comprehensive guide to sporting activities—be it cycling, sailing, hiking, or scuba diving—check in with the departmental tourist offices (Comité Départemental de Tourisme) listed below.

Alpes de Haute Provence
tourisme-alpes-haute-provence.com
Alpes Maritimes
cotedazur-tourisme.com
Bouches-du-Rhône
visitprovence.com
Hautes Alpes
hautes-alpes.net
Provence-Alpes-Côte d'Azur
tourismepaca.fr
Var
visitvar.fr
Vaucluse
provenceguide.com

Ballooning

Hot-air ballooning is a unique and thrilling way to discover the Provençal landscape. Rides usually last from one to two hours.
France Montgolfières
4 bis rue du Saussis
Semur en Auxois 21140
Tel 03 80 97 38 61
france-balloons.com
Montgolfière Vol-terre
Hameau des Goubands
St.-Saturnin d'Apt 84490
Tel 06 03 54 10 92

Bird-watching

The main magnet for serious birders is the Camargue wetlands, home to hundreds of migrating bird species for part of each year. Within the protected area are two facilities offering an introduction to the flora and fauna of the region, as well as walking trails. See also sidebar p. 90.
Maison du Parc Naturel Régional de Camargue
Mas du Pont de Rousty
D570, Pont de Gau
Tel 04 90 97 86 32
parc-camargue.fr
Parc Ornithologique de Pont de Gau
D570, Pont de Gau
Arles 13200
Tel 04 90 97 10 82
parcornithologique.com

Boat Trips

Isles de Stel
12 rue Amiral Coubert
Aigues-Mortes 30220
Tel 04 66 53 60 70
croisiere-de-camargue.com
Boat trips through the Camargue.
Trans Côte d'Azur
Quai Amiral Infernet
Nice 06300
Tel 04 92 00 42 30
trans-cote-azur.com
Glass-bottomed boat trips along the coast.

Bungee Jumping

One of the highest bungee-jumping spots in Europe is the Pont de l'Artuby, 600 feet (180 m) above the water, in the Gorges du Verdon.

Canyoning

Canyoning (aka canyoneering) is an increasingly popular adventure sport that involves the descent of relatively inaccessible mountain streams through the use of climbing equipment and techniques.
AET Nature
Foussa
Breil-sur-Roya 06540
Tel 04 93 04 47 64
aetcanyoning.com
Canyoning, rafting, and climbing in the Roya Valley.
Aqua Viva Est
12 blvd. République
Castellane 04120
Tel 04 92 83 75 74
aquavivaest.com
Aventures et Nature
La Palud-sur-Verdon 04120
Tel 04 92 77 30 43
www.aventuresetnature.com
Base Sport et Nature
Brec
Entrevaux 04320
Tel 04 93 05 41 18
rafting-verdon-bsn.com

Cycling

Cycling is a French passion that ranks up there with (and stands in direct contrast to) the regional *boules* obsession. People are surprisingly helpful when it comes to accommodating bicycles, and most medium-size towns have at least one bike shop, with both rental and repair services. A growing interest in mountain biking (known in French as VTT) has brought about a new spin on the traditional sport. See also sidebar p. 56.
Holiday Bikes
provence-bike.com
French bike rental chain, with numerous locations throughout Provence. They rent both road bikes and mountain bikes.

Le Provence à Vélo
provence-cycling.com
Cycling itineraries in the Vaucluse, including Luberon, Ventoux, Côtes du Rhône vineyards, and more.

Golf

There are surprisingly more golf courses in the region than one would expect, especially given the arid climate. It is a sport that has a long history here, beginning with European vacationers in the late 1800s.

Golf Club Aix-Marseille
Domaine de Riquetti, Les Milles
Aix-en-Provence 13290
Tel 04 42 24 20 41
golfaixmarseille.com
One of the oldest courses in Provence, built in 1935.

Golf des Baux de Provence
Domaine Manville
Les-Baux-de-Provence 13520
Tel 04 90 54 40 20
domainedemanville.fr

Golf du Grand Avignon
Les Chênes Verts
Vedène 84270
Tel 04 90 31 49 94
golfgrandavignon.com

Golf du Roquebrune
D7, Les Issambres
Roquebrune-sur-Argens 83520
Tel 04 94 19 60 35
golfderoquebrune.com

Golf du Ste.-Maxime
Rte. du Débarquement
Ste.-Maxime 83120
Tel 04 94 55 02 02
sainte-maxime.bluegreen.com

Golf de Servanes
Rte. de Servanes
Mouriès 13890
Tel 04 90 47 59 95
golfclub.com

Provence Country Club
Rte. de Fontaine-de-Vaucluse
Saumane-de-Vaucluse 84800
Tel 04 90 20 20 65
provencecountryclub.fr

Horseback Riding

For information on serious horseback riding in the Camargue and other areas, contact the centers below. See also sidebar p. 89.

Centre Équestre de la Ville de Marseille
33 Traverse Carthage
Marseille 13008
Tel 04 91 73 72 94

Centre de Tourisme Équestre Brenda
Mas St. George (Astouin)
Les-Stes.-Maries-de-la-Mer 13460
Tel 04 90 97 52 08
brendatourismeequestre.com

Rafting & Canoeing

Most of Provence's rivers are reined in by at least one dam, if not more. Nevertheless, white-water rafting and kayaking are possible on some stretches in Haute-Provence and are an excellent way to see the Europe's deepest canyon, les Gorges du Verdon.

Aboard Rafting
8 place de l'Église
Castellane 04120
Tel 04 92 83 76 11
rafting-verdon.com

Action Aventure Rafting
12 rue Nationale
Castellane 04120
Tel 04 92 83 79 39
action-aventure.com

Eau Vive Evasion Rafting
Place Revelly
Annot 04240
Tel 04 92 83 38 09
eau-vive-evasion.com

Kayak Vert
La Beaume
Fontaine-de-Vaucluse 84800
Tel 04 90 20 35 44
canoevaucluse.com
For relaxed day trips downstream to L'Isle-sur-la-Sorgue. Fishing supplies are also available.

Kayak Vert Camargue
Mas de Sylverèal
Sylverea 30600

Tel 04 66 73 57 17
kayakvert-camargue.fr
Rents canoes and kayaks for paddling trips through the Camargue.

Rock Climbing

Jagged limestone outcrops and cliff faces make up the majority of the region's impressive climbing sites. The Calanques, the Gorges du Verdon, the Dentelles de Montmirail, Buoux in the Luberon, and the Vallée des Merveilles all have classified routes, some with bolted climbs. A Provençal variant of the sport is the Via Ferrata—a kind of high-altitude ropes course, popular throughout the Alps. Check the following locations for more information, rental gear, and guides.

Association Lei Lagramusas
La Palud-sur-Verdon 04120
Tel 04 92 77 38 02

Aventures et Nature
La Palud-sur-Verdon 04120
Tel 04 92 77 30 43
aventuresetnature.com

Base Sport et Nature
10 rue Fontaine
Castellane 04120
Tel 04 93 05 41 18
rafting-verdon-bsn.com

Club d'Escalade de Quinson
Quinson 04500
Tel 04 92 74 09 95
cequinson.chez.com

Comité Départemental de la Montagne et de l'Escalade
Place Capitaine Arnaud
Mezel 04270
Tel 04 92 35 58 84

Sailing, Windsurfing, & Other Water Sports

There's no shortage of choice along the coast when it comes to renting water skis, Jet Skis, or sailing equipment. The local tourist offices will have a list of the various companies that provide these services.

Cap Kayak
Port Gallice, Cap d'Antibes
Juan-les-Pins 06160
06 62 28 09 54
capkayak.fr

Easy Yachting
Port Gallice, Blvd. Baudoin
Antibes Juan-les-Pins 06160
Tel 04 93 67 75 91
easy-yachting.com

Team Water Sport
Coco Plage
Quartier Pampelonne
Ramatuelle 83350
Tel 04 94 79 82 41
Waterskiing, windsurfing, and
other related water sports in the
St.-Tropez area.

Scuba Diving
There are a large number
of fascinating dives off the coast,
from the shipwrecks surrounding offshore islands to the quiet
and mysterious coves of Les
Calanques. Several schools offer
either certification courses and
first time *plongée baptîme* dives.
To rent equipment on your own,
you will need to prove you are
certified. See also sidebar p. 124.

**Fédération Française d'Études
et des Sports Sous Marins**
24 quai Rive-Neuve
Marseille 13007
Tel 04 91 33 99 31
ffessm.fr
Departmental center for scuba
diving.

Porquerolles Plongée
ZA Porquerolles
Île de Porquerolles 83400
Tel 04 98 04 62 22
porquerolles-plongee.com
A variety of dives for all levels
and ages off the Îles d'Hyères.
They also offer snorkeling and
certification courses.

Skiing
Skiing in Provence's Alps doesn't
quite compare with the larger
Alps farther northeast, although

the lift tickets here are generally
much less expensive. See sidebar
p. 190.

Ancient Spas
Roman customs and natural hot
springs have no doubt influ-
enced the tradition of steamy
relaxation in southern France,
although these days you're
just as likely to find shiatsu,
aromatherapy, and meditation
alternatives on the *carte* in addition to the time-tested saunas
and hot baths.

La Bastide de Gordes & Spa
Rte. de Combe
Gordes 84220
Tel 04 90 72 12 12
bastide-de-gordes.com

Thermes de Dignes les Bains
29 av. Thermes
Digne-les-Bains 04005
Tel 04 92 32 32 92
thermesdignelesbains.com

Thermes de Gréoux
Rue Eaux Chaudes
Gréoux-les-Bains 04800
Tel 08 26 46 81 85
chainethermale.fr/greoux-les-bains

Les Thermes Marins
2 av. Monte-Carlo
Monaco 98000
Tel (377) 98 06 69 00
thermesmarinsmontecarlo.com

Thermes Sextius
55 cours Sextius
Aix-en-Provence 13101
Tel 04 42 23 81 82
thermes-sextius.com

Walking & Hiking
Provence is a great place to
get out and walk through the
countryside and wilderness.
Despite massive development
along the coast, the rugged terrain and growing environmental
concern throughout the region
have ensured that pockets of
wilderness remain intact.

The most spectacular hikes are
along the *calanques* near Marseille,

around the Dentelles in the Rhône
Valley, perched-village hopping
in Nice's backcountry, the rolling
chestnut and pine forests
of the Massif des Maures behind
St.-Tropez, and the Gorges du
Verdon and Vallée des Merveilles
in the Provence Alps.

Hiking trails are known as
Grande Randonée, GR for short.
Tourist offices will have information on the local GRs, otherwise
contact the organizations below
for more detailed information,
maps, and lists of alpine lodges.
Bear in mind that backcountry
hiking is generally forbidden at
the height of summer due to the
threat of forest fires.

Club Alpin Français
14 av. Mirabeau
Nice 06000
Tel 04 93 62 59 99
ffcam.fr

**Comité Départemental de la
Randonnée Pédestre**
4 av. de Verdun
Cagnes-sur-Mer 06800
Tel 04 93 20 74 73
cdrp06.org

Language Guide

Useful Words & Phrases

General

Yes *Oui*
No *Non*
Excuse me *Excusez-moi*
Hello *Bonjour*
Hi *Salut*
Please *S'il vous plaît*
Thank you (very much) *Merci (beaucoup)*
You're welcome *De rien*
Have a good day! *Bonne journée!*
OK *D'accord*
Goodbye *Au revoir*
Good night *Bonsoir*
here *ici*
there *là*
today *aujourd'hui*
yesterday *hier*
tomorrow *demain*
now *maintenant*
later *plus tard*
right away *tout de suite*
this morning *ce matin*
this afternoon *cet après-midi*
this evening *ce soir*
Do you speak English? *Parlez-vous anglais?*
I am American *Je suis Américain* (man); *je suis Américaine* (woman)
I don't understand *Je ne comprends pas*
Please speak more slowly *Parlez plus lentement, s'il vous plaît*
Where is...? *Où est...?*
I don't know *Je ne sais pas*
No problem *Ce n'est pas grave*
That's it *C'est ça*
Here it is *Voici*
There it is *Voilà*
What is your name? *Comment vous appelez-vous?*
My name is... *Je m'appelle...*
Let's go *On y va*
At what time? *À quelle heure?*
When? *Quand?*
What time is it? *Quelle heure est-il?*

In the Hotel

Do you have...? *Avez-vous...?*
a single room *une chambre simple*
a double room *une chambre double*
with/without bathroom/shower *avec/sans salle de bain/douche*

Help

I need a doctor/dentist *J'ai besoin d'un médecin/dentiste*
Can you help me? *Pouvez-vous m'aider?*
Where is the hospital? *Où est l'hôpital?*
Where is the police station? *Où est le commissariat?*

At a Restaurant

I'd like to order *Je voudrais commander*
Is service included? *Est-ce que le service est compris?*
I am on a diet *Je suis au régime*

Shopping

I'd like... *Je voudrais...*
How much is it? *C'est combien?*
Do you take credit cards? *Est-ce que vous acceptez les cartes de crédit?*
size (clothes) *la taille*
size (shoes) *la pointure*
cheap *bon marché*
expensive *cher*
Have you got...? *Avez vous...?*
I'll take it *Je le prends*
Anything else? *Avec ça?*
enough *assez*
too much *trop*
bill *la note*

Shops

bakery *la boulangerie*
bookshop *la librairie*
chemist *la pharmacie*
delicatessen *la charcuterie/le traiteur*
department store *le grand magasin*
fishmonger *la poissonnerie*
grocery *l'alimentation/l'épicerie*
junk shop *la brocante*
library *la bibliothèque*
supermarket *le supermarché*
tobacconist *le tabac*

Sightseeing

visitor information office *office de tourisme* or *le syndicat d'initiative*
open *ouvert*
closed *fermé*
every day *tous les jours*
year-round *toute l'année*
all day long *toute la journée*
free *gratuit/libre*
abbey *l'abbaye*
castle *le château*
church *l'église*
museum *le musée*
staircase *l'escalier*
tower *la tour*
tour (walk or drive) *le tour*
town *la ville*
old town *la vieille ville*
Town Hall *Hôtel de Ville/la mairie*

INDEX

ILLUSTRATIONS CREDITS

All photos by Gérard Sioen unless otherwise noted below.

Cover, Horsche/iStockphoto

Spine, studioportosabbia/iStockphoto

8, Catherine Hansen/Getty Images; 11, Westend61 GmbH/Alamy; 12, Brian Jannsen/age fotostock; 13, Gianni Dagli Orti/Corbis; 15, Laurent Yokel/500px Prime; 26, Stapleton Collection/Corbis; 30, Bettmann/Corbis; 36, "The Starry Night" by Vincent van Gogh/Getty Images; 39, Bettmann/Corbis; 40, Underwood & Underwood/Corbis; 46-7, Artwork by Maltings Partnership, Derby, England; 58, Bertrand Rieger/Getty Images; 68, Peter Groenendijk/age fotostock; 70-71,

Artwork by Maltings Partnership, Derby, England; 78, Juergen Schonnop/Alamy; 82, SIME/eStock Photo; 84, Boris Karpinski/Alamy; 111, DR-IAP/age fotostock; 115, Dominique Hordé; 116, Hemis/Alamy; 118, SIME/eStock Photo; 138, Christina Anzenberger-Fink/Anzenberger; 142, Veniamin Kraskov/Shutterstock.com; 148, Huber/Sime/eStock Photo; 150, LUDOVIC/REA/Redux; 155, Doco Dalfiano/Robert Harding World Imagery; 156, Gianni Dagli Orti/Corbis; 163, Christina Anzenberger-Fink/Anzenberger; 169. Christina Anzenberger-Fink/Anzenberger; 176, Christina Anzenberger-Fink/Anzenberger; 180, Christina Anzenberger-Fink/Anzenberger; 181, Peter Richardson/Getty Images.

National Geographic

TRAVELER
Provence & the Côte d'Azur

Published by the National Geographic Society
Gary E. Knell, *President and Chief Executive Officer*
John M. Fahey, *Chairman of the Board*
Declan Moore, *Chief Media Officer*
Chris Johns, *Chief Content Officer*

Prepared by the Book Division
Hector Sierra, *Senior Vice President and General Manager*
Lisa Thomas, *Senior Vice President and Editorial Director*
Jonathan Halling, *Creative Director*
Marianne R. Koszorus, *Design Director*
Barbara A. Noe, *Senior Editor, Travel Books*
R. Gary Colbert, *Production Director*
Jennifer A. Thornton, *Director of Managing Editorial*
Susan S. Blair, *Director of Photography*
Meredith C. Wilcox, *Director, Administration and Rights Clearance*

Staff for This Book
Kay Kobor Hankins, *Designer*
Moira Haney, *Senior Photo Editor*
Michael McNey and Mapping Specialists, *Map Production*
Marshall Kiker, *Associate Managing Editor*
Mike O'Connor, *Production Editor*
Rock Wheeler, *Rights Clearance Specialist*
Nicole Miller, *Design Production Assistant*
Bobby Barr, *Manager, Production Services*
Rosemary Bailey, Marlena Serviss, *Contributors*

Artwork by Maltings Partnership, Derby, England

The information in this book has been carefully checked and to the best of our knowledge is accurate. However, details are subject to change, and the National Geographic Society cannot be responsible for such changes, or for errors or omissions. Assessments of sites, hotels, and restaurants are based on the author's subjective opinions, which do not necessarily reflect the publisher's opinion.

The National Geographic Society is one of the world's largest nonprofit scientific and educational organizations. Founded in 1888 to "increase and diffuse geographic knowledge," the member-supported Society works to inspire people to care about the planet. Through its online community, members can get closer to explorers and photographers, connect with other members around the world, and help make a difference. National Geographic reflects the world through its magazines, television programs, films, music and radio, books, DVDs, maps, exhibitions, live events, school publishing programs, interactive media, and merchandise. *National Geographic* magazine, the Society's official journal, published in English and 38 local-language editions, is read by more than 60 million people each month. The National Geographic Channel reaches 440 million households in 171 countries in 38 languages. National Geographic Digital Media receives more than 25 million visitors a month. National Geographic has funded more than 10,000 scientific research, conservation, and exploration projects and supports an education program promoting geography literacy. For more information, visit www.nationalgeographic.com.

For more information, please call 1-800-NGS LINE (647-5463) or write to the following address:

National Geographic Society
1145 17th Street NW
Washington, DC 20036-4688 USA

Your purchase supports our nonprofit work and makes you part of our global community. Thank you for sharing our belief in the power of science, exploration, and storytelling to change the world. To activate your member benefits, complete your free membership profile at natgeo.com/joinnow.

For information about special discounts for bulk purchases, please contact National Geographic Books Special Sales: ngspecsales@ngs.org

For rights or permissions inquiries, please contact National Geographic Books Subsidiary Rights: ngbookrights@ngs.org

National Geographic Traveler: Provence & the Côte d'Azur (Third Edition)
ISBN: 978-1-4262-1547-6

Printed in Hong Kong
15/THK/1

Westminster Public Library
3705 W. 112th Ave
Westminster, CO 80031
www.westminsterlibrary.org

© 2015 National Geographic Society